IN HIS SHOES
The Life of Jesus

Based on the Glo Documentary

Written by
Troy Schmidt

Including Interviews with

Max Lucado	Norman Geisler
Joel Hunter	William Paul Young
Avner Goren	Leen Ritmeyer

Complete with *Study Guide Questions* for Small groups

IN HIS SHOES
The Life of Jesus

Copyright @ 2012 by Troy Schmidt
All rights reserved
First edition
Printed November, 2012

Published by: Create Space

Based on the Glo Documentary

Printed in the United States of America

Cover design by Jimmy Huckaby

ISBN-13: 978-1479131235

ISBN-10: 1479131237

Table of Contents

Acknowledgements

In February 2008, **Nelson Saba**, creator and brainchild of Glo, asked me to write a documentary that would be included in a new, revolutionary Bible software he was creating. The idea of an entire documentary being included in software was unheard of and would increase the value of his idea. I set out to write the script over a period of a month. (Nelson has a way of handing you impossible tasks at the last minute then saying "I needed it yesterday.")

Gallons of Starbucks coffee and nearly 200 hours later, I cranked out a 148 page script.

Now the question was—who would be the host?

Our first choice was **Max Lucado**, a friend of mine from the days of collaborating on the Hermie children's series, but Max's schedule does not accommodate the last minute brainstorms. Besides, he already had a trip planned to Israel with his family. Another three weeks in a foreign land would not work.

Nelson called me into his office and I could tell he was about to break some news to me. I couldn't tell if it was good or bad.

It was both.

"I have talked it over with others and we think you should be the host."

"ME!?!" I screamed. "I'm a writer. I hide behind the camera. You don't want me."

Nelson was adamant, but I wasn't convinced. I went home and told my wife **Barbie** about the funny thing that happened to me today.

"You would be perfect." Wives are supposed to be encouraging. Maybe I'll find another opinion.

I called up my director friend **Jimmy Huckaby**, who I've known since our days on The Mickey Mouse Club and who would be handling the directing duties on this documentary. "I think you would do just fine." I couldn't find anyone to say what I wanted to hear.

So I gave in. And I'm glad I did. What a journey it was.

I want to thank everyone who encouraged me to move forward with "In His Shoes: The Life of Jesus." It turned out to be a life-changing experience. And share many memories with those who walked the three week walk with me – Nelson, Jimmy, **Marcio Teixeira, Tony Silanskas, Efrata, B-Gah, Jorge** and **Phil Chen** our financial supporter and cheerleader.

The shooting of the documentary occurred in May, 2008 and the editing occurred through the end of the year and into early 2009. Finally Glo debuted at the end of 2009 and smashed records as the all-time best selling Bible software through 2010 and 2011.

However, there was so much information that we could not include in the final video product. Many more interviews occurred that we had to cut due to time. We had assembled an incredible who's-who of authors and scholars and I hated to see their insights go to waste. That's why I felt the need for this book.

This book is a personal journey that I experienced during the video taping of the documentary. It is also a way to preserve the transcripts of the interviews, so you can read their insights, not only those from the documentary but some great stuff that we could not include.

SMALL GROUP STUDIES

Since the documentary came out, people have sought me out online and asked me if there was a study guide they could use. The requests have come from the United States to as far away as Hong Kong and Turkey.

This book and the "In His Shoes: The Life of Jesus" documentary can be used as that teaching tool for your personal use or small group. The book chapters coincide with the documentary episodes found on the Glo software. You can then use the book and study questions for your group discussion in a classroom setting.

If you do not have Glo, I would suggest you go to **www.globible.com** and download your free copy. There have been over 1 million downloads of the Glo Bible on PC, Mac, iPad and iPhone. To get all the episodes of "In His Shoes," you'll have to pay for an upgrade, but it's worth it when you see how much you can unlock.

Now you can go on this journey exploring the life of Jesus in a new and exciting way, either by yourself or with a group of fellow travelers!

GO!

I also hope the footage you see will inspire you to go to Israel. We got to go with the best guide in town, **Avner Goren**. I've traveled to Israel two times since the documentary and met Avner for lunch. Just walking through Jerusalem to sit down for hummus, always turns into an incredible historical journey. Avner can't help but teach wherever he goes and, boy, am I glad.

If you want to go to Israel, I can't promise you Avner as a guide, but I want to recommend my friends at EO Tours (www.eo.travelwithus.com). They do such an amazing job and will provide for you a trip you will never forget. I have become good friends with the President **Joseph Cavarra** and he'll guarantee you and your church have a wonderful experience.

I look back on the documentary and realize how timeless the lessons were that we captured. This is information that has lasted for 2,000 years and still it manages to challenge and inspire us. Even years after watching "In His Shoes" I'm struck by how applicable and fascinating that trip was…and is.

I hope this book is one more step in your journey into the life of Christ.

With love,

Troy Schmidt
Windermere, FL – February, 2012
www.troyeschmidt.com

The Word became flesh and made his dwelling among us. We have seen his glory, the glory of the One and Only, who came from the Father, full of grace and truth. John 1:14

INTRODUCTION

The Journey Begins

Shoes

I wear a size 13 shoe. It's a pretty unique size. I'm sort of a freak, entering Bigfoot territory, but the size is becoming more and more common as mankind develops into a larger and larger race with a larger and large pace. In fact, all three of my sons have followed in my footsteps, so to speak. I put on the shoes of my youngest son the other day and didn't know the difference until he pointed it out.

"Hey, you're wearing my shoes!"

Payless Shoes goes to a size 13. Some discarded and forgotten 14s and 15s linger around, but nobody buys them. When you get to be my size, you cannot be picky. If the shoe fits, I always say, wear it.

My wife loves shoes. We have a closet to prove it. She's not unusual. It's typical for women to love shoes. I look at her rows of shoes and they all look the same to me. I detect very little variance in a line-up of black shoes with a strap. It's a very prejudicial statement to make around women to say all black shoes with a strap look alike.

"This one is for around the house. This one for the beach. This one a casual shoe. This one is dressy. This one is dressy-casual. Casual-dressy. And this one is for when the President of the United States stops by for a visit."

I don't know why one shoe can't do it all. It works for me and my size 13 sneakers.

While shoes have unique personalities, it's the people in the shoes that have the most distinct personalities. You can tell a lot about a person by looking at their shoes. You can determine their occupation – athlete, nurse, mountain climber, dancer. You can tell their wealth – designer labels, holes in the soles. You can tell their style – funky, sloppy, proper, by the book.

You can tell a lot more about a person by getting into their shoes.

The saying goes like this: if you want to know a person, walk a mile in their shoes.

Understanding a person's life does not come just by observation from a distance, but by getting up close, engaging in the activities, surroundings and people that populate the life of that person. You must see things from their point of view.

Jesus wore sandals, the common shoe of that day. We don't know what size shoe he wore, but we know a little about Jesus' body built and frame. The Bible describes him this way:

3

He grew up before him like a tender shoot,
and like a root out of dry ground.
He had no beauty or majesty to attract us to him,
nothing in his appearance that we should desire him.
He was despised and rejected by men,
a man of sorrows, and familiar with suffering.
Like one from whom men hide their faces
he was despised, and we esteemed him not. Isaiah 53:2-3

An average guy. Not beautiful. Not majestic. Nothing smoking hot about him. Just an average guy. God comes in the form of a man and the only physical description we can find is a prophecy six hundred years earlier and it reads that the Messiah will come as normal looking, every day, indistinguishable man with an average shoe size.

Maybe that was best. When Israel decided to adopt the kingship method that the neighboring countries used, they first chose Saul, described in 1 Samuel 9 as a "head taller" than everyone else. A beyond average giant, with, probably, a size 13 shoe. He didn't turn out very well, proving that looks and size don't matter when it comes to leadership.

David replaced Saul and 1 Samuel 16 describes David as "ruddy, with a fine appearance and handsome features." A beyond average stud. Sadly, his handsome looks and important job allowed him to marry hundreds of women and he caused a great divide in his household. Once again good looks fail.

Judges Chapter 13 tells the story of Samson, the strongest man in the world. A beyond average strong man. Again, he was a big disappointment, hanging around the wrong women and disrespecting his parents.

After all that history, maybe average is the best way to come to this earth, because apparently being above average in looks and muscles only leads to corruption.

Being six foot six, I have no idea what average means in terms of physical stature. But I do understand what it means to be just one of the crowd, another face, a number. Jesus identifies with my "averageness" because of all the bodies he could have chosen, he picked the average frame—not particularly handsome, not too tall, no exceptional strength.

Just average.

But far from average too. ·

An actor before he gets into a role sometimes reads and researches the character he is going to play. He may hang out with cops during their rounds. Or meet with construction workers to hear how they talk. She could visit a part of the world to pick up on gestures, an accent and dress.

Jesus asks us to be like him. He asks us to examine his life and follow him. He wants us to pick up his mannerisms, imitate his works and adopt his heart.

Then Jesus said to his disciples, "If anyone would come after me, he must deny himself and take up his cross and follow me. For whoever wants to save his life will lose it, but whoever loses his life for me will find it. Matthew 16:24-25

He asks that we walk in his shoes. Now those shoes are pretty big ones to fill. To follow in the footsteps of Christ I must deny myself. By denying myself, I must accept something in its place. I must die to myself and take up the cause of Christ.

To truly know Christ, I should have been an apostle. They walked side by side with Jesus every day for around three years, watching him respond and react to common and uncommon situations. They observed Jesus firsthand and all of them (minus one) came back changed.

Only a few people in history got the opportunity to walk side-by-side with Jesus as he walked this earth. The closest I can get to that experience is to walk in the places where Jesus walked. To do that, I must go to Israel.

I visited Israel before, shooting documentary footage for a Bible CD-ROM called iLumina. It featured nearly 30 short vignettes showcasing the locations of the Bible. I went with iLumina creator Nelson Saba, renowned archaeologist Dr. James Strange, and others. We met up with paleontologist Joe Zias, who discovered the tomb of Zechariah, the father of John the Baptist. We shot over eight hours of raw footage in two short weeks.

However, I was so busy setting up shots with a local Israeli crew and creating the segments as we walked, that I forgot to do one thing.

Reflect.

I remember when we walked up to the Garden Tomb and immediately I crafted five shots, examined the inside for proper lighting and assisted in taking photographs.

5

Once it was all over, I stopped and cried. It hit me…

Jesus rose again from the dead very close to here and I was too busy to take the time to reflect on it.

I feel we do that all the time. We are so busy we forget to reflect on the concept of God coming to Earth in the form of a baby, growing up into adulthood, starting a three year ministry with a rag-tag group of men, then allowing himself to die on a cross for our sins.

I was determined not to let that happen again. If I was going to walk in the shoes of Jesus, I needed to commit to the task and spend nearly a month breathing in the air of Israel, walking on the ground Jesus walked and smelling and tasting the foods of the local area.

I wanted to walk in his shoes and understand how Jesus lived, how he faced the problems of life, how he related to others—family, friends, co-workers, how he maneuvered in this human skin and ultimately what he wanted me to learn from his example.

Jesus loved to refer to himself as the Son of Man. The Son of Man? If he wanted to get some attention and respect, why not use the term Son of God?[1] Jesus embraced his humanity, never denying it or hiding it. He lived a human life more successfully than any other human on the planet ever lived.

John 1:14 is a simple verse, yet it has so many ramifications. The Word—the prophesied Messiah spoken of in the Old Testament, the fulfillment of God's written law, the one who speaks and it is—came in the flesh, with skin, bones, blood, hair, eyes, hormones and suffered hunger, exhaustion, disappointment, pain just like the rest of us. The One and Only left His Father and decided to walk the earth and live as we do.

Jesus was God and man in one being. Fully God and fully man. He healed, walked on water, brought the dead back to life like God. He also wept, got angry, hungered like a man.

Sometimes as we talk about Jesus being a man, it feels…blasphemous. How dare we impose humanity on Jesus Christ! But we tend to forget he came as a man, walked in the shoes of first century person and lived as a citizen in society.

Norman Geisler:
Well to deny Christ's humanity is a heresy, it's called Docetism, and it's in fact, we're warned against it in 1 John chapter 4. It says, "anyone who does not confess that Jesus Christ has come in the flesh.' It's in the

---

[1] Son of Man is a term from Daniel chapter 7 that denotes deity.

perfect tense, meaning He came and still remains in the flesh. 'Anyone who denies that is of antichrist.' So it's a heresy. And I think it's because we're overprotective. We like to stress His Deity. His Deity has been denied by so many people that we like to emphasis it and we overemphasis it and neglect His humanity.

While he lived as an ordinary man, Jesus was nothing like an ordinary man. So I had questions. Did his humanity effect his deity? Did his deity give him an advantage as a human? Why would God cry? How did he suffer? How did he balance his human needs with his Godly needs?

So I went back to Israel with the intent of experiencing the life of Jesus, the best I could, using the Bible as my guide and the places where Jesus visited as my inspiration. I was joined on my travels with another film crew and an archaeologist, Avner Goren – a teacher of teachers in Israel. To truly understand the stature of Avner Goren, every time we saw a tour group, the tour guide stopped, crossed to Avner and shook his hand, announcing his arrival to the tourists. Avner teaches all the guides. And here he was, right by my side. A Jew by birth, Avner was an excellent resource to understand the place and context of first century history.

But I still had more questions, so to find the answers, I met up with four esteemed men – all of them writers, a couple of them pastors, one of them a theologian. All of them gave me fresh insight into the life of Jesus from different viewpoints.

- **Max Lucado** – pastor of Oak Hills Community Church in San Antonio, Texas, a prolific author, who has become a friend during our association with the *Hermie the Caterpillar* series which he created. Max's warm, caring, folksy, deep and simple examination of life, faith and the Bible always made the complex seem easy. His books God Came Near, Six Hours One Friday, Just Like Jesus, He Chose the Nails all showcase Max as a man who desires to get into the shoes of Jesus.
- **Joel Hunter** – a pastor at Northland Community Church in Longwood, Florida who has risen to fame because of his work with various Christian Environmental issues and his prayer after the Democratic Inauguration of Barack Obama in Denver, Colorado. He is on the President's Advisory Council on Faith-

Based and Neighborhood Partnerships and prays with President Barack Obama on the phone.

- **Norman Geisler** – a brilliant Christian apologist and author of like seventy books (someday I'll read <u>Systematic Theology</u>, maybe when I'm in prison and I have some time). He is the co-founder and former president of the Southern Evangelical Seminary in Charlotte, North Carolina. He's the apologists of apologists.

- **William Paul Young** – the mega successful author of <u>The Shack</u>. Paul's perspective of God immediately set him apart from the others. I pursued him across America and somehow managed to corner him for a few hours in Knoxville, Tennessee, in the basement of a small Baptist church. Paul proved to be an enthusiastic and unique man of God.

As you can tell, with the perspective of these four thinkers and the guidance of Avner, I was well equipped for this journey into the life of Christ. I needed all the help I could get. Think of it – I was about the step into the shoes of the most revered, the most controversial figure of all of history. The God/Man.

It was a journey that took a year to research and provided me insight that will last a lifetime.

Death
Airplane/Jerusalem

I want to know Christ and the power of his resurrection and the fellowship of sharing in his sufferings, becoming like him in his death... Philippians 3:10

Saying goodbye is always tough, especially when you're going to be gone for so long. It's always hard to leave my wife Barbie, who is so loving, a true companion, wise and beautiful. I do a lot of traveling to foreign countries and just about two days before I leave, I begin to see that look in her eyes, a deep stare that seems to look through me and into my future. She doesn't have to say it. But she's thinking it.

"You're going to die."

I know that's a morbid greeting to give someone, but I've grown used to it. I see that death look when I drive to Tallahassee, fly to San Antonio, or travel half-way around the world to South America or Africa. I get an extra dose of the death look especially when I go to the Middle East.

Westerners perceive the Middle East as the Wild West. Guns fired randomly in the air by lunatics. Suicide bombers going off around the clock, so precisely you can set your watch to them. Religious fanatics kidnapping Americans, holding them for political ransom then separating their head from their shoulders.

However I've never felt any threat during my trips to the Middle East—Israel, Turkey, Egypt—but I guess there is always a first time for everything. I tell my friends I'm more afraid of going to Los Angeles than Jerusalem. Despite my possibly misplaced comfort, I cannot help keep the echo of her stare from my mind...

"You're going to die."

This time, especially, we talked about dying and where all the paperwork can be found to sustain my family line. We discussed the insurance options available and pension stored up. Of all the trips I've been on, I felt I really prepared her for my death this time.

When Barbie hints that I may die on my trip to Israel, I don't lie to her—"I might." I don't want to make a promise over something I don't have any control over. I can't control my death. If planes crash or terrorists attack, it's not my fault. It's fate, freewill, faulty fuel lines or fundamentalist doctrines.

9

But on a trip like this, I have to prepare to die, especially in keeping with the overall theme. When I commit to walk in the shoes of Jesus, I must put aside my life and accept his life—refuse my motives and take his. This trip should be the death of me and the rebirth of Christ in me. So Barbie's fears may come true – Troy may die on this trip.

I actually hope so.

When I fly, I usually like to sit on a plane and just focus on writing and reading. It's the only time I can crank through the stack of books that sit dormant next to my bed. I read eight books once on a mission trip. I must say it was a very productive mission trip. I can't remember any one of the books, but I read them. I'm sure of it.

So when conversations strike up next to me, I traditionally want to cut them short. Since this time I'm starting out my trip to experience Jesus, I reminded myself that Jesus would drop everything and talk to everyone and anytime. I must put aside my shallow desires as soon as I arrive in the airport even if the airplane tires have not departed home soil.

The first leg of the trip I sat next to a wonderful lady named Sue who worked as a church secretary for a pastor in Staton Island and she currently held a top ten ranking in her age bracket for swimming. I especially liked her because she quoted lines from Monty Python and the Holy Grail. Not many sixty year olds are so hip. She was so sweet and very encouraging, wishing me well and anxious to see what would come of this adventure.

Now I'm a rather long guy, so bulk head seats and exit rows are my best friends. The planners of this trip had the gracious foresight to get me those seats before we left the ground, so I didn't have to fight and beg three hours before we left at the ticket counter. As I sat in my roomy seat, I saw a rather large man walk down the aisle and I immediately found myself thinking, "Oh no, I hope he doesn't see next to me."

He did.

"Uh, oh. Looks like they put two big guys next to each other," he said, stating the obvious.

This man needed a seat that was as long as wide. When he sat down, he spilled over the arm rest, our arms permanently rubbing against one another for the remainder of the ten hour trip.

However, my Siamese seat mate couldn't have been a nicer, more interesting guy. And get this—he was a Jewish scribe named David.

David wore the traditional Jewish religious garb—the little black yarmulke that somehow defied gravity and sat precisely over the area of the head known to men as the "bald spot." The tassels of a prayer shawl hung out from the bottom of his shirt. His face was flush with a big fluffy beard that went untrimmed half way up his cheek bone. He acted more like a rock n' roll rabbi and guess what…he was—a former rock musician from Brooklyn turned orthodox Hassidic Jew, with an appetite for food, whiskey and God.

During the trip, David mentioned that it was ordained by God that we sit next to one another and I agreed. We discussed the names of God in the Old Testament, the Bible codes, the process of calligraphy, ancient Jewish mystics, Bible translations, you name it. Exactly the kind of foundation I needed to enter the life of Christ.

I always seem to forget that Jesus was Jewish. My mind associates him as being Christian, not a Jew. So right out of the terminal gate I got to talk about Judaism with a hearty scribe, who laughed like Santa at times, then cursed like a sailor.

I asked him, "Of all the names God could choose, why Jesus?"

"It means 'salvation' or 'redemption.' It comes from the Hebrew Yeshua. Other names like Joshua and Hosea come from the same name. His name means the giver of life through an act of substitution or sacrifice."

This guy was a *Jewish* scribe?

As we went on, David explained, with such robust enthusiasm, the beauty of the Hebrew language and how English (he spoke perfect English being born in New York, if you call a New York accent perfect English) just cannot capture the essence of Hebrew. What fascinated me was David's memory. He quoted whole passages to me in Hebrew and knew his Old Testament, and large parts of the New, as well as any lead singer can quote the lyrics to their hit record, having sung it over and over.

I used the search function on my laptop bible software to talk to him. He used memory, the predominant tool in Jesus' time.

As we opened up the Bible, I asked him to translate the statement Jesus made on the cross, the only Hebrew I could think of in the New Testament – Matthew 27. *Eloi, Eloi, lama sabchthani.* Words of death spoken by Jesus on the cross.

"That's from a Psalm. Psalm 22."

I opened it up and found it. Jesus, like this scribe from Brooklyn, could quote scripture even as died on the cross. I can't quote it sitting in coach with plenty of leg room.

As I read through Psalm 22, I noticed prophecies.

11

But I am a worm and not a man,
scorned by men and despised by the people.
All who see me mock me;
they hurl insults, shaking their heads: 6-7

From birth I was cast upon you;
from my mother's womb you have been my God. 10

My strength is dried up like a potsherd,
and my tongue sticks to the roof of my mouth;
you lay me in the dust of death.
Dogs have surrounded me;
a band of evil men has encircled me,
they have pierced my hands and my feet.
I can count all my bones;
people stare and gloat over me.
They divide my garments among them
and cast lots for my clothing. 15-18

For he has not despised or disdained
the suffering of the afflicted one;
he has not hidden his face from him
but has listened to his cry for help. 24

The prophecies clearly outline the identity of the coming Messiah.

- He will be despised by men
- He will be surrounded by vile people
- His bones will not be broken
- His clothes will be distributed to others

I showed David that. "Oh yeah, Isaiah also says a lot of amazing things about the coming Messiah."

"Doesn't that prove to you that Jesus is the Messiah?"

David shook his head slightly. He liked to look off and gesture with his hand next to his mouth, his index finger pointing up and toddling back and forth. "But it also says that when the Messiah comes, the lion will lay down with the lamb and there will be no more famine. I don't see that happening."

David refused Jesus as the Messiah because Jesus failed to bring political peace to Israel.

As David spouted off scripture and stories and ancient commentaries, I realized how out of my league I was. I boarded the plane familiar with the Gospels and with pages of notes and ideas; however, as I got closer to the center of all major religions, everything I knew was being challenged in my quest to know Jesus.

For one, I didn't know Hebrew.

I had only a basic understanding of history.

Finally, I was not Jewish!

To really walk in the shoes of Jesus, I had to have the Jewish DNA coursing through my veins. Already I was at a disadvantage.

David represented a true, devout, religious Jew and in some ways, he was closer to the shoes of Jesus than I was.

Yet, being Jewish did not make one a follower of Christ. Being dead gave you that privilege. The death of yourself. While I died to Christ years ago in my one room bachelor apartment in Van Nuys, California, David held on to his preconceived notions of the Old Testament Messiah while living in Jerusalem.

David reminded me of the Old Testament world Jesus "flew into" as he decided to leave his home and come to a foreign land called Israel. Jesus departed a place where he was known and accepted, then traveled to a place where was despised and rejected.

Jesus took the trip even though he knew he would die. Little did I know how close I really was to death.

David recommended some restaurants and places to see before we parted ways.

"Are you going to Ashdod?"

I had never heard of it. "No."

"You have to go to the Wednesday market. It's a lot of fun."

Our schedule had no breathing room in it and Wednesday we were going to be north around Galilee, so I nodded and smiled politely. I wanted to meet up with David once again and we exchanged emails, hoping to rendezvous during my time there. It unfortunately never occurred, yet I appreciated the first perspective David gave me on this journey.

That Wednesday we read that someone fired a rocket into that Ashdod market and injured three people. If I walked in David's shoes that day, I may have died.

Death is a reality all around us, no matter where you go.

As the wheels of the jet touched the ground, I thought about Jesus coming to this earth, landing in this country of Israel, ready to die. He came ready to strap on human shoes to his human feet and marched to the cross, never once turning around and heading home. Before His spirit landed inside a fertilized egg, that docked inside his mother's womb, then passed through customs to his final destination, Jesus accepted his fate to receive from God whatever He had planned for him.

I must be ready to do the same.

<u>JOURNEY 1</u>

Birth to Baptism

Birth
Bethlehem

Traveling to Bethlehem is like walking into The Twilight Zone. You are definitely not in Israel any longer. Large, intimidating walls, guarded by frowning security personnel, who seem to suspect everyone, trust no one, and greet you with piercing looks as you enter Bethlehem. I wondered, "Am I visiting a prison or a city?" I'll leave that for politicians to debate.

During my first visit to Bethlehem in 2002, an intifada had been announced, declaring war on Israel, so Palestinians and Jews were not on friendly terms. Bethlehem's borders were closed and impassable. Visitors received a "rocky" welcome, meaning the locals threw rocks at all passing cars. We could not visit the famous Church of the Nativity.

Sadly, here I had access to Avner Goren, the foremost expert on Israel history, and even he could not join us into Bethlehem. Jews were not welcomed. We had to hire a Palestinian guide to take us in. I would have to meet up with Avner later.

As our 15 passenger van creaked passed the gate, our passports approved and identities verified, I was excited to venture into unexplored territory. A new adventure had begun.

Maybe Jesus felt that traveling excitement before he leapt into Mary's womb and gestated for nine months. "Here we go! A new adventure!"

The Church of the Nativity was a busy—how should I say— passionate place. Busloads of pilgrims entered the sacred halls with their faithful tour guides leading the march. Visitors entered the church through a small doorway, which had shrunk over the years, from the Justinian period to the Crusader period to the Ottoman period. The current entrance required me to bend in half, almost touching my knees.

The Lilliputian Door of Back Ache measures 73 centimeters wide and 130 centimeters long, some say, to force people to bow before they enter. Others say it prevented mounted horsemen from looting the place. Either reason, it works. I was humbled and I kept my horse outside.

Pilgrims routinely visited the site after the birth of Christ and, as is human nature, built a small church over the grotto where locals told them Jesus was born. They cut a hole in the top of the grotto, allowing Christians to look inside. In the second century, as the number of Christians visiting here grew, Roman emperor Hadrian destroyed the church and built his own pagan temple on top of the religious attraction to deter Christ worship. From an archaeological standpoint, this was a good thing, since Hadrian, unwittingly, marked the site for future worshippers.

When Emperor Constantine's mother Helena arrived for a scouting trip to mark all the holy sites in Israel, around 325 BC, locals pointed her to the Roman temple. After many years and the changing of hands, the Church of the Nativity became one of the oldest Christians structures in the world.

Today, there are three denominations at the location—Greek-Orthodox, Franciscan and Armenian. A few feet below the main complex sits the Grotto, a small room cut into stone, about twelve meters long and three meters wide. All of this, they say, was once the actual cave where Jesus entered the earth.

People are pretty excited about the site and a line extended longer than Splash Mountain at Walt Disney World, all to visit three small altars – the Nativity Altar (the X-marks-the-spot star where they believe Jesus was born), the Altar of the Manger (where Mary laid Jesus and the shepherds saw him), and the Altar of the Magi (where the magi presented their gifts to Jesus).

When the pilgrims arrive at the star, two or three at a time drop down to take pictures, cross themselves, or kiss the star. Many rub items on the spot, believing the action will sanctify their items and make them holy. The room was tight, hot and smelled like body odor – probably much like a real stable in Jesus' time.

One man pushed me aside as I blocked our video camera from getting knocked over. I was taking too much time in front of the spot (sort of like a 3 seconds violation in basketball). He cursed at me in some language. I just smiled wondering if the shepherds pushed this much to see the actual Christ child.

Camera flashes popped in my face, as I tried to get out of the way. Thankfully cameras were not around during Jesus' time or Mary and Joseph would be seeing spots for days. Frankly, I found the location chaotic and not ideal for reflection.

I did recognize how international this site was. The birth of Christ really unites the world, even Christians and Muslims. Muslims revere Jesus as a prophet, though not necessarily THE prophet. I hoped their visit here would reveal something to them.

Bethlehem, even today, is unimpressive. As you exit Israel and enter Palestinian territory, something changes—the environment, the attitude, the houses, the national pride. I couldn't help but wonder, why was Bethlehem chosen for Jesus' entrance into the world?

The biggest reason God chose Bethlehem was lineage.

Now I have never traced my lineage, but those who do always find a great king or a famous explorer in their heritage. Why doesn't anyone boast of Heinrick the Shoe Cobbler or Louise the Seamstress? We always want to boast of the highlights and brag about the rich blood flowing through our veins and then conveniently forget the lesser important embarrassments to our name.

The lineage of Jesus includes some pretty incredible highlights—Abraham, Isaac, Jacob, Boaz, Ruth, David, Solomon, Uzziah and Josiah—a laudable who's who from the Bible. Then again the genealogies, revealed in Matthew and Luke, speak of others in the line: Rahab a prostitute; Tamar who pretended to be a prostitute and had sex with her father-in-law Judah; Rehoboam, Solomon's son who caused a divisive civil war in Israel; Manasseh, described as the most vile king ever.

Prostitutes and evil dictators wouldn't make it into my biography, conveniently forgotten and misplaced, yet Jesus includes all the best with the worst. The Gospels don't hide who he is or where he came from.

Norman Geisler
Well He chose that family line because it was predicted. God predicted that He would be born of the seed of the woman, the line of Abraham, Isaac, Jacob and from the tribe of Judah, Genesis 49, and as a son of David. So, it was predicted for Him.

God chose the nation of Israel so He could bring His Holy Son and His Holy Word into the world. He said to Abraham, 'Get out of your country from your kindred, from your father's house, unto a land that I will show thee. And I will make of you a great nation and bless you and make your name great, bless those who bless thee, and curse those who curse thee and through you shall all the families of the earth be blessed.' So God chose Abraham and his descendants to be the channel through which He would bring His Son into the world.

19

Max Lucado

The family line of Jesus is a fascinating blend of surprises, people you'd never expect to spot on the family tree of Jesus. There are four women and one of those women is a foreigner, another is a harlot. Another one Matthew doesn't even call her by name, Bathsheba, we know because we read the story. So it's a remarkable blending of people. To me the whole genealogy of Jesus says that Christ comes through dysfunctional people. And that everybody is dysfunctional and yet in spite of it all, and in the midst of it all, Christ comes.

Norman Geisler

Yes you have some interesting people there. You know, He brought Ruth in – she was a Gentile. There were people who had shady characters as you know, from Rahab. You have Gentiles. And I think He wanted to say He's a God of grace, He's a God that wants to reach out to the Gentiles. The Jews weren't the only object of His love, they were the channel of His love and so He wanted to say this is a human, fallible, ordinary blood line but I'm going to do extraordinary things through it.

Jesus' heritage did not make him who he is. While I would hide those names from my past in fear of being associated with them or believing others would think less of me as I carry that tainted lineage in my blood, Jesus seemed to say, "I am who I am" not "I'm a product of my past and doomed to failure."

Jesus rose above his human DNA. That gives hope to us. We don't have to repeat the mistakes of our fathers. Jesus didn't.

His family line wasn't perfect, but whose is? We all have failures and losers who captured headlines and disgraced our good name. Jesus did not want his "perfect" pedigree to be an advantage to his life. He chose to descend from a healthy/unhealthy balance of winners and losers.

Joel Hunter:

None of us have a heritage that is without fault, that there's not some horse thief or some you know, reprobate or some, you know. That's all of our story and so when God chose that, even though there were some people to be very proud of there were also some people whose behavior was very shameful and that's all of our story. So when He entered into mankind, he entered fully into mankind.

20

Jesus was born to two ordinary people in the town of Bethlehem. Joseph, a blue collared carpenter, and Mary, described as a woman favored by God. However, His conception was far from ordinary, for Mary was the first virgin to ever get pregnant.

This certainly got some press by the first century bloggers.

"Did you hear about Mary. She's pregnant."
"And who's the father?"
"Don't know. Maybe Joseph?"
"I hear she said God came to her and she conceived by the Holy Spirit."
"A likely story."
"If I had a dime for every time I heard that one."

Not only was the whole virgin thing a public relations fiasco for her family, but the timing of his birth…please, how inconvenient.

A census created by the Roman government required everyone to return to the city of their ancestors, to register and pay taxes. For Joseph, that place was Bethlehem. So he and a very pregnant Mary packed up their belongings and traveled to the City of David.

Joseph traveled with a pregnant woman across 70 miles of hot, unrelenting wilderness? Does Joseph get all the appreciation he deserves?

And the place…Bethlehem…could God had chosen a better place? During the first century, Bethlehem was a small town living in the shadow of the biggest, most important city around, Jerusalem. Five miles south of Jerusalem, Bethlehem received fame only for being the birthplace of King David, the most revered king in Jewish history. But that was in the past. Even the Christmas carol "O Little Town of Bethlehem" references its obscurity. It could be called "O Little Insignificant Town of Bethlehem That Lived in the Shadow of Jerusalem," but that's too complicated to sing and nothing rhymes with Jerusalem.

If you're going to choose a town to be born in and you want to make a big splash, Jerusalem was the place. Not Bethlehem.

And all of this was planned beforehand? The Trinity sat down and mapped out the ancestors, the time, the place and said, *this is it*? Actually, God knew what he was doing, as seen in the prophecies made hundreds of years before.

"But you, Bethlehem Ephrathah,
though you are small among the clans of Judah,
out of you will come for me
one who will be ruler over Israel,
whose origins are from of old,
from ancient times.'" Micah 5:2

A shoot will come up from the stump of Jesse;
from his roots a Branch will bear fruit.
The Spirit of the LORD will rest on him—
the Spirit of wisdom and of understanding,
the Spirit of counsel and of power,
the Spirit of knowledge and of the fear of the LORD—
and he will delight in the fear of the LORD. Isaiah 11:1-3

"'The days are coming,' declares the LORD, 'when I will
fulfill the gracious promise I made to the house of Israel and
to the house of Judah.
"'In those days and at that time
I will make a righteous Branch sprout from David's line;
he will do what is just and right in the land.
In those days Judah will be saved
and Jerusalem will live in safety.
This is the name by which it will be called:
The LORD Our Righteousness.'" Jeremiah 33:14-16

"'My servant David will be king over them, and they will all
have one shepherd. They will follow my laws and be careful
to keep my decrees.
They will live in the land I gave to my servant Jacob, the land
where your fathers lived. They and their children and their
children's children will live there forever, and David my
servant will be their prince forever.
I will make a covenant of peace with them; it will be an
everlasting covenant. I will establish them and increase their
numbers, and I will put my sanctuary among them forever.

My dwelling place will be with them; I will be their God, and
they will be my people.
Then the nations will know that I the LORD make Israel holy,
when my sanctuary is among them forever. '" Ezekiel 37:24-
28

Norman Geisler
Well I think he was born in Bethlehem because it was predicted in
Micah 5:2 that He would be born in Bethlehem. And it emphasizes in
the prophecy, 'thou Bethlehem, would Judea, though thou be little
among the thousands of Judah, out of thee will come He whose reign
has been from everlasting.' So I think the whole point is summarizing
the passage itself. You're small, you're seemingly insignificant but I'm
going to do great things through you.

As Mary and Joseph pulled into town, the signpost outside of
Bethlehem should have read "Welcome to Bethlehem, the Birthplace of
David." This little town needed some sort of draw, something to brag
about. David was their home boy, their brightest star. But the
prophecies from the Old Testament acted as the real signposts to
Bethlehem's true, forthcoming greatness, especially for those looking for
the Messiah.

God did not hide the mysteries of his entrance into the world like
some Dan Brown novel, pieced together through symbols and ancient
clues. He made it clear to anyone paying attention. David was the
"shoot" coming from the "stump" of his father Jesse. Jesus is the
"righteous branch" from this family tree in the lineage of Judah. God
promised that he would dwell with his people, live and breathe with
them, in the town of Bethlehem, from the line of Judah.

Mary and Joseph arrived late to Bethlehem and you can
understand why. A pregnant woman and a 70-mile trip from Nazareth,
you aren't setting any land speed records. Many passed them on the way
into town and filled up all the rooms.

An owner of a house with spare rooms offered them a simple
place that would at least offer warmth and shelter from thieves. There
were no Holiday Inns in those days, just rooms hospitable people offered
to weary travelers. The place could have been a basement room where
animals and supplies were kept at night, or a nearby cave or even a stable
for animals. Wherever it was, it stunk. Donkeys and sheep turn any
place into a manure-caked stall.

The Church of Nativity just could not capture the real essence of Jesus' original birthplace, so I later found a stable in Nazareth. It was a space about twelve foot by twelve foot. Inside was a stubborn donkey who wouldn't move out of the way no matter how hard you pushed it, a loud sheep who looked me right in the eyes and seemed to say "I hate you" every time he baaa'd and a little goat who never sat still.

All around the floor was straw and crap. That's right. Crap. Animal dung. And it stunk. It was disgusting. Probably the most unhygienic location for an emergency birth I could think of next to the back seat of a New York City cab.

No, I take that back, the cab would be cleaner.

When my sons were born, I had to wear a blue surgical gown, booties and a cap. I can't imagine slipping surgical booties on a donkey before the birth.

Standing in that stable, I couldn't think of a more humble beginning for Jesus than what he experienced. Separated from his grandmothers and grandfathers who could lend a hand. On the road, away from all your belongings, blankets and items that have been handed down for generations. Born in front of obstinate donkeys, annoying sheep and fidgety goats. And Jesus' first blanket was a crude assembly of strips of cloth that came from God knows where.

This was God's plan?

Joel Hunter
There was no mistaking the extent to which He condescended. I think that any of us that have grown up either around a farming community; I grew up in a very small town. The biggest buildings in the town were the corn silos. And so, again that was part of His ultimate condescension into what was common life at the time. It was an agrarian society. They lived with their animals, some of them literally. And so as He came into what was the common life, He was born into a very common dwelling and even once removed so to speak because He wasn't even permitted to be born in an Inn. It wasn't in a house even. It was in the place where other parts of His creation dwelt.

William Paul Young
I don't see this as a demeaning thing. This is a choice. It's not like God says, 'Well let's pick the worst way we can come into this situation', you know. He says, 'Let's go this way because I think this is so beautiful.' And I think it was.

Joel Hunter

His birth was less than common; it was once deducted from common. And again what it shows is God's tremendous humility. That He would empty Himself to that extent and go to the most humble, even to some extent, repulsive. A birth that no one would choose...God chose.

This was humility...more like humiliating.

Born of a virgin with a damaged reputation, with a father separated from his business, tools and favorite clients, and descended from a line of prostitutes and evil villains, Jesus entered this world and his first crib was the feeding trough with discarded food and grain to feed the animal—a manger. There's nothing glamorous or glorious about this scene. We'd like to think that God took the smell away or that Mary glowed in a radiant light and Jesus laid there, no crying he made.

That's just not the case. Mangers stink. Post pregnant women are in pain. And babies cry. They have to. They have no other way to communicate their needs.

Jesus cried. And I would too.

This newborn's name today has become synonymous with God, but back then it was about as common as they come. The name "Jesus" came from the Greek form of the Hebrew name Joshua, which meant, "The Lord saves." It was the John or Bill of the day.

I wanted to name our kids Otto, Zondar or Vaughn (Vaughn Schmidt commands respect...if you're a Nazi my wife would say). I even toyed with Gilligan. I wanted cool names for our kids that set them apart. I think we did pretty well—Riley, Brady, Carson—but I always wanted to go a step further.

Couldn't God have chosen something cool, hip or different? Nebuchadnezzar comes to mind. It sounds like Schwarzenegger and that name did him a lot of good. How about Samson? Zerubbabel rolls nicely off the tongue. Even Ezekiel. His friends could call him "Z".

"Hey Z, what's up!"

But the creator of the universe, the one through whom all life initiated, chose Jesus. It's not by his common name that he would be judged, but by his uncommon life. God not only communicated that name clearly to Mary through the angel Gabriel in Luke 1:31...He demanded it.

25

God wanted his son to have the most common name around.

Jesus entered this world as humbly as you can imagine in order to show that he could identify with us.

Homeless?

Product of an unwed mother?

Poor?

Lost?

Maybe you come from a family line that is despised by others?

Common?

Jesus knows what you're going through.

Face it, if he was born to a king, in a palace, and slept in a crib inlaid with emeralds, only about a handful of Kardashians could identify with him. We would expect him to grow up and become a snobby elitist, looking down on the rest of us.

Instead, he chose to enter the world looking up from a manger, while everyone else looked down on him. Even the stubborn donkeys were upset he was blocking their feeding trough. They had no idea this little baby created them to be stubborn.

The family line, the unwed mother controversy, even the stench of the manger did not defile Jesus. He wouldn't allow it. He entered life sinless and refused to permit the world around him to contaminate him.

Nothing at his birth said he was better than us.

All of it says he's one of us.

Max Lucado

He'll go anywhere to touch His people; He'll do anything to reach His people. That's the big announcement of the humility of Christ's entrance into the world. Every person has a more noble birth than Jesus had. It's hard to find one more ignoble. What, what else could be done? Even if you're born in the back of the greyhound bus like that old song, you know, it's more hygienic than a stable. If you're born into poverty, so was Jesus. If you're born into anonymity, well so was Christ. If you're born in a map dot town, so was Jesus. If you're born on the far reaches of a remote part of an empire that's out of the radar screen of any civilization, so was Christ. His birth says he'll go as far as it takes and do whatever it takes to reach every single person.

TIME TO JOURNEY

1. **Watch "Birth" from "In His Shoes: The Life of Christ"**

2. **Discussion Questions**

- Have you ever traced your family line? What did you find?

- Who would you like to find?

- What did your parents do for a living when you were born?

- What would your parents be like if you could choose them? What would be their status, wealth, career?

- Why did God choose Mary and Joseph of all people?

- Where were you born?

- What was your hometown like?

- How did others perceive your hometown?

- Why did God choose Bethlehem?

- Would you rather be born in a small town or a big city?

- Why are prophecies so important in the birth of Jesus?

- Have you ever been to a stable/barn? What are your impressions of that place?

- Why would God choose to have his son born in a place where they kept animals?

- Why did Jesus choose such a humble beginning? Would you?

- What does this choice say to you about God?

King
Bethlehem/Herodian

The political system of Jesus' time was a little complicated to explain to a newborn, let alone a fully grown adult. Rome controlled the region under their mighty evil empire. They allowed the puppet Jewish kings to look like they were in charge, as long as they did everything Rome told them to do.

Keep the peace was the Roman mantra.

One of those kings was Herod, whose self-proclaimed title was Herod the Great. Subtle. Herod enjoyed being king of Judea and ran unopposed when it came to his reign. He stayed in power from 37 to 4 B.C.

An Idumaean by birth[2], Herod did not come from the line of David, so the Jews did not consider him a true king. He became a power-hungry, paranoid-driven monarch, running the country on fear and power.

When I asked Avner about Herod, he grinned widely on the subject, unable to contain his mockery over such an insane despot.

"Herod was crazy. He was really sick and had paranoia, being sure that everyone around him wanted to kill him. So much so, he was awful with his people and his own family. He killed his most beloved wife. He killed his own children. He was also very powerful so people were afraid of him as a king. The others around him didn't like him at all, including his masters and the Roman emperor. At the end of his career, Gustav said it is better to be a pig in his court rather than be one of his sons."

Under Herod's reign, another kingdom began its quiet invasion, through the birth of its ruler. A little baby. Jesus Christ entered the frontlines of Bethlehem as the newborn king. God did not fear the complicated political opposition of Herod and Rome. In fact, He publicly announced Jesus' arrival in scriptures, hundreds of years beforehand.

---

[2] Idumaeans were descended from Esau, the twin brother of Jacob. Jacob's family line produced the Israelites. Esau's family line produced the Edomites, the enemies of Jews throughout the Old Testament. That's why the Jews hated Herod. The enemy was in charge.

"Woe to the shepherds who are destroying and scattering the sheep of my pasture!" declares the LORD.
Therefore this is what the LORD, the God of Israel, says to the shepherds who tend my people: "Because you have scattered my flock and driven them away and have not bestowed care on them, I will bestow punishment on you for the evil you have done," declares the LORD.
"I myself will gather the remnant of my flock out of all the countries where I have driven them and will bring them back to their pasture, where they will be fruitful and increase in number.
I will place shepherds over them who will tend them, and they will no longer be afraid or terrified, nor will any be missing," declares the LORD.
"The days are coming," declares the LORD,
"when I will raise up to David a righteous Branch,
a King who will reign wisely
and do what is just and right in the land.
In his days Judah will be saved
and Israel will live in safety.
This is the name by which he will be called:
The LORD Our Righteousness. Jeremiah 23:1-6

These words from Jeremiah point the finger at a bad king and welcome a good king. It describes kings as shepherds, watching over their flocks, making sure they are well cared for. Just as a shepherd serves the sheep, so should a king serve his people.

Herod would never do such a thing. He only slaughtered his people.

I visited a real shepherd's field in Bethlehem, on a hillside in the center of the city. The shepherds, as I imagine they were in the first century, were hard-working, unkempt people, but very humble and sweet, with ragged and mismatched clothes and many missing teeth. They had to be the lowest class in town.

Surrounded by sheep who nibbled on the green plants sprouting from the mountain rocks and standing with real live Bethlehem shepherds on a hill overlooking this little town, I could feel the moment two thousand years ago.

Maybe it was the sights and smells. Maybe it was the expanse of the Bethlehem sky, the stage for that holy night when it was populated by the Angelic Men's Choir. Maybe it was the proximity of the Church of the Nativity, in clear walking distance from my location. Whatever it was, I felt like I was standing in the place where God invited his first guests to the birthday party of the newborn king.

And there were shepherds living out in the fields nearby, keeping watch over their flocks at night. An angel of the Lord appeared to them, and the glory of the Lord shone around them, and they were terrified.
But the angel said to them, "Do not be afraid. I bring you good news of great joy that will be for all the people. Today in the town of David a Savior has been born to you; he is Christ the Lord. This will be a sign to you: You will find a baby wrapped in cloths and lying in a manger."
Suddenly a great company of the heavenly host appeared with the angel, praising God and saying, "Glory to God in the highest, and on earth peace to men on whom his favor rests."
When the angels had left them and gone into heaven, the shepherds said to one another, "Let's go to Bethlehem and see this thing that has happened, which the Lord has told us about."
So they hurried off and found Mary and Joseph, and the baby, who was lying in the manger. When they had seen him, they spread the word concerning what had been told them about this child, and all who heard it were amazed at what the shepherds said to them. But Mary treasured up all these things and pondered them in her heart. The shepherds returned, glorifying and praising God for all the things they had heard and seen, which were just as they had been told.
Luke 2:8-20

I could imagine God lighting up the sky with a spectacular sound and special effects show, like a proud papa, proclaiming the arrival of his son into the world. The simple shepherds, who maybe saw a shooting star once a week, suddenly stood here, with mouths agape as God put on a private concert, just for them.

The shepherds normally found themselves overlooked, especially by royalty. Herod would pay them no mind. Pay your taxes and shut up. Not much has changed, I thought as I watched them direct wayward sheep, trying to escape the flock.

But God invited these shepherds to the birthday celebration of his son. Not only because Jesus came to shepherd simple, hard-working people like the shepherds, but to draw parallels between their profession and the reason of Jesus' arrival.

Shepherds and kings are very similar. Jeremiah 23 says all kings are shepherds. They must:

- Protect their people
- Gather and unite them
- Live righteously
- Live in unity, without fear

Jeremiah 23 also points to a "righteous branch" coming from the line of David, who came from the line of Judah and was also a shepherd. This unique king from David's seed will:

- Reign wisely
- Do what is right
- Bring salvation through the line of Judah
- Bring safety to Israel
- Be called righteous

The parallels with shepherds did not stop there. David was instrumental in getting the temple built, where the sacrifices of lambs would occur. Many suspect that these Bethlehem shepherds raised sheep used for sacrifices at the temple, since they were so close to Jerusalem. If so, it seems fitting that these shepherds were notified first. Maybe to warn them that their job would soon be outsourced to the ultimate, perfect lamb.

John the Baptist would proclaim thirty or so years later that a lamb of God had come to take away the sins of the world.

Shepherd imagery filled this moment. These guys were more important than they thought.

But the birthday announcement for the newborn king didn't stop here.

At eight days of age, according to Jewish custom, Mary and Joseph walked over to Jerusalem and made sure Jesus was circumcised. A purification offering was given one month later. While there, people began talking and proclaiming Jesus as Savior. Simeon, an old man about to die, and Anna, an elderly widow, both praised God for a glimpse of the promised King.

The elderly and widowed were not the concern of Herod the King either. He concerned himself with architecture and longevity, not dying old men and barren widows. Once again, we see a clash of the kingdoms.

Next on the birth announcement list, wise men. These astronomers from the eastern land of Iraq or Iran, once known as Persia, came by to see the one prophesied in Micah 5:2. They had been reading the scriptures of a coming king, spotted a gigantic star in the sky one day and didn't want to miss the event.

They packed up their things, gathered birthday presents and made a huge trek hundreds of miles from home.

Max Lucado
The angels know something is up and they cannot help but have a party with these common shepherds. And who else shows up at the celebration but the wise men who somehow perceive what's happening by reading the stars. They have more faith than the religious leaders 10 miles away in the city of Jerusalem who, because of the wise men's questions, go back and reread the prophecies and yet they don't think it's worth connecting the dots to even travel to Bethlehem, the 10 miles, just to see if this happens to be someone worth checking out. And so it's full of ironies that the Persian star gazers or wherever they came from, they came from so far, travelled such distance on such a tiny shred of evidence. And those who were closest, who had prophesies and scripture didn't take the journey. So, it's full of ironies, messages and powerful teachings. It's just the most dramatic entrance. No one could have scripted this kind of entrance.

Herod didn't like what he heard from these wise men.

No future king could interrupt his current reign. Herod still had things to do, mansions to build. People to oppress.

Here were a number of intelligent foreigners bearing gifts of great value, showing up in his kingdom with presents for some other king.

Standing at this location, I couldn't help but notice how close the Church of the Nativity sat to Herod's opulent home, the Herodium. It was a huge monolith, impressive to the eye, that dwarfed the town of Bethlehem, undoubtedly making the residents feel insecure, oppressed and scrutinized.

The Herodium was built in 20 BC and acted not only as a fortress, but a home and retreat for King Herod. Many of the sites I've seen in Israel were places of worship. I wondered if that was the intention of this place too. Was this a place to worship King Herod?

Archaeologists like Avner live for finds like the Herodium and its cousin in the south, Masada. Walking through both of Herod's homes filled me with awe and sadness. So much time and effort that has turned to dust.

Avner captured that theme perfectly in his description. "Herodium was a fortress in the middle of nothing. He built an artificial mountain that was topped by a wonderful fortress. Below that was a huge area of palaces and towns, administration center, garden, a huge pool full of water in the middle of the desert."

I hung on Avner's words… "Nothing…artificial…desert…."

"What made Herod so great?" I wondered.

"Herod was a great builder. A massive architect. He was great in terms of taking a very small place and making it an important entity in the world at the time. He was the greatest of the builders of that time."

I thought back to that stinky barn I visited earlier. Herod would never step foot in such a "common" place. His kingly feet only touched marble.

Herod erected monuments to himself all over the region. He had extensive renovations done to the Temple, building it up so he could gain the approval of the people. Greatness, for Herod, came through rocks, stone and architecture.

Jesus had no monuments made in his honor. His temple was his body, which He promised to tear down and build back up in three days. Herod concerned himself with the physical, his efforts torn down or disintegrated over time. Jesus focused on the spiritual, salvation and eternal life, things which can't be destroyed by human hands.

Why was Jesus born so close to the "greatest" king in the region?

Norman Geisler

I think God is saying that He wants to get the glory. He wants to get the credit. He wants to show the humility of His Son born on humble ground. He wants to show He's truly human, He's truly ordinary, He's truly normal and there's nothing ostentatious or showy about this whole thing.

Jesus came proclaiming the kingdom of God—one that welcomed all people, one that promised provision and a life free from worry. Most of all, Jesus offered all those who believed a place in his heavenly kingdom, awaiting believers on the other side of death.

Herod could never promise any such thing.

Jesus' earliest years, maybe his earliest recollection, was of Bethlehem and maybe of Herod's opulent palace that sat high up in the sky. What a shame, even a small child would think, that a man as sinful and as corrupt as Herod could ever call himself "great."

Norman Geisler

Herod was wicked and Jesus was sinless. Herod ruled by human power, Jesus ruled by divine power. Herod ruled the way the others of this world do and that is through the use of the sword, Jesus ruled by changing people's hearts. I mean, you couldn't get two more opposite kings.

In an attempt to block the new king, Herod, true to form, and paranoid too, ordered all babies two years old and younger to be killed on the spot, thanks to the information offered by the wise men. Joseph, warned in a dream, packed up the family and left town, the sound of babies crying and women screaming behind them.

Herod did not care about the shepherds, the elderly, the families of men, women and children. They only stood in his way toward greatness.

Jesus did care and built his kingdom, without walls or boundaries, on the foundation of love and became the greatest figure in all of history.

One thing you notice in Jerusalem today is that everything is political. The tension always looms around the West Bank and Gaza strip, barricaded by huge walls and checkpoints. Everyone has an opinion about the political situation and feels very strongly about it. They are happy to let you know their opinion.

Driving through the checkpoint to get into Bethlehem, we passed a painting, or maybe political graffiti, depicting a dove of peace wearing a flak jacket, with crosshairs pointed at its heart. Peace...ha...it seems to say.

Underneath the Church of the Nativity, Dr. Qustandi Shumali, a Professor of Arabic at Bethlehem University and a Palestinian, took me on a tour of a small room, called the Chapel of the Innocents, then to a series of tombs behind steel bars. In those tombs he showed me stacks and piles of bones.

"The monks here believe these (bones) belong to the children killed by Herod. They were unearthed during the building of the church." Dr. Shumali spoke in such hushed tones about the massacre of the innocents, out of profound reverence, in such a sacred place.

While there is very little proof of their authenticity, since the monks won't allow them to be examined, the sight was staggering. Tiny femurs and small arm bones scattered about like some morbid game of pick-up-sticks. Skulls stacked one on top of another. Whether they were the bones of young boys two and under who were killed by Herod's horrendous political positioning, it didn't matter. They represented a cold, evil act and laid it out for your eyes to see and imagine.

"What do you think when you see this," I asked.

Dr. Shumali did not hesitate to make his point. "These bones represent the brutality going on all around us. As Palestinians, we are being oppressed by an enemy. Our children are being killed too. We live under the domination of Herod, even today. These bones are a political statement."

"So I guess politics and religion will always be mixed in this area."

"Always."

Herod's politicking never left Israel.

Jesus was born into a hotbed of political domination and a deadly dictatorship. He spoke to people in spiritual terms. They wanted him to speak in political terms. Jesus spoke of a heavenly kingdom, but the people thought he meant an earthly kingdom. For his whole life, whether before the Roman army or the Jewish Sanhedrin, Jesus faced political and religious tension.

Not much has changed two thousand years later.

Political kings, though, rise and fall, then fade into dust.

Only one king reigns forever.

Joel Hunter

The difference between the kingship of Jesus and the kingship of Herod was night and day. Herod was paranoid; he was what we call hard power. It was a kingship by coercion, by force, by money. He wanted all of the adulation the world had to offer. Jesus on the other hand had a kingship of servant hood. It wasn't at all coercive. It's what we call soft power. It was a kingship of influence, of example. It was a kingship to lift others up, not to elevate oneself. Herod was always paranoid that someone would have more power and Jesus was always concerned that people get more power.

TIME TO JOURNEY

1. **Watch "King" from "In His Shoes: The Life of Christ"**

2. **Discussion Questions**

- What was going on in the world when you were born?

- How did the political climate effect your childhood?

- As a kid, who did you invite to your birthday parties?

- Are any of those parties memorable?

- Why did God invite shepherds to the birthday party?

- Why did God invite angels to the birthday party? Why so many?

- Describe the mood of the angels.

- Why were Simeon and Anna invited to the birthday party?

- Why were the Wise Men invited to the birthday party?

- What do you think of Jesus being born so close to the ruling king of the area?

- What makes someone "great"? What makes a leader "great"?

- If Herod accepted this new king, would he have lost his greatness?

- Do you think it's fair that so many children died for Jesus to live?

- What do those bones in the Church of the Nativity say to you about sacrifice?

- Why do people reject a new king in their life?

Escape
Bethlehem/Egypt

Growing up as a skinny young string bean, I have to admit, I got picked on a lot. I stood at least a head and shoulder over everyone else in my grade, but I weighed as much as a #2 pencil. So the other kids, struggling with their own feelings of inadequacy, decided to push me around, throw things at me or tease me to make themselves feel superior.

It was the least I could do.

It's normal human behavior: find the biggest target, take it down and crown yourself a giant killer. It worked for David, why not the kids at the bus stop on Cherry Blossom Road?

Every time someone picked on me, I remember the great debate – do I stay and fight or do I run for my life? If you stay and get knocked out, you're a loser. If you run, you're a chicken. I usually stayed and did my best to use humor to disarm the situation.

The kids would punch me, but at least they were laughing as I went down, so it wasn't a complete waste of effort.

In every conflict there is the question of fight or flight? Jesus' family faced that impasse.

King Herod just ordered the death of every newborn male child between the ages of 0-2. His army marched through Bethlehem stripping crying babies from the arms of wailing mothers, then spearing the children in their fragile chest or smashing them to the ground.[3]

So what could a poor carpenter, his wife and newborn child do? Go up against King Herod and his armies? Joseph was no Chuck Norris and Mary far from an Angelina Jolie. They had no self-defense tactics or karate skills. They needed to run.

If you think about it, they were carrying the most powerful weapon in their arms. The newborn child was Jesus Christ, who spoke the world into existence and could speak Herod's armies out of existence. But at such an early age, Jesus could not speak. Maybe he uttered the Jewish words for "mama" or "milk" or maybe even "dada," as a tribute to his earthly father.

Certainly not the words "King Herod, I banish you and your armies to hell!" That's a mouthful, especially for a toddler.

---

[3] Since Bethlehem was such a small town, experts that I talked to believed the number of babies between 0-2 in the town probably numbered around 70-100. While still tragic, it's hardly a massacre in the thousands.

Jesus had not come into his own power and cognizance yet, so all Joseph and Mary could do to save Jesus from death was to escape. An angel of God came to Joseph and told him to go to Egypt and to stay there until further instructions were given. Joseph complied and that action saved the savior of the world.

Joseph made the right decision. We have to thank Joseph for running away and saving the life of the one would save the lives of millions to come.

Coming to Egypt had its symbolism. God led Abraham to Egypt for protection from a famine, then led Jacob's family there through another Joseph's captivity, slavery and rise to power. Then God safely led the Israelites out of Egypt through Moses.

Now Jesus, just like his Old Testament counterparts, came to Egypt from Israel for safety.

This is what God wanted to happen. In fact, it was prophesied in Hosea 11:1.

**"When Israel was a child, I loved him,
    and out of Egypt I called my son." Hosea 11:1**

Maybe this action was not so much an escape *from* something, but an escape *to* something. God clearly wanted Jesus and his family in Egypt. It was no Plan B.

So maybe there was something Jesus could learn in this country or maybe God could connect the dots between the Old Testament and the New, proving that Jesus was his son.

Jesus spent his early formative years in Egypt, possibly from the age of two to maybe six or seven...the Bible isn't really clear. It says in Luke 2:19 that they stayed in Egypt until Herod's death, which history tells us happened in 4 B.C.

Egypt was not an unusual, isolated place for a Jew to go. Egypt was a multi-cultural crossroads for trade, much like New York City is today. Plus, the Jews felt an Old Testament kinship to Egypt. Their historical roots and dramatic flight from Egypt fueled their passion for God, his temple and the laws they now lived by.

Colonies of Jews lived there in the first century, a result of previous Assyrian and Babylonian invasions into Israel, causing Jews to scatter to Egypt for one thing - safety. Their historical roots and dramatic escapes to and from Egypt always connected them to this ancient land.

God seemed to be saying through Jesus' flight to Egypt, "I am still a God of the Old and the New Testament. I am a God of the Jews in Israel and afar. I am a God who is willing to travel to other nations." These "scattered" Jews were not left out or forgotten by God. Jesus affirmed his Old Testament ties and his connection with nations outside the border of Israel.

So later, when he tells his disciples to go to all the nations, Jesus could at least say he'd been to one.

Joel Hunter

I think the trip to Egypt set at a very early stage in His life that He would operate beyond the Jewish culture. That He would not just be the Messiah for the Jews only. I think that this was both symptomatic of what was to come and it was symbolic of His Lordship for all cultures, in all countries. And so I do think that God's course in taking Him to Egypt, God's sovereign travel, so to speak, was preparing Him for a much broader view of the world than if He had simply been raised in one small town in His home country.

Max Lucado

It was just one of the many things how Jesus had this tendency to cross borders and speak to the Samaritan woman. How he included people from Cana in his teaching how he didn't turn away the woman from Cana who came with a prayer request. You begin to stack all of these up and the picture of a Messiah for the world is presented. So I think even the early escape into Egyptian captivity is one of God's ways of posturing Christ to be a messenger to people all over the world. I think it also postures and presents Christ as he understands what it is like to be a victim, to be caught in a political system that is cruel and harsh and, boy, people in third world countries need to hear that.

During his ministry years, Jesus drew parallels between himself and Moses, at the Sermon on the Mount and the Transfiguration. Coming to Egypt positioned Jesus as a new shepherd, leader and law giver…a new Moses.

Passover originated in Egypt. Every Passover celebration the Jews rehearsed and remembered God's miraculous Egyptian intervention.

41

It even pointed to the coming Messiah, as seen in Exodus 12.

The LORD said to Moses and Aaron in Egypt, "This month is to be for you the first month, the first month of your year. Tell the whole community of Israel that on the tenth day of this month each man is to take a lamb for his family, one for each household. If any household is too small for a whole lamb, they must share one with their nearest neighbor, having taken into account the number of people there are. You are to determine the amount of lamb needed in accordance with what each person will eat. The animals you choose must be year-old males without defect, and you may take them from the sheep or the goats. Take care of them until the fourteenth day of the month, when all the people of the community of Israel must slaughter them at twilight. Then they are to take some of the blood and put it on the sides and tops of the doorframes of the houses where they eat the lambs. That same night they are to eat the meat roasted over the fire, along with bitter herbs, and bread made without yeast. Do not eat the meat raw or cooked in water, but roast it over the fire—head, legs and inner parts. Do not leave any of it till morning; if some is left till morning, you must burn it. This is how you are to eat it: with your cloak tucked into your belt, your sandals on your feet and your staff in your hand. Eat it in haste; it is the LORD's Passover.

"On that same night I will pass through Egypt and strike down every firstborn—both men and animals—and I will bring judgment on all the gods of Egypt. I am the LORD. The blood will be a sign for you on the houses where you are; and when I see the blood, I will pass over you. No destructive plague will touch you when I strike Egypt. Exodus 12:1-13

The parallels are amazingly clear:

- Just like Passover marked the beginning of the New Year, the arrival of Jesus marked the beginning of a new era (A.D.). Jesus changed time and his place in history became the preeminent marker on our calendars.
- Just like the blood of the lamb protected the home from death, Jesus is the Lamb of God that takes away the sin of the world, protecting believers from an eternal death, separated from God.
- Like the unblemished, male lamb, Jesus came as a human man without sin.
- Both Jesus and the Passover lamb had to die and spill their blood.
- God will bring judgment to all people who do not believe in God's provision. Both the lamb's death and Jesus' death covered the believer's life and kept them from death.

Jesus fulfilled the Passover qualifications and, by coming to Egypt, he identified with God's Old Testament plan.

God could have been making another significant statement by bringing Jesus here. The pyramids.

The pyramids take your breath away. On a visit to Egypt, I remember seeing the pyramids in the distance and thinking, "They're not as big as I thought," until I walked to their base. They're huge, especially the pyramids of Giza.

I asked Avner Goren, former Chief archaeologist of Egyptian Antiquities what significance the pyramids played during that time. Egypt was very much Avner's second homeland and talking about, I could tell, brought back fond memories. He spoke of Egypt with the familiarity of the Temple in downtown Jerusalem.

"Pyramids signify the huge power of Egypt and how centralized it was. The Pharaoh was considered to be a deity who would take all of his hundreds of thousands of people and to put them into work to build something that would serve as a tomb to himself. So he was the only one who had connections with the deities of the gods and through all that the gods sent to humanity, in their eyes, came. No proper person had access to God. Only Pharaoh."

"Did they believe they would be resurrected?"

"Not technically. They believed they could travel between this world and the other. The afterlife was a continuity of the life on earth. Whoever moved to the afterlife still needed to dress, food to eat, games to play with and so on. And we know that looking at the tomb of Tutankhamun with all the things he possessed in life, including his toys as a kid."

"So the pyramids are just storage units for their stuff?"

"The pyramid was a storage unit first of all for the body so this spirit could come back to the body and to all the necessities, all the goods over there."

Norman Geisler
Well I think the contrast between Pharaoh and Jesus is incredibly opposed. Pharaoh was trying to build big monuments to leave in memory of him. Jesus left no monuments behind whatsoever. Pharaoh was trying to make himself of a great reputation. Philippians chapter 2 says, 'Jesus made Himself of no reputation whatsoever.' He didn't leave anything behind. He wasn't there to make a reputation. He wasn't there to announce that He was a king, that was done later by John the Baptist. These two are totally opposed.

The magnitude of the pyramid's architecture speak of the time and human effort and earthly resources needed to construct them. No Pharaohs have yet shown up to collect their stuff. The museums around Egypt display piles of unclaimed items. The Pharaohs are still quite dead, mummified and on display.

What would have gone through Jesus' mind if he saw these tombs all over the Egyptian landscape?

Joel Hunter
I think it was sad for Him to look upon this preparation for death and all of these efforts and all of the gold that was stored and all of the food and all of the preparation to go into the next world. Servants and everything. And then later on Jesus would say, "Don't store up treasures on earth, store up treasures in heaven". To know that you couldn't take any of that because rust sets in and moth. And so all of it was ultimately degraded and that had to inform later on His understanding of what was really valuable, what you really could take into the next world. And it wasn't any of the stuff in the pyramids.

44

The Egyptians had monuments of death. And death was very much a preoccupation of the Egyptian culture, especially of the kings of the culture. And preparation for death was very much on the mind of those kings that built those pyramids. And so Jesus would have been thinking, "look at these monuments; look at all of the effort and all of the riches it took to be buried". And growing up with this living God, this history of a God who was a God of life, a God of history and a God who was one, who called all of us to something beyond what was simply a human life, that would hope for something beyond death. I think that had to have an effect on the mind of Jesus and certainly the mind of His family. Why this great spectacular monument that would enshrine literally death and hope for the life beyond? And I think it may have peaked His interest at that age about facing the monumental specter of death and how, what a big deal that is to those that can afford to think of it.

One day, Jesus would find himself in a tomb, but for him, it would be only temporary. A mere three day stop on the way to eternity.

God drew distinct parallels and bridged the gap between the Old and New Testament by bringing the Messiah to Egypt, uniting both testaments in the one life of Jesus Christ.

Finally, the Egyptians were considered to be Pagans and Gentiles, ostracized by serious Jews. Jesus, for a short time, lived among them, showing his heart to reach out to those outside the Hebrew system.

In the land of false gods came the one true God. Nobody paid him any attention nor did anyone erect a pyramid in his name. But Jesus does not ask us for monuments, only our hearts and it is there that he wants to make his eternal home.

Joel Hunter
I think the family stories of His flight to Egypt left an imprint...His family knew what it was like to be an immigrant family. His family knew what it was like to have fear and to have the potential of being discovered and living in danger. His family knew what it was like to live in a culture that was not their own. And so, therefore, they had to form relationships with people who were very different, had a different culture, different values, different language. But yet, they adapted for the safety of their son. And the other thing that really fascinates me about this trip is how absolutely, utterly dependent on God they must have been. Joseph was a hard worker, everybody knew that, and so he

had to make a living in a strange culture. But even so, how much more faith, how much more dependence on God would you have to have when you weren't around family, when you weren't around your own culture, and so I think that He learned a lot about how to relate to outsiders and how to consider outsiders as part of your dependency network when He heard those stories of how He was raised in the early years.

TIME TO JOURNEY

1. **Watch "Escape" from "In His Shoes: The Life of Christ"**

2. **Discussion Questions**

- As a kid, what were your earliest memories? What landmarks do you remembering visiting?

- As a kid, were you ever in a fist fight? Who started it?

- Did you ever have to run from a fight?

- Do cowards always run from a fight?

- What options could Joseph have chosen in this situation up against Herod?

- What would happen if this were an action movie?

- What would you do if your family was threatened?

- Why would God send Jesus to Egypt of all places?

- Why did God send people to Egypt in the Old Testament?

- What comparisons can you see between Moses and Jesus?

- Have you ever seen the pyramids? What was your impression of them?

- Why did the Pharaohs build pyramids?

- Do you have a storage unit? What do you have in it? What does it say about you?

- If you knew you were coming back to life, what item would you want with you?

- As you think about leaving all your stuff behind one day, do you get sad or excited?

- As you leave this earth one day, what will you be escaping from and running to?

Home
Nazareth

I was born in Cleveland, Ohio. Many from Cleveland understand the look that they get from outsiders who hear what city they're from. "Cleveland!" It's as if Cleveland is the punchline to some silent joke that everyone's been telling.

Cleveland's a great town. Drew Carrey's from there. So are the Indians and Browns. It's the birthplace of rock n' roll. Give Cleveland a break.

Other towns suffer the same sarcasm—Toledo, Peoria, Barstow, Buffalo, Newark, or really any city in Jersey. Everyone has preconceived notions of the quality of living and the type of people who live there.

Frankly, I didn't have much choice in being born in Cleveland. It's where my parents chose to live and where I found myself emerging. Later, at the age of three, when we moved to Philadelphia, my status increased. Philly is a cooler town, or so people think.

Jesus knows about towns like Cleveland. He grew up in Nazareth, the Cleveland of Israel.

After Jesus started his public ministry, word got out about this carpenter's son from Nazareth. Nathanael, one of Jesus' apostles, made this comment after his introduction to Jesus by Philip.

"Nazareth!" exclaimed Nathanael. "Can anything good come from there?" John 1:42

Cue rim shot.

I asked Avner how others would perceive Nazareth and why it carried such a reputation.

"Well Nazareth in the first century was a rural village, not very sophisticated, maybe, of hard workers. Those tough, rugged mountains around made life quite hard. I don't know how much people would really pay attention to Nazareth then. It didn't have a special importance."

Driving into Nazareth, you immediately recognize that you are going uphill, along tight, winding roads filled with traffic. It's not easy to get to Nazareth.

Nazareth was a place of isolation then and now. The mountains provided protection. Jesus would be safe here from outside influences

49

and marauding armies. Off the beaten path, nobody passed through Nazareth. Young Jesus could incubate slowly and quietly away from all the chaos of the world, in a location few ever visited.

This is precisely the kind of town where God wanted his son for the next twenty plus years.

After Herod died, an angel of the Lord appeared in a dream to Joseph in Egypt and said, "Get up, take the child and his mother and go to the land of Israel, for those who were trying to take the child's life are dead." So he got up, took the child and his mother and went to the land of Israel.
But when he heard that Archelaus was reigning in Judea in place of his father Herod, he was afraid to go there. Having been warned in a dream, he withdrew to the district of Galilee, and he went and lived in a town called Nazareth. So was fulfilled what was said through the prophets: "He will be called a Nazarene." Matthew 2:19-23

God established an incredible line-up of qualifications for the Messiah so everyone could spot him.

1. He would come from the line of David.
2. He would come from the line of Judah.
3. He would be born in Bethlehem.
4. He would live in Egypt.
5. He would be called a Nazarene.

The move to Nazareth completed another prophecy of Jesus' origin and birth. God orchestrated genealogies, travel plans and birthplaces so no one could say a person manipulated the events to qualify himself as Messiah. What child can determine his bloodline and force his parents to move to three different cities?

So early in his young life, Jesus had already moved around so much – born in Bethlehem, hidden in Egypt and relocated to Nazareth. Finally, his family could settle down.

Returning to Nazareth ended a long, disruptive run for Joseph, Mary and Jesus. They finally set up their home, accumulated belongings, established friendships, reconnected with family, built a business and started their normal life.

During this time, Jesus had to overcome any leftover stigma attached to his teenage mother's suspicious pregnancy. People don't forget such things, especially in small towns, but Joseph and Mary bravely faced any opposition head on. Their lives spoke of their sincerity and righteousness.

Maybe the locals worried about them disappearing so long and greeted them warmly, happy they were still alive, putting aside the past. Either way, they returned to some degree of "normalcy," back home, moving into a permanent house with a permanent address. Finally.

So what happened during those twenty or so years in Jesus' life after he returned to Nazareth? The Bible gives only one clue.

And Jesus grew in wisdom and stature, and in favor with God and men. Luke 2:52

This verse says very little, but then again it says a lot. Jesus simply grew up. He did not enter the world with a 30 year old mind, with all the thoughts of God on his brain. He didn't learn to talk at two months old, speaking complete sentences. He didn't walk around all pious at the age of five and refused to engage in any activities for fear of corruption. Nothing extraordinary was mentioned in any Gospel.

Jesus pursued a normal life. What would that normal life look like for Jesus, a boy in the first century?

First of all, the verse says, Jesus grew in wisdom.

Like any person born on this earth, Jesus began life as a blank slate. Over time, through teaching and the retention of information, his mind filled with facts, figures and truths.

Joel Hunter

I think His growth in wisdom and stature was both linear. But, I think there was a dawning, the dawning of insights periodically. You know there's a phrase used in biology called "punctuated equilibrium". And it means that you don't just grow learning more and more each day. You don't just grow by accumulation. There are huge spurts of growth. And anybody who's raised kids knows that there are times when you think, "Is this kid ever going to learn anything?" And the next day they walk in and you go, "Where did that come from?" I think He had a normal life, as much as is possible for the son of God. But, I do think He had insights that were from the Holy Spirit. And I think that there was a special closeness and a special bond there that informed His growth and shaped His growth that was not completely normal.

Norman Geisler:
I think Jesus had a growing realization. Obviously when He was one years old He had no human consciousness that He was the son of God. In fact, you don't even have self-consciousness until you get to be one and a half to two years of age. So Jesus in His human nature grew in consciousness of who He was and I think that consciousness continued to grow and I think He even continued to learn because it says in Hebrews, ' He learned through the things He suffered.' So you can't deny that there was a growing consciousness but never did He doubt, never was He uncertain of who He was it was just a greater realization of who He was and all the implications of it that He experienced.

I find it difficult to imagine Jesus going to school, studying for his education, both academically and religiously. Jesus learned to read and write in both Hebrew and Greek. Think of it – the God of all languages and races learning to enunciate with this slowly developing mouth and tongue.

I'm sure his retention of information and his understanding of all things eternal blossomed, but I wonder if he was a math genius or a geography wizard or the spelling bee champ at the age of six years old.

Norman Geisler
Jesus is totally human. And I think one of the things we neglect as evangelicals is His human side. We know He is God and He claimed to be God and He proved to be God. But He also is human, He had a human birth. He had a superhuman conception but He had a human birth, a nine month pregnancy. He was dedicated like anyone else, circumcised like any other Jewish boy of the day. His mother and father taught Him at home. Taught Him the scriptures. They took Him to the synagogue, it says, 'as His custom was', in Luke 2. He went to Sabbath school as it were. He learned the way any other human being would learn. He didn't come as a human being with all the knowledge of scripture already memorized in a photographic memory. He had to learn scripture. He had to memorize scripture. He had to do what any other human being would do to learn.

Including the Bible. Jesus was not born with the entire Old Testament pre-loaded into his brain. He had to learn it like everyone else. But Jesus must have found an intense interest and passion for the word of God. It rang true to him, drew him closer, made him feel at home, peaceful, content, connected.

As time went on, Jesus discovered why.

Like any son, Jesus would adopt the skills of his father, who pulled Jesus into the shop or on the job to watch him work. It was easiest to take on your father's job, with all the tools and clients were readily available, than to start your own company, with new overhead and resources needed.

If you really want a sense of first century living, you have to visit Nazareth Village located in Jesus' hometown. Nazareth Village recreates the buildings, farmlands and local community a first century Nazarene would understand. If you can ignore the high rise buildings and cell phone towers on the horizon, you can get a pretty good sense of life in that time.

Locals dress as first century people, acting as background and giving the area a living component. They weave, prepare food, press olives and stomp grapes just like Jesus experienced.

If you watched any documentaries on Jesus, you know Nazareth Village. It's the backdrop for every History Channel, Discovery Channel, NOVA special I have ever seen. So naturally I needed to go there too.

Backstage you see the people are very much twentieth century people, smoking cigarettes and flirting with each other. It's kind of like of the feeling you get when you go backstage and Disney World and see Snow White cussing up a storm.

But the presentation they put on is the best you can find to get a feel of the first century.

I was especially impressed by the carpentry shop, the realism of the setting and the crudeness of the tools, a couple steps up from stone-age.

Carpenters of that day were more like handymen, with skills in all areas—masonry, construction and wood. Like any good son, Jesus adopted the trade of his father, picking up odd jobs around the neighborhood and house.

Here was Jesus, the builder of the earth, building a simple table. Here was Jesus, the lamb of God, designing a door frame, where Jews spread the blood of the Passover lamb once a year in remembrance of God saving them from death.

If the neighbor only knew who wielded that hammer.

Carpenters are creative types, problem solvers, who look at a stone or a block of wood and figure out where it fits. They see something broken and find a way to fix it.

They build up and make sure things run optimally.

Carpentry is the perfect metaphor for Jesus. God takes broken lives and fixes them. God will make a way, when there seems to be no way. He's an architect, a creator, a fixer. As the creator of the universe, Jesus made the Milky Way galaxy so a simple end table shouldn't be a problem. "Next Wednesday?"

Joel Hunter

First of all, He was educated both in the Torah and vocationally at the same time and you would see both of them later in His teachings. He was educated as every Jewish boy was, to know the history and the prophesies and the sayings of Judaism. And so yes, He was very much educated by both His parents and the local religious leaders to understand what it is to be a Jew.

At the same time He was being educated in His father's workshop. He was being educated as a poor craftsman...And He knew what the precision was like that had to be taken by a carpenter. When He said for example, "Who builds a tower without first sitting down and considering what it will require?" You know, all of that training came back to Him when He was presenting His teachings later on in life.

Now the third component of this was where He was spiritually. He must have heard all of the stories by this time. The stories of His birth. The stories of His exile into Egypt, "Why would we have to go into Egypt? Well, because they were after you, because they thought that you were a king and they were killing, you know and so on and so forth". And so He's hearing all of these stories. He's putting all of them together. He's spending time with His father. He's getting these insights that will later amaze the people at the temple and He's twelve years old. And so, yeah, He had education from the Jewish teachers, from His father vocationally and directly from the Holy Spirit.

Secondly, the passage in Luke says Jesus grew in stature. This speaks of Jesus' normal human maturation from boy to man.

54

Puberty is probably the most awkward time for us humans. During this change, we find ourselves at a crossroads, trying to figure out our path in life, what direction we are going.

Since Jesus had a normal human body, the body of a boy, that means he had to go through puberty, that conflicted time of hormonal awakening when a young man realizes his sexuality. For many guys, this is a troubling period of temptation and sexual struggle.

Not for Jesus. Since he was sinless, he managed those signals his body sent out with relative ease. His body did not dominate his thoughts and emotions. He dominated his body.

Joel Hunter

I do believe that Jesus had normal sexual temptations because I think to identify with all of us that would have been necessary. To walk in the flesh as we do. The Bible says He was tempted in every way as we are yet didn't sin. Whether or not He as a celibate went through His life longing to be married or He settled that early on and just never went there, you know. Discipline in His mind or it was a gift from God so that He could concentrate on His ministry? I don't know. But I do know that growing up with a physical body you face normal temptations of every sort and He had to go through it just like we do.

Max Lucado

I know he was thirsty because He drank. I know He was tired because during a storm He took a nap. I don't feel like were demeaning Jesus on earth to say that He felt everything that we feel in being a human being. I really don't. I think that's the reason He became flesh. And that figures into this discussion of Jesus as an adolescent. Did He have pimples? Did He watch His body mature? Did He go through growth spurts? Did He look twice at young ladies? Was He puzzled by the way His body reacted? Yes. I think everything I have felt He felt. I think He faced it with more courage. And He did lead a sinless life. You know sin is not the presence of a temptation. Sin is the caving in to a temptation. And so He felt everything that an adolescent boy feels. He didn't respond the way adolescent boys did. Which then begs that earlier question, how did He not, what did He know, and what did He have? But yeah, otherwise the word did not become flesh.

55

Jesus had no difficulty with puberty since at a very early age, twelve to be exact, Jesus in the temple announced clearly his relationship with God, his Father. These realizations protected him from the awkward floundering that occurs during the ages of 12 to 18.

Jesus spent these teenage years focused on his mission and waiting for his ultimate calling.

Third, Luke 2 says He grew in relationship with man, developing friendships and playing with other kids.

His relationship with his own family grew. I wondered what Jesus' family life was like. What were the conversations around the dinner table? Were they like most families? What they did today…who they saw at the well…who they talked to on the road…problems they faced with a stubborn goat…something funny that happened on the way to the synagogue…

And how did Jesus respond to their conversations? Did he listen to the needs of his brothers and sisters[4] with compassion and interest or was he the kind of guy who constantly sermonized?

> *"Let me tell you what I would do…"*
> *"You know in my experience…"*
> *"I remember Moses faced a problem like that…"*

Did Joseph and Mary really keep all of Jesus' secrets deeply in their hearts, never divulging them to others? Even family? I can hardly contain myself when my kid gets on the honor roll or wins a track meet. Imagine what Mary felt!

> *Proud mother: "My son Caleb got to read the Torah at school today."*
> *Mary: "My son wrote the Torah."*

I imagine their family dynamics were pretty normal, yet this was not a normal family. You thought soap opera families harbored secrets. Nothing like The Josephs.

The neighbors certainly would have thought them crazy if they announced that their son was the Messiah. Joseph and Mary probably

---

[4] Matthew 12, Mark 3, Luke 8, John 2 all indicate that Jesus had brothers and sisters. Some faiths believe these were cousins, but "siblings" and "cousins" are two different Greek words.

thought themselves crazy at times for even believing such a notion. God had moved into their house!

Sibling rivalry occurs in any family, but who in Jesus' house would compare to him? He had to be smarter, a better carpenter, more knowledgeable of spiritual affairs, kinder, nicer, happier than anyone else in his family.

Did Mary or Joseph say his brothers and sisters over and over again: "Why couldn't you be more like Jesus?" Ouch. That would be unfair.

Face it. Jesus was the ideal son. He understood the concepts of parental obedience because of his Trinitarian relationship. He obeyed his Father in heaven, so he was prepared to obey his father on earth. Besides, honoring mother and father are number five on the list of Ten Commandments. Jesus respected his mother and father even though he was God.

Growing up in Nazareth, I imagine a young Jesus running through the streets with friends, climbing rocks and chasing goats. Certainly he didn't sit in the temple all day and read scrolls. Jesus loved relationships and had to make lots of friends. He was probably the most popular kid in school, always smiling, always encouraging the others.

Paul Young

I think He developed like a regular boy in terms of growing in wisdom and stature. For me He grows like a boy and He goes through the questions and He goes through the relationship issues that happen with family and all of these things. And He does it as a human being except without sin, without this self-centered independence.

Where do we think laughter came from? Where do we think fun came from? Do we think that it kind of showed up after everybody messed the world up, you know, and it's part of what the fall is? No, I don't think so at all. I think fun and laughter and those elements of relationship that are so deep and so beautiful and so wonderful they exist within Father, Son and Holy Spirit before the incarnation. And they're exhibited in us.

And so I don't see Him becoming a 'holy man' who needs an ascetic kind of existence in order to portray the severity and holiness of God. I think He loves life and He loves everything about it. I see a total exuberance in His experience. I would see people that would look at Jesus as a boy

57

growing up and they would say, 'I don't know what it is about Him but there is something that is so alive about that boy. I wish you kids could be like Jesus.' You know, I could see that kind of conversation happening. He's so respectful and yet He's so fun. You know, I just see Him as an embracing of life because life is a manifestation of what God has created and His Father, He's going to see His Father everywhere. He's collecting the stories that He's going to be telling down the road.

Thinking of Jesus' kindness, exuberance for living, wisdom, his helpfulness around town, willingness to serve others, that warm smile and concern for other's wellbeing, you would have to think that Jesus attracted some attention from the opposite sex.

There were certain expectations of a young Jewish man. Avner agreed with this point. "Getting married in the first century was almost a must. It would be unusual for man not to be married."

Nazareth had to be where, as a young adult, neighborhood girls checked Jesus out, finding him quite desirable for marriage. I imagine friends dropped hints to Jesus about marriage proposals, all of them he denied, but emphasizing what a good friend they were and what a wonderful wife they would make for someone, some day.

Did Jesus break hearts?

Norman Geisler
Well, we know He was tempted in all points like as we are but apart from sin. But you also have to remember Isaiah chapter 53 says, 'He was a man of sorrow and acquainted with grief.' Then I think He was pretty sober. He was pretty goal directed. He set His face as a flint to Jerusalem. And I don't think Jesus had what we would call 'sex appeal' today. I think that girls are attracted to guys who are putting out the flag saying, 'Hey, I am here.' I don't think Jesus would put out the flag saying, 'I am here.' So no, I don't think they mobbed Him and I think because of His demeanor, because of His sobriety, because of the seriousness of His mission, He didn't intentionally try to attract any.

Wouldn't Mary, a good Jewish mother, turn to this twenty year old still living at home and say "When are you going to give me some grandchildren?"

Norman Geisler

You have to remember in Jesus' case that Mary knew who He was. She knew that He was virgin born. She knew He was the Messiah and so Mary is going to be conscious of His mission, conscious of who He was and she's not going to be putting any pressure on Him to move Him in another direction.

Jesus knew his heavenly purpose and an earthly marriage would only complicate his life, tie him down, force him to focus on his wife and children instead of saving the whole world. He needed to stay single, so he could prepare his "bride," the church, for the ultimate marriage - God with man for eternity.

Finally, during this time, Jesus also grew in his relationship with God. He began to relate to God, seeing ultimate truth in the physical world around him and in his relationships of others.

Nazareth is where he watched and learned the premises of many parables.

He examined the ground and saw what soils were ideal for growth.

He watched the interaction of Samaritans and Jews and sensed their prejudices.

He saw persistent widows bang on the doors of local authorities demanding to get their way.

He saw the dedication of people seeking a lost coin, lost sheep or a lost son.

It is in Nazareth where Jesus witnessed the pain of sick friends and the death of close relatives. It is believed that his father Joseph died in Nazareth after Jesus was twelve years old. But since his ministry had not started, Jesus could do nothing but watch loved ones pass and mourn with the others.

How troubling to stand by and not be able to resurrect the one you love.

Jesus had to keep the secret about his true identity. Even Superman steps out of his Clark Kent shoes at times to save a toddler trapped under a burning car.

But Jesus stayed silent.

He had too.

Max Lucado

Jesus was reserved about announcing who He was before He became public, but there are even those occasions afterwards that he would perform miracles and then He would tell people "Don't tell anybody what has happened or what you have seen". I think the best answer, from my perspective to that question was that the ultimate reason Jesus came was to give Himself as a sacrifice. And nothing was going to deter Him from that. Nothing was going to take Him away from that. He said that the Son of man came "to seek and save the lost". The Son of man came "to give himself as a ransom for many". Along the way he was a teacher and a healer which made Him a public figure. But His big job was at Calvary and His big job was Easter Sunday. So, those were the big things. And He knew that if He could accomplish what He came to do and that is to be the Lamb of God who takes away the sin of the world, if He could accomplish that then everything else would fall into place. So, it makes sense to me that there were times in which He wanted to protect His Messianic secret because it could deter Him from what He came to do.

If word got out that this little kid in Nazareth claimed to be the Christ...the anointed one...the Messiah...Jewish rulers would have him stoned before his ministry even started.

Nazareth became a hideout for the Messiah until God called him center stage. A secluded, average, blue collar town, of no importance, where no great figures of history ever came from. God picked a perfect address for his son.

All in all, Nazareth had some wonderful memories for Jesus. It was here he spent most of his time on Earth. While the greater events happened outside these city limits, the normal day-to-day occurred here, where Jesus matured as a man and prepared for his unveiling as God.

Max Lucado

He chose to lead a very normal 30 years of life. There was nothing about His first 30 years that caused Him to be an historic figure. Because when He did come to prominence, at least according to the Gospels they were saying, "Is this not the son of Joseph?" No one said, "Is this not the superstar? Or is this not the hero of Nazareth? Or wasn't He voted best personality in His high school?" You know there wasn't any of that, so apparently He was content to lead an unassuming life, out of the lime light.

TIME TO JOURNEY

1. **Watch "Home" from "In His Shoes: The Life of Christ"**

2. **Discussion Questions**

- What kind of a child were you growing up?

- What kind of a child do you imagine Jesus was?

- How did you grow in stature? What was puberty like for you?

- What word describes your teenage years?

- What big events happened in your teens that were life changing?

- What do you think other parents and kids in Nazareth thought of Jesus?

- How did you grow in wisdom? What schools did you attend?

- How do you think Jesus did at school?

- How did you discover your choice for a career?

- Did you ever visit your dad at his work?

- Why is the job of carpentry ideal for Jesus?

- What boyfriends/girlfriends did you have? Was there pressure to marry?

- Do you think Jesus was "desirable" for marriage?

- Did you like your hometown? Why or why not?

- What did your hometown teach you about life?

- What did Nazareth teach Jesus about life?

Temple

Jerusalem

We identify certain emotions and feelings with our home. It's always depicted as a place of completeness, where one feels unified with their past and their family, a place of comfort where one remembers the love expressed, the holidays experienced and the provision that came in the form of food, clothing and shelter. At least homes should express those feelings.

While I was in my house growing up, I must say I was an independent thinker, a safe way of saying...a rebel. I wanted things my own way, had my own opinions about things and generally fought the system. At the age of twelve, my mind was consumed with baseball cards, girls and pimples. Church was a thing we had to do once a week, but I sat there bored throughout the service, not finding anything applicable to me. Eventually I wanted an excuse to get out of there, so I chose to serve in the children's department as a way to escape church. (I'm sure that comforted many parents reading this, to hear that bored teenagers who hate church are teaching their children about God.)

Jesus, when you think about it, was away from his real home during his time on earth. Nazareth and Israel had become a place where he lived, but his true home was with his heavenly family.

So the best place to meet up with his family was in his Father's house—a home away from home.

The temple.

Joel Hunter

It's difficult for me to imagine what Jesus thinks when He looks at the temple or what He's feeling. On the one hand all of us have had the experience of growing up in a place where we feel God inhabits. Most of us have grown up in a church and we have this sense when we walk into the church of reverence, of this is where I meet God, this is where I come into the presence of God, this is where God belongs...But I think for Jesus there must have been something even more personal than just, "This is the temple and I go there because this is where the Jews go." I think there was a sense of, "I was born in a manger, I've been in Egypt, I've lived in Nazareth but this is kind of my home. Because of my calling and my ultimate sacrifice, this is who I am." And, so I do think there was something very striking in that visitation.

The significance of the temple and his visits there with family on a regular basis must have unleashed a flood of information, feelings and questions to a young Jesus' mind.

"Why am I drawn to this place? Why do I feel warm and comfortable here? Why does it feel like home? Why am I looking for my father?

Coming to the temple put Jesus close in touch with God and, over time, he realized why.

The Southern Temple Mount is one of the most stunning sights in Israel. Its staircase was a pathway that led right into the first century temple. It's a place where God Himself touched down on earth, His glory filling the Holy of Holies, his own personal address on Earth. Seeing those stone walls of the Old City is an unforgettable experience, your spirit crying out "I'm here" when you first spot it. This was once God's House!

Coming here stirred many emotions for me, as it must have for Jesus, especially during the Passover in Jerusalem when he was twelve years old.

The temple was the centerpiece of Jerusalem, dating back to King Solomon in the 10th Century BC. It was the only place where sacrifices could occur, so it became very crowded during three significant feasts every year. Worshippers would first cleanse themselves in baptismal baths called mikvahs (which you can see today), ascend the stairs and enter through the double gates to worship in the temple, as Jesus would have done 2,000 years ago.   Avner and I walked the large staircase leading up to the temple mount.

"Are these stairs first century?" I asked.

"These stairs are first century and are part of much larger staircase that was twice as wide and partially destroyed and led to the temple. There were gates to the temple in one side and in the other side. And people would come up and go through the far side to the temple praying, offering their offerings and so on. And at the end would come out from here. And the large staircase could serve as a great gathering area. And people would talk to each other. Maybe even studying and spending time here."

Wow, I thought. Two thousand years ago Jewish scholars sat here to discuss, debate and dissect scriptures. It's where religious leaders engaged in question and answer times with inquisitive minds. Maybe even the mind of a twelve year old boy.

And here I was with one of Israel's most renown scholar doing the same. With all of Avner's knowledge, I felt like a twelve year old boy.

"Why is that temple so significant to Jewish people?

"The temple is a very significant place to Jewish people because of many things. Because at the very beginning it says in the Book of Psalms that this is the very place where Abraham bound Isaac. And that was the ultimate test of faith. And Abraham is the father of all believers.

"The other point is that this was the place of worshipping God. This was the center of institutional religion.

"The other reason why the temple is so important is because that's supposed to be the only place where Jews sacrifice to God and therefore the only real connection of the people to God. It was an ongoing worshipping place and so it became also the magnet that puts the Jews all together and physically they would come here each one of the three high holidays and gather. Many Jews from all over the country and all over the world. It was built at the end by Herod to be able to accommodate about a quarter of a million people. Jerusalem is a very large city yet more than twice that number of people would come here during the high holidays. Therefore the temple still stands as the place that people relate to even though there is no temple anymore here. But the location is still celebrated."

It's true. Later, on a Friday night, we joined the celebration of the Shabbat, the Jewish Sabbath. Hundreds of Jews gathered by the Wailing Wall to dance, pray and sing. As I put on my yarmulke and walked among them, I was swept up into their celebration and joy. It was a moving and powerful experience. One of the few times I cried on this trip. They have a passion for the temple and everything it represented to them.

Jesus must have felt this too.

"So what sort of emotions would come up inside of a person as they approached this temple? Was it like what we saw Friday night?"

"Well the emotional feeling of coming to the temple is probably coming to a climax, coming to a time that you dreamed all your lifetime about. If you're not living in Jerusalem it might be the only time they would come to the temple. But you prayed to the temple, you talked about the temple, you sent your contribution to the temple, you sent your prayers across to the temple and so on. The temple is the place that people identify with the core of the faith. And, so it's really moving.

Even today and even for secular people today, I can remember myself being far from Jerusalem during this time of the war of '67 when the Israelis came back and reached the Wailing Wall and it was in the news and I was far away but I burst in tears because I was so excited."

For so many people, at so many times in history, this city, these walls, these steps had deep meaning for people, who arrived here feeling connected to God. It only seems fitting that this is the one place where the Bible gives a clue into the youthful days of Jesus, at the age of twelve years old.

Every year his parents went to Jerusalem for the Feast of the Passover. When he was twelve years old, they went up to the Feast, according to the custom.
After the Feast was over, while his parents were returning home, the boy Jesus stayed behind in Jerusalem, but they were unaware of it. Thinking he was in their company, they traveled on for a day. Then they began looking for him among their relatives and friends.
When they did not find him, they went back to Jerusalem to look for him. After three days they found him in the temple courts, sitting among the teachers, listening to them and asking them questions. Everyone who heard him was amazed at his understanding and his answers.
When his parents saw him, they were astonished. His mother said to him, "Son, why have you treated us like this? Your father and I have been anxiously searching for you."
"Why were you searching for me?" he asked. "Didn't you know I had to be in my Father's house?" But they did not understand what he was saying to them.
Then he went down to Nazareth with them and was obedient to them. But his mother treasured all these things in her heart. Luke 2:41-51

Jesus' parents did the correct Jewish thing every year. They kept very current with the feasts held at the temple in Jerusalem, seventy miles from Nazareth. They probably felt an incredible religious burden to go to temple. I mean the Son of God was staying at their house! They were giving his real Father visitation rights.

The Jew considered Passover one of the most important of the feasts. It represented God's power to save his people. The miracles displayed during the Exodus still rank as some of the most magnificent. Leviticus 23 outlines all the Jewish feasts, including Passover:

"'These are the LORD'S appointed feasts, the sacred assemblies you are to proclaim at their appointed times: The LORD'S Passover begins at twilight on the fourteenth day of the first month.
On the fifteenth day of that month the LORD'S Feast of Unleavened Bread begins; for seven days you must eat bread made without yeast.
On the first day hold a sacred assembly and do no regular work. For seven days present an offering made to the LORD by fire. And on the seventh day hold a sacred assembly and do no regular work.'" Leviticus 23:4-8

After following all the regulations for the seven day feast, the family packed up and traveled home with friends and family from Nazareth. The group could get large and someone could easily get left out. One did.

The Son of God.

At the age of twelve, according to Jewish custom, Jesus would be considered a boy entering manhood. Today Jews mark that event with a Bar Mitzvah (12-13 years old).

I can't imagine Mary and Joseph leaving Jesus behind (and there all sorts of metaphors for this act that we could apply to our lives), but I think Jesus was a pretty responsible kid, a "young man" by Jewish standards, and his parents always expected him to be at the right place when he was needed. An honest oversight. Don't call the Department of Child Protection yet.

His parents, one day journey outside of Jerusalem, turned around and went back to look for him. They found Jesus sitting calmly and coolly talking to the teachers in the temple courts. A twelve year old!

The text says: When his parents saw him, they were astonished. His mother said to him,

"Son, why have you treated us like this? Your father and I have been anxiously searching for you." Luke 2:48

Were they shocked that the very responsible Jesus did an irresponsible thing by not joining the group? Did they feel his disappearance dishonored his mother and father, breaking the parental commandment? Were they amazed that he kept company with such learned scholars?

What caused their astonishment?

Norman Geisler

They were astonished because they just assumed He was in the big group until they found out He wasn't there. They knew who He was and that He wouldn't do anything that He shouldn't be doing. So it astonished them. Two fold, one that He wasn't there and two that it was unlike Him to do anything like that unless there was something really important. And they went back and they found out it was something really important. He was about His Father's business.

Mary and Joseph must have been amazed by how quickly Jesus was developing and how boldly he acted. Since the incident is mentioned in Luke, this must have been a significant moment for some reason—maybe Jesus' first outward, verbal recognition of his divine calling. All the previous announcements about his identity came through angels, prophets, political leaders, wise men.

This, according to the Gospels, was the first time Jesus acknowledged it himself, the revelation coming from his own lips—*he gets it*!

Whatever sparked their shock, Mary and Joseph seemed relieved they had not misplaced the Savior of the world.

Now a Son of God should keep a low profile, especially in this volatile religious community. Why did he risk getting so close to the Jewish leaders, men who could have him killed if he divulged any information about his identity? Jesus probably desired some spiritual exercises and the best sparring partners he could find were in the temple. Probably his local synagogue had tired of his endless questions. Jesus tapped that reservoir and now he moved on to the big leagues. The temple priests and scribes.

It's interesting to note that Jesus asked questions. I always thought he taught the religious leaders. Instead, he seemed to be probing into areas that many mature adults don't even venture. So what kind of questions was he asking?

He could have been questioning them, trying to find out whether they had a genuine faith to hold such a prestigious office. Maybe he wanted to explore their hearts.

He could have been seeking answers to some questions about the thoughts swirling around in his brain. Like…who is the coming Messiah?

Norman Geisler

Jesus asked two hundred and thirty some questions during His lifetime. He always had a good purpose for His question. It was always to draw out other people. It was always to somehow covertly reveal who He was without ripping His shirt open and seeing the big "G" on his chest, you know. He never did that. He was questioning them on their knowledge of prophesy and trying to draw them out to see if they were really expecting the Messiah or if they even had any idea that, you know, the Messiah might be there.

But, could Jesus be questioning his role, doubting his true nature? The question continued a fascinating discussion between myself and Dr. Geisler.

Norman Geisler

I don't think Jesus ever doubted and needed reassurance. I think doubt of who He was would be tantamount to sin and so I don't think. We know Jesus didn't sin and I think doubting who He was would be a sin because it would be a distrust of God. In Romans 14 it says, 'What is of doubt is not of faith.' So I don't think Jesus ever doubted and needed assurance. I think He was severely tested and the test was from the outside in not from the inside out. There was nothing in Him as in us because when we're tempted, first of all we have that desire that leads us away. He never had any internal desire to sin and He never had any internal desire to doubt.

Troy

If Jesus began to doubt that he was the son of God, that would be a sin. But was there a time when He questioned, 'Am I the Son of God?'?

Norman Geisler

I think it's different from asking the question, "Is there a time when He didn't know He was the Son of God and did He doubt He was the Son of God." He never doubted, but there was a time when He didn't know. Some time in his early development whether it was four or five, certainly by twelve years of age in the temple, He knew He was the son of God. So He had to come to that growing realization.

Troy

How does God learn?

Norman Geisler

God doesn't learn anything in His divine nature but Jesus is both God and man and He learned things in His human nature. You've got to remember that Jesus was divine and human at the same time. Two natures, one person. Two sets of consciousness. He had a divine consciousness and a human consciousness. As God He never got hungry, as man He did. As God He knew everything, as man He didn't; He didn't know what was on the fig tree, He didn't know the time of His second coming. So, His human nature was limited, His divine nature was unlimited. And you can't confuse the two natures, that's another heresy called Monothacidism or Utikianism where you blend the two natures of Christ. They're distinct natures and they're different. He has both of them. And He had divine consciousness and human consciousness all in one person. But the divine side never leaks over to the human side and the human side never leaks over to the divine side.

Troy

So it was the divine side slowly being revealed to the human side of Jesus?

Norman Geisler

Right, the divine side of Jesus is slowly being revealed to the human side as He grew.

Troy
So it's almost like there's a veil over it and He's allowed to sort of peak in, see, understand?

Norman Geisler
Information is coming across from the divine side but not attributes. Revelation is coming from the divine side to the human side but no attributes are being transferred from the divine to the human side. See some people have a wrong view of Christ, they have a view that, you know, while He was man He could just kind of pull on these divine attributes all the time and pull this stuff, well no He was truly human. He said I don't do anything the Father doesn't tell me to do. I don't teach anything the Father doesn't tell me to teach. So, He's constantly getting revelation from the divine side but He's never pulling rank.[5]

Whatever questions or dialog occurred between Jesus the religious leaders, it was highly unusual for a twelve year old to think these thoughts. Then again, this is no ordinary twelve year old.

The incident revealed Jesus' rapid development and his understanding of himself. This could have been the pinnacle of his self-revelation. Maybe the temple leaders helped him to seal his understanding of himself once and for all, so when Mary and Joseph showed up and Jesus announced "I know who my real Father is," it's the first time he's ever expressed it to them.

And what better place for it to happen then right here at the temple.

"Why were you searching for me?" he asked. "Didn't you know I had to be in my Father's house?"

What is Jesus saying? "Where else would a son be, but enjoying time at his father's house? Everyone goes home for the holidays."

I remember moments of self-revelation in my life. One occurred in English class, seventh grade, when our teacher asked us to writing anything we wanted for an entire period. Most kids moaned and complained.

---

[5] Times like this helped me to understand what Jesus felt like as a boy sitting at the feet of certain learned scholars.

"What do we write about?"

"Anything you want," the teacher responded. That blank slate of creativity frightened most of the students. Not me. I was on to page two while they just started putting pencil to paper. It was during that time I realized I wanted to be a writer.

I remember as a child watching "King Kong" (1933) on TV and thinking, "I want to make a movie like that, so I got into script writing.

We all have those rare but meaningful moments that help us understand who we really are – our future, our purpose, our goals.

The temple, before this time, was a place where Jesus' family went to perform their obedience before God. Now, it appears, the temple took on a new significance. Jesus saw this not as a temple, but a house. His father's house. I asked Avner what that could mean in the context of the first century.

"There are two levels to relate to the temple as Jesus' Father's house. The first one is that temples were always considered to be the house of God. But it was also the house for the people that felt they belonged to the God. Therefore everybody would relate to it as an intimate place."

"I guess for many Jewish people it's really a place of security, and protection and provision that we would all associate with a home?" I asked.

"All along the history and especially along the last two thousand years, the longing to the temple was a longing for home and homeland and the place that we all came from, the place that we all belonged to. So the temple, even in ruins, symbolizes very strong link to a real home. And therefore coming back to the Holy Land was coming back home."

Jesus had to be reminded of the long course it took to get this temple built – the struggles with Abraham, Isaac and Jacob, the Exodus, the desert trek with the Israelites, the tabernacle, the ups and downs in the Promised Land under Joshua and Judges, the rise and fall of David, Solomon and the rest of the kings, the political divisions, the enemy takeovers, the destructions of the temple, rebuilding and rebuilding and finally the cries of the prophets, still echoing in these hallowed halls.

Norman Geisler

Well it stirs very deep emotions. It is His Father's house, all the way back to the tabernacle where God dwelt there on the day of Atonement, on Yom Kippur, when God came down in the Shekinah Glory and the mercy seat when the blood was offered up and of course

He is the lamb slain from the foundation of the world and He fulfilled the Passover, First Corinthians, chapter 5, 'Christ our Passover lamb is sacrificed for us.' So, it stirred deep emotions and it was very disturbing to Him that they had commercialized it, that they didn't realize the true significance of the temple. And that, 'Greater than the temple was here', as He said to them as well. So, I can't even totally empathize with how deeply this must have hurt Him.

Here Jesus sat in a newly refurbished temple, a place of sacrifice that represented him—a flesh and blood temple that would offer the ultimate sacrifice…his life.

"Or haven't you read in the Law that on the Sabbath the priests in the temple desecrate the day and yet are innocent? I tell you that one greater than the temple is here. If you had known what these words mean, 'I desire mercy, not sacrifice,' you would not have condemned the innocent. For the Son of Man is Lord of the Sabbath." Matthew 12:5-8

This house was his father's house, but it was his house too. Since Jesus had some ownership of this "house" he felt a need to protect it too. Jesus would later condemn the priests, some of whom he encountered at twelve years old, for desecrating this house. He would tip over the tables of the moneychangers, desiring honor for this house. Jesus got defensive. Look what these "thieves" were doing to HIS house too!

At the age of twelve, Jesus understood his identity and his true father. By this time, wouldn't a teenage boy shrug off his earthly parents and rebel like most twelve year olds?

"Who do you think you are, Joseph! You're not my father!"

In my father's house, at the age of twelve, I rebelled against my father. At church, I rebelled against my heavenly Father. It's what twelve year olds do! Not Jesus.

Jesus understood who is real father was, but it didn't diminish his love and respect for his earthly father. It's important to see that Jesus did not act condescending or superior once he realized his status. Verse 51 of Luke 2 says he was obedient to Mary and Joseph in Nazareth.

73

Jesus never flaunted his title or disrespected his parents, even though he was God.

He acquiesced and willfully submitted himself to Mary and Joseph.

I come to the temple in Jerusalem with complete respect for Jesus who never rebelled against his father, earthly or spiritual. He never acted like a smart aleck, twelve-year-old know-it-all even though he knew it all.

He loved both of his fathers and acknowledged their roles in his life.

TIME TO JOURNEY

1. Watch "Temple" from "In His Shoes: The Life of Christ"

2. Discussion Questions

- How many different places did you live as a child? As an adult?

- Which place do you consider your home? Why?

- When you think of your home, what words describe it?

- Describe the holidays at your house.

- What was on your mind at the age of 12 (6-7th Grade)? Were you thinking of the things of God?

- Have you ever lost a child in a crowded area? Were you ever lost as a child?

- What feelings were going through the mind of Mary and Joseph looking for Jesus?

- If you have children, did they ever do anything that "amazed" you?

- What do you think "amazed" Mary and Joseph about Jesus?

- What questions do you think Jesus was asking?

- Why did Jesus respond the way he did?

- As a child, describe what it was like going to church.

- How is attending church different now than when you were a child?

- Why don't you call church "your Father's house"?

Spotlight
Jordan River

I wonder if I should go on a reality show. I think my first choice would be "Survivor," a show I've loved since Season One. "Amazing Race" would come in second, since I love to travel. However, I get cranky without food and under stress.

It's not a side of myself that I'm proud of and I certainly don't want all of world to see the "real" me played over and over on YouTube. As I come to think about it, being in the spotlight doesn't seem so interesting.

Exposing our true selves, warts and all, takes a lot of guts, since it opens you up to praise, criticism or ridicule. Where once you hid in the shadows of obscurity, now you lay wide open in the spotlight of notoriety.

So why would someone want to go on a reality show?

Notoriety. They are willing to expose their real self for all to see. They allow cameras to capture every mistake, every hiccup, every fall, then allow others to point out their failures.

Celebrities who become stars experience a kind of death. Their old life is over. Their new life, now lived in front of cameras with blinking lights and flashbulb strobes, begins. They die to themselves so to speak.

When Jesus came to the river Jordan in order to be baptized by John, he stepped out into the spotlight, risking it all. Jesus stepped out into the spotlight to die for everyone who accepted his reality.

During the morning of our arrival at the Jordan, the river looked particularly inviting especially with the 100 degree temperature. Its cool, crisp water flowed rapidly, more ideal for tubing instead of baptizing. A 98 pound convert would get swept away once they went under:

"In the name of the Father, the son..." WHOOSH "Where did he go?"

Avner took us to a national park along the Jordan River, a more pristine location where many Israelis like to camp. It sort of reminded me of the Jewish holiday, the Feast of Booths or Tabernacles, when God called the nation to go camping outside the city limits to remember the forty years they spent in the desert. I saw nearly one hundred tents. Apparently camping is in the Israeli's blood.

There are a few traditional locations for the baptism of Jesus, one the Allenby Bridge near Qasir al-Yahud on the West Bank (part of an Eastern Orthodox monastery) and the other is in Jordan called Al-Maghtas which fits well with the John 1:28 passage that says it occurred in Bethany beyond the Jordan. Because of political reasons, we could not visit these places with Avner (a Jew) so we decided to find any spot along the Jordan, preferably one that was camera-worthy, since we really don't know the precise location.

The Jordan River is a flowing metaphor. Its sources begin high in the mountains of Hebron in the north, gather together, then spill into the Sea of Galilee, streaming south below sea level to the Dead Sea where it stops in a murky dead end. It's a symbol of life to death, from heavenly highs to the extremist of lows, extending nearly the entire length of Israel.

For Jesus, the Jordan represented a transition from life to death. He was dying to himself. His old life was ending. His new life beginning. A fresh start. Figuratively, he was traveling against the current, upstream. Most lives flow to death. Jesus moved towards life.

The Jordan's history also made it perfect for the symbolism of baptism. As Avner and I relaxed along the banks, he elaborated on this thought.

"It was a very common practice in Judaism at the time of Christ to immerse in water in order to be purified. People really felt they were about to approach the last judgment, the Messiah is about to come. The basic idea was we should be ready and prepared and being prepared meant being pure.

"The fresh start would be considered also when you clean yourself from your sins and impurity together. And since the Jordan was a place that the Israelites crossed and got this fresh start, Jordan would be a preferred place for this baptism."

The Jordan represented a place where the Israelites began their new life as a nation—thanks to Moses—and through baptism, where believers began their new life dedicated to God—thanks to John the Baptist—who led this campaign for spiritual preparation.

John preached the coming of the Messiah in this wilderness area between Jerusalem and Galilee. John fulfilled a prophecy himself in Isaiah 40:3 which said:

"A voice of one calling:
'In the desert prepare

the way for the LORD;
make straight in the wilderness
a highway for our God.'"

John became that voice, preparing people for what was to come. God had been silent for 400 years between the Old and New Testament during which he inspired no prophet to speak for him during that time.

Then Jesus walked up and John's whole purpose for being came to a climax. He pointed to Jesus and cried, "Here he comes, the lamb of God who will take away the sin of the world."

No longer hiding in Nazareth obscurity, playing the part of a 30 year old, unmarried handyman still living at his widow mom's house, Jesus now became known as the subject of John's mysterious desert ramblings.

The Messiah. The lamb. The chosen one. Elijah...had come.

Jesus entered the spotlight finally revealing who he really was.

Jesus was thirty years old at the time of the baptism. Luke tells us that.

Now Jesus himself was about thirty years old when he began his ministry. Luke 3:23

It was the minimum age all Jews could enter ministry.

Count all the men from thirty to fifty years of age who come to serve in the work in the Tent of Meeting. Numbers 4:3

For thirty years, Jesus kept quiet and humble, then he swung open the doors and announced his true identity.

Most superheroes conceal their identity for good reason. They cannot live a real life once everyone knows who they are. They would receive knocks on the door late at night. Phone calls throughout the day. They would get besieged with requests.

"Superman, can you open this jar?"
"Spiderman, my cat is stuck up in a tree."
"Flash, I need this letter taken to the post office ASAP!"

Jesus did not hide under a costume any longer. No secret identities. No longer was he Jesus, the son of Joseph the carpenter, but Jesus, the son of Joseph the carpenter who CLAIMED to be the son of God. He now exposed his dual nature, altering his whole life.

Baptisms were not the latest craze or the newest thing. Gentiles were baptized when they converted to Judaism. Jews routinely cleansed themselves before entering a holy place like the temple or as a sign of forgiveness. John preached a message of repentance which naturally influenced those who heard it to repent and be baptized.

Max Lucado

Jesus did not need to be baptized. That's the beauty of His baptism that He did not need to. He's the only one who has ever lived who did not need to. Because baptism celebrates forgiveness of sins and Jesus was a sinless person. So He was baptized then to relate to us to show us that where He calls us to go He has already gone Himself.

While Jesus did not need baptism—a sinless man does not have to come clean—he established some primary guidelines for his ministry—repentance, cleanliness, forgiveness—by agreeing with John's overall message of baptism, an outward expression of an inner decision.

Joel Hunter

Jesus was baptized because He lived His life as an example. Most of His life when He was walking along with His disciples He was showing them what was important in life as well as teaching them intellectually what was important in life. Did He need to be baptized for the remission of His sins? Obviously not, the Bible says He was tempted in all matters but sinned not. So, He didn't, that part was not the purpose.

Then, in a rare family portrait, Jesus posed with the Trinity—father, son and Holy Spirit—all showing up in support and unity. The Holy Spirit descended upon Jesus, offering a fresh touch to him. As that occurred, the father spoke, offering words of encouragement and more support.

"This my son with whom I am very pleased."

"This is my son…" is a statement of fact. God wanted everyone around to understand the facts. Jesus is God's son.

The second part, "with whom I am very pleased," conveys words of affirmation. God could be saying he's pleased with the way things

80

were working out, or he's pleased with the way Jesus acted, or just saying before everyone, he loved his son.

I am a son. I have three sons. I know firsthand the need every male has for affirmation from his father. Was Jesus any different?

William Paul Young

You know, part of the beauty of the life of Jesus in terms of His relationship with His Father, with Abba, part of the beauty is that, He doesn't do anything for so long. I mean we think we're in such a performance oriented culture, you know and it's all about making sure you get the education because then it's going to lead to you doing something significant and leaving your mark in the world. This is God who is incarnate in human flesh. This is God who is growing up. He's a twelve year old. He's a fourteen year old. He should be getting married by now. I can hear His mother saying, 'It's about time, you know, I want grandkids', you know.

And you've got this God who's in a world that is lost and hurt and damaged and He's not doing anything. I mean He's just growing up. And He's now twenty and He's twenty-four and He's twenty-eight and He's thirty and the first thing the Father says, He's thirty, He's done nothing, and the first thing the Father says ,'Look at my boy, I love this kid, this is my Son in whom I am so pleased.' He hadn't done anything. Which is a beautiful picture for us. It wasn't the next three years, now, that made Jesus significant in the eyes of His Father. See it was who He was, not what He did. And yes, it is significant to us but in the love of the Father He was significant the whole time and He didn't need to do anything to have the affection of the Father.

How long had Jesus lived without hearing those words of affirmation from his father? Maybe Joseph never said such a thing. Maybe Joseph never felt the right to say such a thing. Jesus technically wasn't his son. Joseph could have felt conflicted. Maybe Joseph routinely affirmed his son, but his death created a void over the past five or ten years.

Whatever happened, those fatherly words of encouragement happened not only to establish the facts for those that heard it—Jesus is the Son of God—but possibly those words were for Jesus too. We all like to hear our father's words of support. Wouldn't Jesus relish such a verbal touch?

Some suggest that Jesus needed to hear those words from God to confirm his true identity.

Joel Hunter

It was the demarcation from His growth and preparation period to actually taking full responsibility as the Messiah for all the world. But it must have occurred to Him every once in a while, "Am I really the son of God, am I really the Messiah, am I really…? You know I'm gaining all this insight, I believe I know what my purpose is but do I really know?" When He came up from that and there was this epiphany and there was this voice and all heard it. That must have been the pronouncement. Not only did it announce to them but it announced to Him, the confirmation of who He was.

It's not that doubt is a demerit; it is that doubt is a process of faith. And so, God is building up in His own Son's faith. Uncertainty is not a negative. Uncertainty is what is required in order to have faith. And so, all of this, if He has these incidences of uncertainty, which I think He does, then for God to finally pronounce who He is, is the capstone of the certainty that He has felt in His spirit but maybe not admitted in His mind up to that point.

There must have been a sense of relief on Jesus' part to finally expose the truth about himself. What would it be like living thirty years as a carpenter's son—your secret identity—waiting for that moment when you would be called to step out in your superhero role? For thirty years, Jesus could have multiplied food, but looked the other way when the homeless begged. Jesus had the power to heal, but could not help the hurting. Jesus had the power to bring others to life, but he stepped back at funerals and mourned.

He had the power, but it was not the time.

I find it significant that the entire Trinity showed up. Many claim that the Trinity is never found in the Bible. While it's true the word "trinity" is not found in the text, the members of the Trinity show up together a couple times. The Jordan River was one of those places.

82

Norman Geisler

Well, the here and now is the time for the Trinity to show up at His baptism because in the Old Testament the Trinity was only implicit. You have the Father talking to the Son in Psalm 110:1, 'The Lord said unto my Lord' and He indeed used that in Matthew 22 as one of His passages to affirm His own Deity. You have the Trinity in Isaiah where it talks about Yahweh, the angel of Yahweh and the Holy Spirit all in one passage. You've got the angel of the Lord, who is worshipped, who talks to the Lord in Zechariah chapter 8. You've got all of these tantalizing implications there so now the time is to make it explicit and while He was there being baptized, the Father 's voice spoke, so they know it's God. That's one person. Another person is there, the Holy Spirit descends on him. All three persons are going to be there because they were all part of the plan. They were all part of the prophecy that was predicted and now they're all part of the fulfillment.

Jesus the son, received confirmation and love from his Father, being touched with the Holy Spirit, anointing him. The word "Messiah" or "Christ" means "the anointed one." Here was Jesus' spiritual anointing, receiving immersion not only into the water, but by the spirit too. This moment foreshadows Jesus' discussion with Nicodemus.

Jesus answered, "I tell you the truth, no one can enter the kingdom of God unless he is born of water and the Spirit." John 3:5

Since the Jordan represented a transition, I wonder if, while standing on the banks of the Jordan, Jesus also felt a moment's hesitation. Jesus knew this moment was not only the start of the great redemption of mankind, but the beginning of the end of his life on earth. From here on, Jesus became a target for death on this ultimate and fatal reality show. Jesus opened himself up to opportunities to help, heal and lead, but also to the attacks of Pharisees and religious leaders.

This baptism at the Jordan mixed feelings of relief and dread. Relief, that Jesus could finally show everyone who he really was. Dread, as he opened himself up to rejection, betrayal and hate.

There's always a risk exposing ourselves and our dreams to the world. Jesus understood what that felt like, as did his cohort in baptism,

John, who would be dead in a couple years, his head separated from his body, the victim of a simple dare.

That's probably why the entire Trinity paid a visit—a spiritual family reunion—as the three persons of the Godhead offered their support to the one who had sacrificed so much and been away from their fellowship for so long in order to fulfill the ultimate cleansing to those that believed.

Jesus stepped out into the spotlight and risked it all, for you and for me. If he had stayed in the shadows, quietly and comfortably, we would all be destined for darkness.

Max Lucado
It's unlike anything but that moment, the baptism of Jesus and then the Mount of Transfiguration are I think two of the most mystical moments in scripture...It's like heaven cannot stay away any longer. It shows us that heaven is watching, heaven is participating in the life of Jesus. And at the great launching of the ministry of Jesus the Father has to affirm verbally what is happening. So, I believe that must have meant everything to Jesus, especially during the next 40 days as He's about to go into the wilderness and battle the temptation, the hunger, the isolation. I would imagine He thought a lot about that phrase, "This is my Beloved Son in whom I am well pleased". And I think it's important for us to know that God says that to us too. He is pleased with us...We're still His masterpiece. We're His workmanship...He's pleased with His children. We don't always do what is right but we never step out of His love.

TIME TO JOURNEY

1. **Watch "Spotlight" from "In His Shoes: The Life of Christ"**

2. **Discussion Questions**

- Do you want to be a celebrity? Why or why not?

- Was there ever a moment that you made the headlines, television news or were honored for some noteworthy performance?

- Would you go on a reality show? Which one?

- When Jesus stepped into the Jordan River, everything changed for him. What changed?

- Why did he need to go public with his identity?

- What did he risk?

- Is there a body of water that means something to you?

- When were you baptized?

- What did your baptism signify for you?

- Why didn't Jesus need to be baptized?

- Why did Jesus need to be baptized?

- Describe your family reunions.

- How do you think Jesus felt being reunited with his spiritual family?

- What words of encouragement did your father say to you?

- How important is/was your father's approval?

- How would you feel if God spoke out loud in front of others and said, "This is my adopted son/daughter with whom I am well pleased"?

- What moment in your life was a pivotal cross-over point in terms of your faith?

JOURNEY 2

Temptations to Demons

Temptation
Wilderness/Mount of Temptation

As we prepared to go to the desert and experience Jesus' time of temptation, I became acutely aware in the morning of all the temptations coming my way. I wanted to be pure as I headed into the desert, strong, ready to take on whatever Satan threw at me. No such luck.

As I prepared to eat at the hotel's breakfast spread, my timing coincided with a busload of tourists. Tourists take their time, like they're on vacation or something. I grew impatient as they blocked my way to the yogurt and fresh fruit.

Strike one.

As my group hit the road, someone in the vehicle announced that we should stop off and get coffee at a place Avner introduced us to— Aroma, the closest we could find to a Starbucks experience in Israel. The smell of a double cappuccino picked me up. We had not driven five blocks from the hotel and already I was panting for my biggest temptation—coffee.

Strike two.

Inside Aroma, I spotted probably the most beautiful girl I had ever seen the entire trip. A tall, slender twenty-something year old beauty, very elegant, with blondish streaked hair. Probably a model, if not, she should be. Immediately I could understand King David's attraction to Jewish women.

Strike three.

Maybe Jesus had a good idea disappearing into the desert. I too needed to get out of the city.

We drove forty minutes outside of Jerusalem to an area on the way to Jericho. No billboard advertisements. No people. No food stands or coffee shops. No tourists or buses. No beautiful models hanging out on the side of a dusty road. Nothing. We saw what Israelis call true wilderness.

They name this arid, mountainous region a wadi or valley that compares to a mini Grand Canyon, except for the absence of many colors that paint the landscape of Arizona. These vast stretches of dusty brown mountains are mind boggling as to their size and undulation. They looked like something out of Lawrence of Arabia. I could see myself wearing the white head gear, riding a horse with a long sword in my hand.

Uh, oh…was that another temptation?

These wadis were excellent places to visit and wonderful backdrops for a Kodak picture moment, but to live there for any period of time—no way. Within thirty minutes, my breakfast-filled, coffee-soaked body began to succumb to the heat.

The desert sun has one goal—to kill whoever or whatever dares to challenge it. The heat felt like a vise, squeezing every bit of energy out of me. Since we were under sea level, the air pressure was greater and the heat more compressed. The car was always within eyeshot, though I began to remember we were low on water.

After Jesus' Jordan River extravaganza, a publicist would have told Jesus, "Get out there and hit the talk show circuit. You're the subject of water cooler conversations. Do meet-and-greets at the synagogues. Hold a conference at the temple. You need to be interviewed by Oprah."

No such thing. Instead, Jesus retreated to the desert for forty days, as far away from the spotlight as you could get. What a momentum killer. You don't want to disappear in the desert. People have short term memories and forget things after forty days. You want to press palms and kiss babies in downtown Jerusalem!

But fame brings with it tons of temptations. You're given the best seats and the best food. You're granted favors and expected to grant favors. Jesus needed to prove something before his popularity increased and with it the temptations of the world.

So he went to the opposite of notoriety. He went to nothing.

Deserts are desolate and frankly a bit boring. They are brutal places that offer very little comfort or sustenance or distraction. In some ways, they are the worst places to go if you want to remain strong.

But Jesus didn't choose this place:

Then Jesus was led by the Spirit into the desert to be tempted by the devil. Matthew 4:1

William Paul Young

It says, 'ekballō.' He was cast out by the Holy Spirit. It's the Holy Spirit that said, 'This is where I want you to be.' So He's there again because of relationship and because of obedience.

Standing in the vast arid desert, I wondered why Jesus came here to be tempted. What is there in the wilderness that is particularly tempting? I felt I had left all the significant temptations behind in

Jerusalem. Was Jesus going to lust out here after a crusty old rock or covet a dried up bush? You go to the desert to escape temptation…right?

Maybe picking the wilderness had something to the do with the symbolism. The Bible speaks of the wilderness when the Israelites crossed it to reach the Promised Land. Moses fasted and retreated on a mountain to prepare for his reception of his most divine orders—the Ten Commandments and the Mosaic covenant. Jesus also was getting ready to receive his orders for the next three years, when he would reveal to the world new commandments and a new covenant.

The Israelites, during Moses' stay on the mountain, caved in to temptation and worshipped a golden calf. The desert then became their prison for forty years.

Jesus identified himself with the Old Testament out here by fasting like Moses and refusing to be tempted in the wilderness. Jesus became a new representative taking on the Old Testament sin and refusing to succumb. He's clearly the God of the Old and New Testament.   Deserts also signify purity. Avner, having spent a lot of time in the Egyptian wilderness, knew a lot about the experience of crossing such difficult terrain. And he has grown to love them.

"We know that the Essenes, who wrote the Dead Sea scrolls, disappeared into the desert to escape worldly contamination. The desert for them was pure, untouched, unscathed by human hands. It represented purity and caused purity at the same time."

William Paul Young

It's a very stark place but things become clear in stark places. Part of the value of fasting, for one, is that it takes away some of the things that cling to us. They drop away and our focus becomes a little more clearer about the things which are real, especially in terms of the Spirit. And so He's in a place where there is nothing to depend on.

Standing alone in the desert, I felt vulnerable. While there's nothing there to tempt you, there's nothing here to hide behind either. No means of support. You are all alone.

No comfort food.

No encouraging chats with friends.

No hammock.

No temple, church or synagogue.

No entertainment.

No mommy to tuck you in at night.

91

No prisoner would ask for solitary confinement. Jesus accepted it obediently.

This moment also became a showdown of epic proportions. A cage match. God versus Satan.

Fair fight? This is the Son of God versus a mere creation, a renegade angel. God certainly had the advantage and the Vegas odds go his way.

So to make the fight more fair between Satan and Jesus, Jesus came in the form of a man, wearing a vulnerable skin suit that historically attracted sin since its first inhabitant, Adam.

That's a little bit better—more even—but not enough.

So God picked the arena—a barren desert. Okay, but still Satan didn't have a chance, so Jesus did one more thing…he fasted from food.

Now, with the odds more even, and Jesus weak, Satan took three tactics to trip up Jesus. He went for what he thought were Jesus' weaknesses, as a starving human, all alone, in the desert.

After fasting forty days and forty nights, he was hungry.

The tempter came to him and said, "If you are the Son of God, tell these stones to become bread."

Jesus answered, "It is written: 'Man does not live on bread alone, but on every word that comes from the mouth of God.'"

Then the devil took him to the holy city and had him stand on the highest point of the temple.

"If you are the Son of God," he said, "throw yourself down. For it is written:

" 'He will command his angels concerning you, and they will lift you up in their hands, so that you will not strike your foot against a stone.'"

Jesus answered him, "It is also written: 'Do not put the Lord your God to the test.'"

Again, the devil took him to a very high mountain and showed him all the kingdoms of the world and their splendor.

"All this I will give you," he said, "if you will bow down and worship me."

92

Jesus said to him, "Away from me, Satan! For it is written: 'Worship the Lord your God, and serve him only.'"

Then the devil left him, and angels came and attended him. Matthew 4:2-11

First, Satan went after the physical component by offering Jesus something to eat. It was a cruel trick. A piece of bread would taste good after forty days of starvation. Jesus, though, focused not on the physical, but the spiritual. Jesus made a clear statement: man needs spiritual food, like the word of God, not buffets and power bars.

I fasted once for forty days. I felt called to take on the ultimate spiritual discipline by refusing to eat and focusing on prayer. While some would not call my fast real since I drank juices, soup broth and chocolate milk, I must admit—I WAS HUNGRY! I did not have pasta, hamburgers, pizza, doughnuts, peanuts, all my comfort foods. I ate no whole foods for forty days and when the fortieth day was over, I nearly killed myself as I gorged on cheese and sausage. My gall bladder protested, putting me in the hospital.

I remember the physical weakness I experienced throughout, in addition to the spiritual power I felt. But if someone offered me bread— steamy, soft warm bread—all alone with nobody looking, it would be tough. I would have killed for some butter too.

William Paul Young
The first temptation about even turning stones to bread is about necessity. Don't you need necessity? I mean this is food , these are the necessary things. Surly you could just supply the necessary things? And He is saying, 'There is nothing necessary except this relationship, this word, this communication that I have with the Father. That's what's necessary.'

Jesus' physical body was at the brink of death. Satan's offer of bread had to look tempting. While eating bread was not a sin, forcing someone to stray from a commitment they made to God is. The Holy Spirit led Jesus into the wilderness for a forty day fast and Satan wanted to disrupt it by catering the event before its time had been fulfilled.

Second, Satan took Jesus to the highest point of the temple and told him to jump. "Don't worry. The angels will catch you." Jesus probably felt vulnerable and all alone in the desert for all that time and the security of angels would feel nice right now. A sort of angelic group hug. Jesus told Satan not to test God with frivolous acts.

William Paul Young
You know, there was a Jewish legend that that's how the Messiah would show up, He would leap from the temple and land in their midst. So this was a temptation to independently make the expectation happen.

Satan correctly stated that angels could catch Jesus if he jumped off the temple tower. But Satan cannot tell God what to do. It might have felt good for Jesus to have a heavenly touch, but not at the expense of becoming Satan's servant.

Finally, Satan took him to a mountain and showed him all the kingdoms below. "Wouldn't it feel good to control all of this? Just worship me and I'll hand it over." Jesus, the King of Kings, now weakened and drained of physical power, spent forty days in the desert, taking the position of the king of nothing but a bunch of lizards and stones. Without exerting any authority for so long, certainly Jesus would succumb to the temptation of power. "God needs to be in charge," Satan thought. "He feels inadequate without something to rule over. He'll take this offer."

William Paul Young
'I'll give you all the kingdoms of the world. We can short cut this', you know, 'It doesn't cost much, just a little worship in my direction. This is what I've been wanting the whole time.' But again, it's to act independently of the relationship. And I think that's the core of the temptation.

We all seek power and significance in some way. Satan offered to allow Jesus to become king over a few cities. Quite a demotion, especially when Jesus already ruled the whole earth by title. It would be like someone coming by your house and offering to sell you your house, when you already pay the mortgage or hold the title. But at the time, feeling weak, isolated and abandoned without human contact, the offer could have been tempting. Again, Jesus did not cave in.

By defeating Satan's triple temptation, Jesus presented himself as the perfect substitute for the first man who ever lived. The temptations Jesus received were no different than the ones Adam and Eve succumbed to.

Lust of the flesh, lust of the eyes and the pride of life. All three were there in Adam's temptation – he saw it was good for food, good to taste, and desire to make one wise. So there you have the lust of the flesh, the lust of the eyes and the pride of life.

While the themes of Adam's and Jesus' temptations were the same, the circumstances were drastically different. Adam had a beautiful garden with mild temperatures. Jesus had a desert. Adam had all the food and drink he needed. Jesus had nothing. Adam had Eve, a companion to watch his back. Jesus sat all alone.

Through this, Jesus emerged qualified to substitute for the first man's sin. His life was a direct contrast away from unrighteousness and towards righteousness.

For if, by the trespass of the one man, death reigned through that one man, how much more will those who receive God's abundant provision of grace and of the gift of righteousness reign in life through the one man, Jesus Christ.

Consequently, just as the result of one trespass was condemnation for all men, so also the result of one act of righteousness was justification that brings life for all men.

For just as through the disobedience of the one man the many were made sinners, so also through the obedience of the one man the many will be made righteous. Romans 5:17-19

Jesus came to the desert wanting to get himself physically, emotionally, relationally, spiritually down to the bare bones. No friends to help. No strength. No one in his corner. Just a bunch of wild animals that he helped create. He lived as a primitive, wild man, completely and totally exposed for Satan to tempt.

The model prayer that Jesus told his disciples contains the phrase "And lead us not into temptation." It would seem to me that avoiding temptation is the key to a Godly life. Yet Jesus tempted his own rule. He went to be tempted.

This was a risky move on Jesus' part. To open himself to temptation was like inviting the invading army into your city gates and giving them a head start. If Jesus failed in this showdown, after he evened the playing field, his whole purpose of coming to earth and living as a man for thirty years would be for nothing. Once he sinned, he no longer fulfilled the credentials for a sinless offering, spoken of in Leviticus.

All sacrifices were spotless. Sin stains our soul. Jesus had to be spotless and sin free. He could not fail in this temptation exercise.

I wonder how fragile the balance existed between God and man. Being fully God and fully man meant Jesus was not 80% God and 20% man. Or even 50-50. Jesus lived 100% God and 100% man. He had all the senses, all the organs, all the needs that come with humanity.

Two of the three Gospel accounts of the desert experience in scripture talk of the angels coming to minister to him after the temptation slugfest ended. I find that statement odd at first. Why would Jesus need attendance by the angels? Were they acting as an angelic paramedic team, rushing to assist the patient? Maybe. I could understand why being in the wilderness myself for a couple hours.

I see in that angelic rescue the vulnerability and weakness Jesus felt in a human body. Jesus stayed as strong as he could, putting on a tough exterior, keeping a stiff upper lip, taking on Satan with what little strength he had left in him. He reminds me of Rocky in the final round, staggering and frail, collapsing as the bell rang in his trainer's arms. Jesus was weak after the temptations and those angelic arms finally wrapped around him for comfort.

So why did Jesus put himself through all this? And why now?

It seemed clear to me that at the very beginning of Jesus' three year ministry, Jesus wanted to establish some boundaries with Satan, who sat poised and ready for this moment to bring down God. Jesus made a statement in the desert that even in his weakest state he would not be tempted, so don't even bother later on, Satan.

From the wilderness location, our group packed up and traveled to Jericho where we saw the most ancient ruins of our whole trip, which dated back to the years 2,000 BC. There is some indication that these were the walls of Jericho. Jericho is mentioned occasionally in the Gospels, most famously for the wee-little Zacchaeus incident and his sycamore tree.

Next we took a cable car up to another traditional location of the temptations, the Mountain of Temptation, which spurred all kinds of jokes for those of us traveling. Suddenly everything became a temptation – ice cream, gift shop trinkets, water.

Even the restaurant at the base of the cable car was named Temptation Restaurant. We didn't give in here. We had to stick to our schedule.

The tradition holds that Jesus sat inside one of the mountain caves during his 40 days of temptation. It makes some sense for a couple reasons. One, it's far more hospitable to sit in the coolness of a cave, then the extreme heat of a desert. From that location Satan could easily have tempted him with bread, then taken him to that high mountain peak and showed a view that could have included the city of Jericho (where Zacchaeus lived) and, on a clear day, Jerusalem the home of the temple, way off in the distance.

The mountain sits high over Jericho and the cable car is in the Guinness Book of Records as the highest cable car under sea level (quite an honor). It took us to a monastery where we climbed a huge amount of stairs.

Pilgrims climb this mountain to reach the top, retracing the supposed steps of Jesus. We saw old women struggling up the mountain, while healthy men like us took the cable car up.

When we got to the top, the monk who ran the monastery decided to lock the doors. Other pilgrims began to line up, some saying he does this all the time, closing the doors when he feels like it. The monk only did what most holy places do – lock up for religious afternoon siesta. However, one person in our group said he heard a woman talking inside the monastery.

Scandalous! Did the monk of the Mountain of Temptation have a little fling going on? We gave the benefit of the doubt to the monk and hoped he used his quiet time to watch religious programming or maybe reruns of "Touched by an Angel."

We waited in the shade while a salesman dangled jewelry in front of us. Temptation never ends…even on the Mount of Temptation. He pushed his wares on us, a captive audience stuck between 100 stairs and a locked door.

"Are you the tempter on this mountain?" I asked.

The salesman smiled, I must say, rather devilishly, holding his jewelry up to me. "This would look good on your wife."

"I don't have any money." Honestly I didn't.

"No money, no honey," the tempter grinned, rubbing his thumb and index fingers together in my face. I don't know what that meant, but he seemed to enjoy the English rhyme.

97

The tempter explained. "I have two wives. One in Jericho and one in Jerusalem."

"Do they know about each other?"

"Sure. No problem. No money, no honey."

It seems no one on this mountain can overcome temptation. Maybe indeed this was the place Jesus visited.

At 2:00 p.m., the monk opened the door. He looked like a wild and crazy John the Baptist. Long grey beard and hair. A robe that was stained from years of use and no laundry service. Dirty old sandals and yellow, unclipped toenails. He yelled at us in Greek, but nobody understood him. Then he switched to English. We entered and walked into the church, then he started to yell at us again!

He told us to get out, walked away, then apparently had a change of heart and returned to see our permits. He allowed our director and one other to go in to film. The rest of us stood outside and waited. I tried to talk to the man and thank him, but he would not listen or make eye contact. Slowly my opinion of the man turned to pity. He was so lonely.

If I were all alone on the mountain, twenty-four hours a day, seven days a week, I think I would welcome guests. However the absence of relationship seemed to strip him from the need of relationship. Visitors became a nuisance. All he really needed was a friend. Our guides told us that there used to be 25 monks who lived there. All of them have left. Relationships give us hope and connect us to the world. Living like a hermit stripped the monk from all the benefits of community.

I now understood how difficult it must have been for Jesus to be alone and fight off temptations. Loneliness attracts all kinds of demons.

But did Satan ever really have a chance to tempt to Jesus, God himself? Was this temptation moment unnecessary because of its improbability? It brings up the whole question of whether or not Jesus had the freedom to sin.

Norman Geisler

That's a debated question among theologians. There are two views. One says that Jesus could not have sinned and the other one says Jesus did not sin. The first one is called Impeccability; the second view is called sinlessness. I think Jesus was sinless but not impeccable. As God He couldn't sin, as man He could have but didn't. As God He couldn't get hungry, as man He could get hungry and did. So He was 100% human and He was 100% God and every time you ask one question of

Jesus you have to ask two. As God did He know everything? Yes. As man? No. As God did He grow in knowledge? No. As man did He grow in knowledge? Yes. As God could He have sinned? No. As man could He have sinned? Yes, but He didn't.

Paul Young
If He is fully human, He had the same choice that Adam did in the garden. That He could have declared independence. And I think that's the basis of what those temptations are.

Max Lucado
If Jesus did not have the freedom to sin, then He was not tempted. It seems to me that temptation is temptation because there is the choice to sin. So, yes I believe that Jesus had opportunities throughout his life to either disobey or disregard God which to me is a pretty good workable definition for sin.

Norman Geisler
Temptation was real. It was not like somebody approaching a battleship in a canoe with a pea shooter. You know, there's no chance to sink it, so no it was real. It was real but again it was external. It didn't come from within, from His lust. It came from without but, it was a tremendous power, a tremendous force upon Him, especially when you haven't eaten. C.S. Lewis said, 'His greatest temptations came after a physical low or a spiritual high.' Well you have a physical low after forty days of no eating and drinking. And Jesus was as weak as a human being can ever get and yet He resisted it. Yes, He could have, no He didn't sin.

We all experience temptation. Every day. It is impossible to be a human being and escape the reality of temptation, whether we're alone or with a group.

Ever since the first humans were placed in the most ideal place on earth, temptation found its way to ruin the party. The power of temptation is so strong it destroyed paradise and led to the destruction of God's handiwork.

Temptation, though, is not sin. It is the suggestion to sin. It lays the pathway for sin. Temptations to sin are the same for everyone, though they take on different forms in different places. Some would find

99

a bar tempting. Others a mall. Still others get tempted in church, of all places.

For Jesus to be walking in human flesh, temptation was a real invitation to sin. By overcoming these three temptations—physical, relational, spiritual—Jesus established his dominance over sin in every situation he would find himself for the next three years.

After these forty days, Jesus walked around cities and the temple. If Jesus could defeat Satan here, in the condition he was in, Jesus, well-fed and surrounded by friends, could defeat Satan anywhere.

So Satan changed his tactics and tempted others for the next three years—the weak minded, the weak willed, the weak of spirit, including the Pharisees, who, just miles from here, sat in palatial mansions, gorging themselves on the best food and drink, a direct contrast to Jesus' current situation. Satan's efforts through the lives of others brought Jesus to the cross, but even that was by God's design and set up Jesus' triumph over death.

Jesus came to the desert to shut down all distractions and focused on one thing—his relationship to God. I would choose to retreat in a mountain cabin or an ocean villa, blocking out the usual distractions, but never *all* distractions and *all* relationships.

A barren desert would expose my weakness. Instead, it exposed Jesus' power over temptation and his power over the human body.

The more we say no to temptation, the less power Satan has to tempt us. Jesus had been tempted all throughout his childhood, adolescence and adulthood, but the wilderness was an extreme showdown to show Satan and us that Jesus truly had the power over sin.

William Paul Young

And so I think the wilderness temptation is a beautiful time. And He comes out powerful, contrary to the old Hollywood movies remember where He comes out looking kind of beat up and just about destroyed, you know. It says that 'He comes out full of the Holy Spirit' and it becomes a very precious time. A lot of us have gone through wilderness times where God shows up.

TIME TO JOURNEY

1. **Watch "Temptation" from "In His Shoes: The Life of Christ"**

2. **Discussion Questions**

- What food is your greatest temptation?

- Have you ever fasted? How long?

- If you haven't, would you fast? What for?

- Have you ever been in the desert? What was that like?

- If you were gone for 40 days, who would you miss the most?

- If you are gone on business trips, what's your biggest temptation?

- What about being away from home encourages temptations?

- If you could rule one city, which one would you choose?

- What's the most power you've ever held?

- What temptations come with power?

- What kind of a person would you turn into if you cut yourself off from humanity?

- What is the difference between temptation and sin?

- What do you think of Jesus going to the wilderness to overcome temptation?

- Does Jesus' victory in the desert give you encouragement to overcome your own temptations?

- To build your resistance to temptations, you need to experience temptations. Is that a good idea?

Called

Sea of Galilee/Capernaum

I've received some pretty important phone calls in my day.

One day in 1997, our pastor called me, asking me if I wanted to join the staff at our church. It came as some surprise since I had no formal training in church education or a seminary degree. It didn't seem to matter. They just saw something in me that they liked. I have continued to be involved in our church to this day. That call changed everything.

I remember a phone call from a producer asking if I wanted to write for an animated series based on a story by Max Lucado. "Max Lucado," I cried. "I have all of his books." That relationship spawned the Hermie series and has given me so many great opportunities. That was an important phone call for me.

I also remember the phone call from my mom telling me my father had died. It was Valentine's Day. Though I knew it was coming, he had been sick for years with MS and cancer, it didn't take away the shock. I didn't like that phone call, but it was milestone, a life-changer, nonetheless.

Calls do that to us. They can completely redirect your whole life in an instant.

"You've won a million dollars."

"Your son has been arrested."

"You got the job!"

"We need you to relocate."

"I want us just to be friends…"

Opportunities have a way of calling us up when we least expect it. What would you do, right now, if someone of great importance walked into the room, looked at you and said, "You're the person I've been looking for"?

Now that could be bad news if it's Dog the Bounty Hunter or good news if the person is a Hollywood casting agent, Publisher's Clearing House or the President of the United States.

We have to be ready for those life-changing moments because sometimes we do not get a second chance to say "yes."

As Jesus began his ministry, he needed to call people to join him. They were faced with a crises decision that would dramatically change their lives.

Let's start by looking at the list of apostles:

Simon (whom he named Peter), his brother Andrew, James, John, Philip, Bartholomew, Matthew, Thomas, James son of Alphaeus, Simon who was called the Zealot, Judas son of James, and Judas Iscariot, who became a traitor. Luke 6:14-16

Not an impressive group. No formal education. No seminary degrees. Not even any staff experience at the local synagogue. At first glance you notice some redundancy with the names, which always causes headaches during roll calls—two guys named James, two Simons and two Judases. One guy was a zealot, or a political rebel, which meant he had an independent don't- tell-me-what-to-do, Tea Party spirit. The other was a traitor, quietly harboring negative, ill-feelings. That's always good for team dynamics.

On the northern side of the Sea of Galilee sits a large, busy fishing village called Capernaum. Many call Capernaum the ministry home of Jesus—the place where he recruited many of his apostles and hung out during their down time. It was there that we visited.

As we walked amongst the ruins of Capernaum, Avner and I leaned against a railing overlooking the excavation site of the ancient city, near a synagogue that they believed Jesus visited in John 6, when he declared "I am the bread of life" to the Jewish leaders. The foundation for the fourth or fifth century ruins beside us could have been the first century synagogue Jesus spoke in.

"The name of the place Capernaum comes from the Hebrew, Kefar Nahum. Kefar is a village and Nahum is Nahum, a name that we are familiar with from the Bible, the prophet Nahum. Yet we don't know who this Nahum was."

"Now if you're going to pick a ministry area like Jesus did," I asked, "why would Capernaum be significant?

"The people of Nazareth act differently than the people here. These people were open to listen, open to follow. And the people of Nazareth, maybe, because of being in the community where Jesus grew up in just turned their back towards Him and were not open at all to hear His message."

"Why was Capernaum important in the first century?"

"In the first century Capernaum was an important area because it was quite a dense area with rural communities. People who lived here made their living from fishing and from cultivating the area around.

People who seek after a normal life, for a real connection with God, and probably were much more open to listen than other people in the cities. Very family oriented people. Yet, the people in cities, especially in the big cities would see them as not sophisticated and not so engaged in the big things that were in Jerusalem."

I looked out over the location. Capernaum had a slightly elevated, seaside view of Galilee, prime real estate in a seller's market. "Now Capernaum would be key, I think, strategically because you have the sea and you have a main road here, right?"

"Yes. Capernaum and the lake are within the Rift Valley. The Rift Valley allows traffic here from north to south and was the main road of the ancient world. Not only for the land of Israel but for the whole ancient world. This road passed by here very close to Capernaum. So Capernaum was enjoying the proximity of such an important route that trade went through. But not only trade, because also ideas where exchanged among people and being next to the road is like being exposed to main radio station today, to the media today."

That road in the Roman highway system was called the Via del Mar, the Road by the Sea. A ruin of an unassuming ancient road sign sits in the Capernaum site.

"So when Jesus says to these followers, 'take my message to the world', Capernaum really is connected to the world, right?"

"Capernaum is connected to the world. When one would go to the communities in Ephesus or any other place, one would take this road."

So Capernaum was the right place to call disciples, but did Jesus call the right people? Fishermen? When I think of fishermen, I see hard working, blue collar laborers, with some limited education, who smell like fish. They don't immediately come to mind as people I want to give the responsibility of my worldwide mission to.

And just because fishermen may be good at catching fish, does it mean they are good at catching people? Since when do we throw out nets to get people to accept Christ?

I walked with Avner along the pebbly shoreline of Galilee in an area called Tabgha, near the Church of the Primacy of St. Peter, a Franciscan church built in 1933 to highlight Peter's reinstatement into ministry after denying Christ three times. A simple statue shows Peter on his knees accepting Jesus' call to feed his sheep. I asked Avner if he felt these would be the kind of people Jesus would need for his team.

"There are a few things. Being exposed to the nature is being exposed to who created it. They were probably strong, well-built people.

There is also something very symbolic about people who take things out of the water. For us human beings, getting into the water is to die. But fishing out people is like bringing them to life, bringing people to the air, to expose them to heaven."

So Jesus needed people who saw God in the world around them, who were hard working and could withstand the rough road ahead of them. He also saw symbolic parallels in their current job with their future job.

Jesus knew who he was calling.

I decided to talk to a modern day fishermen, so I met up with Menachem Lev, a fishing manager for a Kibbutz called Ein-Gev on the Sea of Galilee. Menachem is a stout, gruff, salt of the sea, as they say, kind of guy. Exactly the type of exterior I would want a fisherman to be. Menachem surprised me with his wit, charm and acute wisdom.

"Not everybody can be a fisherman. You have to be patient. You have to work as a team. Somebody has to say what to do. Somebody has to be the captain at this time. So I think some things come together to say, 'I want these people to come with me...'"

So Jesus needed patient people who could persevere despite setbacks and dry seasons. He called team players and people who respect authority. Once again, fishermen appear to be the right people.

I met Menachem's wife, a beautiful woman with a big smile.

"This is your wife," I said, trying not to sound too surprised. I didn't think fisherman got the good-looking girls.

Menachem smiled, winking at me. "It is very romantic being a fisherman."

Maybe fishermen were good at attracting people.

Jesus saw something in them I would miss. I would ask for seminary degrees, church recommendations, statements of faith and testimonies. All the things that people thankfully never asked from me.

Jesus saw these fishermen's willingness to work hard and to get dirty as positive traits. Their physical strength would come in handy for the long days and long nights, the prison stays and arduous journeys. I never liked fishing because I don't have patience. I hate sitting for long periods of time doing...nothing.

The patience required to land a fish is really no different than the patience needed to attract a person to Christ. You have to know their environment, what time of day is ideal, the mind and motivations of your catch, and when they are hungry.

Then...wait for them to bite.

Since the fishermen owned their own businesses, Jesus saw self-motivation and endurance to get up every morning at go to work.

All it takes is someone to redirect their previous interests into a new interest.

And think of it—Jesus called these men and they weren't even saved! That would come later, after the resurrection.

Like Peter, Jesus also met Matthew at work. Jews considered those who took the job of a tax collector equal to a traitor. The Romans gave Jews the job of collecting taxes from other Jews. The Jewish tax collectors charged the normal Roman tax then added a hefty rate or fee to cover their own effort. It sparked greed in those that practiced it.

We still don't like tax collectors today because they want our money.

That didn't seem to matter to Jesus. He asked Matthew to join his posse. Again, I would require a certain amount of trust and I wouldn't want to disrupt my team with someone no one else liked. I'm also, face it, very concerned about my image. If I bring a tax collector onto my team, it would reflect poorly on me.

But Matthew's appointment spoke to those who felt unworthy to be a disciple. If Jesus liked him, certainly he would accept anyone. He still does today.

I would miss so much if I just looked on the outside of people or even at their resumes. I wouldn't have the confidence in myself to invest the time and effort in such a ragtag group of repetitious names.

Jesus wanted the common, the untrained, uneducated, disliked so he could demonstrate his power to make them uncommon, skilled, wise and loved. Jesus wanted teachable people without a strong agenda. That's a tall order to ask. Jesus must have had confidence in his ability to rally and educate this unconventional ministry team. No rabbis or Pharisees were approached. No professors or scholars. Just every day guys.

One account in Matthew 5 says he asked them to follow him and they immediately dropped everything to go. That's a bit hard to believe. Can you imagine someone walking up to you and just saying the words, "Follow me" and you dropping all your plans and dreams to pursue their plans and dreams?

The other account in Luke 5 tells of a miracle Jesus performed in correctly predicting a spectacular catch of fish. A miracle might change my mind, but it had better be very good trick.

So what made the apostles drop everything and follow him?

Joel Hunter

It is a mystery why people would just say "all right" and go along. But we get some hint of it when we hear the Jewish teachers say "This man has a sense of authority". How does He have the authority that He does? And in the Bible it's in the tone of His voice, He speaks not like other men. So there was a sense of authority and confidence I believe that just came through Jesus. And when people heard, first of all, I believe that God prepared people to hear Him. And just as He does, I mean, when God finally calls us it's not because all of a sudden we've lived this reprobate life and now we're surprised...When that voice comes, and it comes through Jesus. I believe that there was a confidence, an authority, a movement of the Spirit that left no room for any kind of doubt on the part of the hearer as to who was really calling them.

Norman Geisler

It looks quick but it wasn't. There's indication that He had contact with them previously and that He was just saying, 'Okay, now the moment has come', and it wasn't just a spur of the moment thing. Although I have no doubt in my mind that the power of Jesus' personality and His divinity would show through and could easily convince somebody on the spot to do that. It seems to me by studying a passage clearly and knowing that we have a three and a half year period here we're talking about and you can summarize all that in a few minutes. There are a lot of other things that took place and I think He knew these people before, He had met them, they had already been attracted to his ministry, and He's just now calling them to follow Him on the basis of what they already knew.

There is some thought that word of Jesus had spread after the dramatic Jordan River moment. Maybe one or two of them were followers of John the Baptist and present at Jesus' baptism.

I like that Jesus met them at work. For a man, work is everything. It's where a man gets his focus, his encouragement, his structure and his success. Jesus invaded their work space and showed these fishermen, Andrew and Peter, something he could do that they could understand. Now I personally don't read this story of a miraculous catch and immediately think "that's it...I'm following Jesus" and begin to pack my bags for Africa. So they made a catch of fish...big deal.

But I'm not a fishermen.

Catching fish is unpredictable, even for the most experienced. The miracle, for them, occurred in the where and the when and the how Jesus predicted that catch. The time of the day. The place in the sea. The amount that came in. This meant something to fishermen. It, admittedly, doesn't do much for me.

For me, Jesus could show up in my office and say "Look under your chair and you will find that completed manuscript you've been wanting to write for fifteen years." NOW THAT WOULD BE AMAZING!

As I think about it, Jesus has met me at work. The Hermie series and the church job both came at a time of financial crises. We had very little money or prospects in "our nets." Suddenly they were full. God always provided us with work when we needed it. As a result, I find myself serving him more out of appreciation and amazement for what He did and does for us through His provision.

He asked the fishermen to re-examine their work and offered them more fulfilling work. Maybe the frustration of fish-less nets caused them to think, "I've got to get out of this business. I wonder if there's something else." Then, in walks Jesus.

But once Jesus performed the miracle, wouldn't the tendency be to stay and profit off that catch? Suddenly their fishing business promised a pretty steady income. Following Jesus did not. In fact, Jesus made no promise of profit or paycheck. The fishermen needed to quickly make a choice—trust the fish or trust in God.

Once again, something about Jesus…his charisma…his confidence…his personality caused them to walk away from their full nets. People are attracted to these qualities. We follow people with vision and direction.

William Paul Young

He is a person of substance. Just like in cosmology, the denser the substance the greater the attraction, the greater the gravitational field. And so almost in a human sense, you're dealing with somebody who you can't see through. This person is a real person. This person loves life. This person, there's something about the way they love children, the way they love people. The way they're open, there's something about. And His reputation is already preceding Him, I mean, it's getting out there already. So as He begins to show up well, one, He's asking people, they would never been asked to follow a rabbi, I mean there's something about that. You know, 'You're asking me? Me, I'm a fisherman? What do I? I'm past the age of following a rabbi.' All of those things are part of this. It's part of the enigma and the subtlety of all this and the difference. And He's pulling out of people stuff that is resident within them. Some of them, they see Him as an opposition to the religious system that they can't speak for themselves, you know, that they're not comfortable declaring for themselves. Some of them, it's just the fact that He would ask them. Maybe that was enough. You know, who knows what's in the heart of man but there was something about Jesus that is just absolutely unusual, absolutely spectacular and attractive and I think they're just drawn to that.

We cannot overlook, nor hardly imagine, Jesus' appeal. Remember, Jesus had no physical features that made him fashionably attractive, so his attitude, his love, his heart had to radiate from his words, eyes and touch. His most significant appeal could have been his determination, authority and confidence. People want to follow leaders who know where they are going.

Norman Geisler
There are people that when you meet, you just somehow are attracted to them. So Jesus no doubt had charisma but, He must have had super charisma because He was a perfect man. He was the son of God. He was somebody who was totally innocent. You could look at Him and see right through Him. So I have no doubt that that was a factor that played in the role of convincing people of who He was and that combined with the fact that they had Messianic expectations, they knew He was doing miracles. Nicodemus himself said, 'Nobody can do these things, these miracles that you do unless God be with him.'

I asked Menachem Lev how it would feel if someone came up to him and said he couldn't' fish any more.
"I feel like somebody ripped my head off. I tell you it's a part of me, but it's not only me, it's my family."
When those apostles walked away from their jobs, they walked away from their identity and their family. Yet, Jesus asked from them only what he was willing to risk. He asked these men for their lives, complete and total surrender to the cause. Jesus gave up his possessions, his time, his relationships for the cause.

110

These are not easy demands. We should always read the fine print before we commit to something. Did the apostles really know what they were getting into?

Then he said to them all: "If anyone would come after me, he must deny himself and take up his cross daily and follow me. For whoever wants to save his life will lose it, but whoever loses his life for me will save it. What good is it for a man to gain the whole world, and yet lose or forfeit his very self? If anyone is ashamed of me and my words, the Son of Man will be ashamed of him when he comes in his glory and in the glory of the Father and of the holy angels. I tell you the truth, some who are standing here will not taste death before they see the kingdom of God." Luke 9:23-27

Deny yourself.
Grab your instrument of execution.
Lose your life.
Give up the world.
Get ready to taste death.
Later on, Jesus added more exciting perks.

As they were walking along the road, a man said to him, "I will follow you wherever you go." Jesus replied, "Foxes have holes and birds of the air have nests, but the Son of Man has no place to lay his head." He said to another man, "Follow me."
But the man replied, "Lord, first let me go and bury my father." Jesus said to him, "Let the dead bury their own dead, but you go and proclaim the kingdom of God." Still another said, "I will follow you, Lord; but first let me go back and say good-by to my family." Jesus replied, "No one who puts his hand to the plow and looks back is fit for service in the kingdom of God." Luke 9:57-62

Oh, by the way, you'll be homeless.
Say goodbye to your family.
Don't look back.
Yes. Jesus made it clear.

111

I like that Jesus didn't sugar coat or hide the demands of the calling. "Many of you will be killed." That's pretty blunt. Some disciples turned away. Others stayed. Jesus weeded out the casual from the serious.

Jesus offered these men the opportunity of a lifetime, giving them a chance to learn firsthand from God himself. Along the way, he made friends with these men. He invested in them. He saw things in them everyone else missed.

I turned again to Avner, "Now Jesus asks His followers to give up so much, to deny themselves, to take up the cross, to follow Him. And I have to wonder, are these the kind of people that would really be the kind to say, 'yes we would follow'? And be that passionate about something?"

"Well I would say that during that period, everybody was quite passionate and there was a feeling that the Messiah's about to come...There were so many different groups. Many of them were very highly sophisticated and were so much into the philosophy behind the understanding of the faith. Where here people were much more down to earth with two legs on the ground. And when somebody came and convinced them, 'I have the right way', they were more than ready to follow Him. And it seems the sense of something coming in, giving up daily life was very a small thing."

"So of all the areas," I asked, "you have Nazareth over here which rejects Jesus. You have the Gentile area over here. Then you have the people of Jerusalem who are all the religious types, the scribes and Pharisees. This is kind of it for him right?"

"Capernaum is really about it for Jesus. I'm sure that whenever Jesus went to Jerusalem, He passed through this area and got to know the people around. And indeed those people were rural people, not very sophisticated; they didn't go to the university. And therefore they didn't deal with the very complicated theology and philosophy.

"But they did share the idea that the Messiah's about to come...And therefore they were like everybody else, preparing themselves to the coming future. And in their way they needed some guidelines and when somebody came and was convincing to them, 'here I have the true way', they were more than happy to leave everything and follow Him to this road."

While being called into ministry can change everything, it doesn't mean it changes it for the worst. In fact, Jesus' call changes everything for the better, giving the one called new direction, new hope, new purpose and new life.

He came to the right place, called the right people, at the right time.

At the site in Capernaum, you cannot miss a huge flying saucer that sits suspended over the ruins. A bizarre visual contrast of modern and ancient. Avner confides in me that it's a disgrace to put such a structure over a key archaeological location.

This is the Church of the House of Saint Peter, also built by the Franciscans in 1990. Aptly named, it is a church that sits over, what they believe, the house of Peter, the place where Jesus healed Peter's mother in law.

Inside is a quaint church, inlaid with rich woods and magnificent carvings all along the walls. It's a more modern contrast to the 2,000 year old stones sitting outside.

Since my mind was on calling and apostles being called to follow Jesus, I noticed a petite nun working quietly and diligently inside the church. Her name was Sister Rebecca Dangeran, all the way from the Philippines. I asked her if she had a few moments to help me understand how one could completely give their entire life over into ministry.

"I feel this calling of Jesus since I was a child. Six years old."

Wow, I thought. I felt a calling to the swing set at six and she was feeling called to ministry. "You left everything, haven't you? Your home town"

"Yes, of course. My mother. My brother. Nieces. Nephews."

"Do you have any hesitation or regrets?"

"As of now, no."

"Why did he call you here?"

"Just for a mission. To serve. We are not married. Wherever our mother tells us to go we will go. If she tells us to go to America, I go to America. If she says go to Italy, I go to Italy. I will sacrifice because it is not my own way."

Sister Dangeran responded exactly like the apostles and disciples whose homes sat underneath the church she served at. She was a modern day example of the kind of sacrifice required for people who are called into ministry.

Being called was an honor to her, but a sacrifice too.

Am I doing that?

That question bothered me the entire trip. I responded to my calling, many times, on my terms and my schedule. To drop my net and completely, totally and sacrificially follow Jesus Christ...am I doing that? Am I really a disciple?

113

TIME TO JOURNEY

1. **Watch "Called" from "In His Shoes: The Life of Christ"**

2. **Discussion Questions**

- Can you think of a phone call that changed your life?
- Has anyone ever asked you to be a part of a ministry?
- What do you think of Jesus' ministry team?
- What was it about the fishermen that were ideal evangelists?
- What other trade would be good at evangelism today?
- Do you think the disciples were special?
- Who would you have called?
- What qualities in your line of work would Jesus find appealing to be on his team?
- What event/crisis/request would be significant enough for you to drop everything?
- Who could get you to drop your net?
- What would convince you to follow someone into ministry?
- What about Jesus would you find appealing upon meeting him?
- If you called a pastor to your church, what would you expect to see on his resume?
- What qualities does Jesus require on a resume?
- Would you follow someone who asked you to take up his cross and follow him?

Teacher
Mount of Beatitudes

I love to teach. It's the one thing you don't have to force me to do. Setting up chairs, planning budgets, baking cookies...shoot me now. A simple invitation is all I need to teach and I'll be there, fully prepared. I have sermons and lessons in my back pocket, but I'm always excited to explore new territories and teach new things.

In 2011, I took on the challenge of teaching the entire Bible in one year. It's forced me to read, study and know the entire Bible. Three times a week I taught the same lesson. Three times a week I can't wait. I even taught a class at 6:30 in the morning. I woke up at 5:00 too excited to sleep.

One of Jesus' primary tasks for coming to this earth was to teach. The world had strayed from Old Testament law and Jesus needed to bring a New Testament reboot to the previous teachings. I really believe Jesus enjoyed teaching—he did it so much. The pages of the Gospels are filled with lessons, sermons and anecdotes that explained a significant truth—God loves his people!

As I ponder the teachings of Jesus, I am struck by the volumes of material he communicated off the cuff. Jesus taught wherever he went, to whatever audience was listening, both friendly and hostile. No notes. No prepared lessons.

As I walk in the shoes of Jesus, I found myself at the traditional site of the Mount of Beatitudes where Jesus taught his most famous lesson. Marking the spot was a nice little chapel, built in 1939 right on the shore of the Sea of Galilee, commemorating Jesus' most famous sermon. This structure, a collaboration of Franciscan Sisters and, of all people, the Italian dictator Mussolini, stands as a monument to the power of Jesus' teaching. By coming here, I wanted to reflect on those qualities that made Jesus an incredible teacher and why people of that time recognized his authority.

This time of year, every site in Israel felt quite packed with people. The workers at this location, like the Mount of Temptation, take a lunch break, but they decided to open a little early since nearly 70 buses were heading their way. Think of it, as many people that heard Jesus that day speak on the topic of the Beatitudes, drive up to this monument in one hour.

Jesus can still pack them in.

115

However, all was not beatitude-like on this little mountain. It appears Mussolini himself dictated that a certain Nazi nun oversee the complex. When our film crew showed up, we were greeted by screaming from nearly 100 yards away…

"No film! No film! You do not have the proper document! Let me see your permit!" When our producer tried to talk to her, she would have nothing to do with him.

"Permit!"

The Beatitudes came to mind…

Blessed are the merciful,
for they will be shown mercy.
Blessed are the pure in heart,
for they will see God.
Blessed are the peacemakers,
for they will be called sons of God. Matthew 5:7-9

I know we were clinging to the next verse.

Blessed are those who are persecuted because of righteousness,
for theirs is the kingdom of heaven. Matthew 5:10

Her tone and behavior changed our name for this location: The Church on the Mount of Bad-Attitudes. "Read the beatitudes, sister," we wanted to cry. Eventually the permit satisfied her, we were shown mercy and Avner and I began our tour around the location.[6]

When Jesus taught, he preferred a number of locations.

Again Jesus began to teach by the lake. The crowd that gathered around him was so large that he got into a boat and sat in it out on the lake, while all the people were along the shore at the water's edge. Mark 4:1

---

[6] During a return visit in 2012, I was sad to learn that three nuns from the Mount of Beatitudes died in a car wreck on Christmas Eve. I fear one of those nuns was her.

In a world without microphones or sound amplification, water provided excellent acoustics, which was why Jesus, at times, spoke from a boat or near water. His voice traveled along the surface, spreading out like sounds waves to their ears.

While standing on the Sea of Galilee, I heard what sounded like someone speaking into my ear. I knew no one was behind me, but I still turned and there, about 300 yards off the coast, was a boat. Though I could not see her, I heard a woman speaking Mandarin Chinese to those on board, the sound traveling clearly across the water. I didn't understand Mandarin Chinese, but our sound man did and immediately translated. Water is an excellent acoustic.

Jesus also taught in synagogues, the local Jewish "church."

They went to Capernaum, and when the Sabbath came, Jesus went into the synagogue and began to teach. Mark 1:21

It was customary for a visiting rabbi to be a guest speaker and Jesus used that opportunity to teach indoors.

Finally, Jesus liked to teach from a mountain. The shape of a mountain filters the sound down and out, through the audience. There he could speak over the heads of the people, so no one would block the sound of the person behind him.

As I walked around the Mount of Beatitudes with Avner, we avoided the stare of the Nazi nun, who even had the guts to shush Avner as he explained the significance of the symbols inside the chapel to me. Here was a teacher trying to teach a student, but the chapel master enforced protocol. "No teaching at the place where Jesus taught," she said by her actions.

So we stepped outside, into the shade, away from the others to talk. I wondered what it took to be a rabbi, a Jewish teacher, in the first century.

"When Hosea was renovating the temple and the [Old Testament] was found there, the scroll was brought to him. And when it was read he said 'Wow, what can we do? We are all in sin because we did not know.' Meaning, we couldn't learn. We were not familiar with the text. And since then rabbis have become more and more important because they were the people who could teach, who could explain the text.

"At the time of Christ, they were more and more respected and could have come from different backgrounds. The main thing is the devotion and being a teacher, having the capability to understand and to give that understanding to others."

"How many rabbis," I asked, "would there be in a town?"

"Probably there could be quite a lot of rabbis in one town."

"And no education was required?"

"No formal education," Avner continued, "except for knowing the Torah and the Scriptures well."

Now when he saw the crowds, he went up on a mountainside and sat down. His disciples came to him, and he began to teach them… Matthew 5:1-2

During the Sermon on the Mount, Jesus probably sat down first, turning everyone's attention to him. Sitting traditionally signified that the rabbi was about to speak. Even in our services today, we say "Be seated" and everyone sits knowing a teaching or sermon is coming. The difference is our pastors and ministers remain standing, while everyone else relaxes. Back then, the rabbi would sit on a step or on a rock, above the heads of his listeners as they sat.

Jesus began a lengthy sermon that covers three chapters in the book for Matthew, but scholars believe it was a compilation of teachings from days of speaking. Jesus may have spoken for thirty minutes at a time or maybe for hours, we don't know. One of the reasons scholars believe Jesus felt the need to feed the gatherings of the four and five thousand was that he had been teaching for so long. Imagine being that interesting that thousands would want to hear you and not once would they complain about the length of the sermon or focus on their rumbling stomachs.

When Jesus had finished saying these things, the crowds were amazed at his teaching, because he taught as one who had authority, and not as their teachers of the law. Matthew 7:28-29

The greatest compliment Jesus received from listeners was that he taught with authority, something the first century listeners had not heard before.

What sort of qualities must a teacher exhibit to be received as one with authority? What made him such a wonderful master teacher?

Max Lucado

During the time when Jesus taught, the authority was based on the teaching of the preceding rabbis, from what I understand. They would quote the rabbi – "Rabbi so and so said...." But Jesus, remember in the Sermon on the Mount would make statements like well you have heard it said but, I say unto you..." Well where does He get the right to say "I say unto you?" I think that's what they meant. He teaches with authority. He doesn't have to have footnotes or references or quotes. He doesn't have to quote anyone. He stands on His own legitimacy.

For starters, Jesus taught with *insight* that others didn't see, using the Bible to support his statements. He established new twists on the old teachings. Jesus did not reference other teachers in his sermons. He established precedents when he spoke that others were to follow. All of this without a formal seminary degree.

As Jesus taught, he made *promises* too, unlike teachers before him. In Matthew 6, Jesus promises that God will take care of them, their food, clothing and housing. He promised the listeners that if they acted "in his name" that they would succeed. Only one in authority could make such a statement. I personally can't tell you what God will do unless the Bible says God will do it. Jesus made promises without precedent and spoke in the first person, saying he himself will fulfill those promises, thereby taking on the role of God.

Jesus spoke from *experience and knowledge*. He knew truth and it showed. He had answers to tough questions, never once stammering or fumbling for an answer. His eternal experience and Godly knowledge spilled out in every word. The Pharisees only had second hand knowledge.

People are drawn to speakers who speak with *passion*. Unfortunately, some have been led astray by such teachers who fervently teach a false doctrine. When used for good, a passionate speaker can change a world.

Surveys say one of people's greatest fears is speaking in public. I only experience trepidation when I don't know my subject. When I know what I'm going to say and how I'm going to get there, I'm less afraid. Jesus felt *confident* with his subject matter, never having to draw from notes like I do. He taught with illustrations, points and a

119

conclusion in mind. He relied on the Holy Spirit to give him insight as he spoke.

Jesus on the Mount of Beatitudes and in other sermons talked of *feelings and emotions* like blessing, happiness and joy. One thing I have found over time is if you can't express it, don't profess it. If I'm a dour, sour, moody speaker and I say, "Accept Jesus and you'll be so happy...like me," I've destroyed that message. I must exude the emotions that I speak of, being a living example before their ears that the message really works.

That means Jesus overflowed with love and joy in his sermons. He expressed his heart and everyone around him knew it.

Norman Geisler

There are speakers, that just the tone of their voice, their demeanor, they come across with authority. Quite often it's a combination of some human factors like they have a deep voice. I doubt if He had a squeaky voice. *"(in a squeaky voice) I doubt He went around talking like this",* that He'd get too many followers. So He had a deep voice. He had a life that exemplified what He said. You lose all authority, all moral authority to teach when people know your life doesn't correspond to your lips. So He had a couple things going for Him there.

A teacher must sustain the interest and energy level of his audience through his *presentation*, especially for long periods of time. Jesus varied the levels of his volume, using emphasis, shifting from strong and forceful, to loving and compassionate. He may have moved, standing for emphasis, using his hands, referencing people and items in the audience.

Jesus tackled the *tough topics* and was unafraid of offending his audience. A few times they wanted to stone him or throw him off a mountain. Jesus walked into the temple and appeared to pick fights over the issue of truth. Negative reviews did not stop him.

Jesus spoke with *integrity*, living up to the standards he told others to live up to. I fear being called a hypocrite, so my solution is to avoid those topics that I haven't fully mastered. If I can't speak from conviction, then let's move on to another series. Jesus succeeded in every category he spoke on—greed, lust, loyalty, prayer. He believed, lived and breathed every lesson he ever taught. If he failed in his integrity, he failed as a teacher.

Jesus was *interesting*. I cannot fathom a moment of boredom during those lessons. Jesus had so much to draw from, not just the experiences he saw in thirty years of living as a man, but the eternal truths he knew, saw and established as God. I rely on the internet, books and my limited forty-some year perspective on life as a basis for my stories and examples. Jesus drew from unlimited resources.

Joel Hunter

As a teacher I believe that Jesus was absolutely riveting. He was, I believe, the best teacher of all time and let me tell you why. First of all, He taught in stories. The Bible is a story and it's a long narrative. And Jesus learned the art very early in His teachings. The Bible says "He taught them not without a parable". And so people love stories, people are made for stories so He taught them stories. Secondly, He taught them in ways that their spirit responded; it didn't just record in their brain "Oh this is a good religious teaching". As a matter of fact, in much of His teaching there was even a correction of what they'd always been taught, "You've always heard it said, but I say to you"...And so there was this radical kind of teaching that he had that just kind of smacked people with a spiritual two by four, so to speak. And at the same time I believe this tremendous compassion came through His voice. You know people can tell when you care about them and they want to listen when they know you care about them and you're speaking for their sake, not for your sake and you're not just pushing an agenda. You're pushing their growth and their closeness to God and you're doing it for some, and in ways that will help them live the abundant life that He promised. And so I just think that He had all of those things going for Him.

Humor and stories draw a listener into your sermon and vary the mood. Jesus used his stories to draw parallels to his message, forcing the listener to think and solve his own questions.

Parables were stories that drew from real-life experiences of human behavior and natural phenomena. When we hear a story of a persistent widow knocking on the door of a local mayor, we get it. We know people like that. It's kind of a funny scene. We all have the "nagging neighbor." To relate that to prayer does more to underscore the truth than just to say, "Keep on praying. Never give up!"

Or to relate different soils to the condition of our hearts immediately sinks in since we see parallel truths happening in our natural world as in the spiritual world.

Or to tell the story of the Good Samaritan resonates deeply with an audience who cannot imagine a person from Samaria doing any good. The parable spoke of kindness despite prejudice. They immediately got the point.

Not many of you should presume to be teachers, my brothers, because you know that we who teach will be judged more strictly. James 3:1

Teaching the Bible is the highest honor but one that comes with a higher standard of judgment. If anyone teaches, they will be judged by what they teach when they die. Teaching is very difficult because it addresses tough subjects that don't have easy answers. If you mislead others to sin, Jesus taught, it was better to tie a rock around your neck and drown in the water. Die now, before you sin much more. (That illustration alone proves Jesus' effectiveness and boldness when he taught)

Jesus desired *transformation* when he spoke. He wanted them to change the way they thought, the way they lived and interacted with others. He wanted them to change their worldview. I think it's the opportunity to change a heart that motivates a teacher most. To present stories and truths, then to see that lesson alter someone's preconceived notions and take them a step closer to God…that's what it is all about.

Jesus desired to make *followers and disciples*. He wanted them to become leaders who would lead others. He wanted hearts to repent and accept God's mercy, then see them go out and tell others the good news.

Norman Geisler
He was the master teacher as we know. People have written books on the laws of teaching. Jesus was the perfect example of every one of those laws. We have hints of it because even His enemies said, 'Never a man spake like this.' They were impressed. Even His enemies recognized that he's a man who calls it like he sees it.

For three years in the ministry, Jesus saw life change happen, but he also saw stubbornness, deception and hate—hearts so calloused and hard that even he could not break through. Many disobeyed, rejecting truth from the truth-giver himself, standing right before them.

He hurt when he faced stubborn hearts that would not budge.

Max Lucado

When He looked over the city of Jerusalem and said, "O Jerusalem, Jerusalem how many times I would have gathered you like a hen gathers her chicks but, you would not let me." There's no silver lining in that statement. I mean that's not a positive mental attitude sermon. He is distraught. He's sad. It broke His heart. It literally broke His heart.

Jesus saw the eternity those faced from such a heart condition, but he continued to *persevere*. Jesus experienced the same ups and downs we all do. He refused to be sidetracked by the deceivers and pressed on for the receivers.

I'm always blown away that not everyone accepted Jesus' message. It's sad, but comforting too. If Jesus couldn't convince them, then I can't convince everyone who hears me. I just have to present the truth, drawing from Jesus' proven teaching methods and showing the same passion for my subject just like Jesus did.

Avner and I moved down the mountain to see the natural terrain. I looked behind me, awaiting the nun to yell out, "You kids get off my lawn!"

It was a hot day and a very arid, shade-less area we descended into, with rocks and prickly plants. Not the kind of location I pictured from artists, who saw this as a grassy, manicured lawn, comfortable and lush, with maybe a sprinkler system and a maintenance man. Jesus did not choose this place for comfort.

"So why would Jesus pick this location to deliver this sermon?" I asked Avner.

"I think that a mountain has a very strong meaning here. It is like Moses getting the Ten Commandments on a mountain. The message is coming from heaven and that is the foundation from now on. It is to say Mount Sinai was just a pre-figuration of what is happening now."

"So the imagery here is that when God wants to speak and give a new message, a new covenant to the people, he seems to do it from a mountain."

"Yeah, and not only does the mountain reach high and up to heaven, but it stands also for the power of God in creation."

I see clearly standing here on the Mount of Beatitudes, looking over the beautiful valley and the Sea of Galilee, that Jesus came here to hand down a new law, the Sermon on the Mount, to his followers. This was far more than just teaching. Jesus laid out a new covenant or a new testament. The Mount of Beatitudes became the new Mount Sinai. Bringing a new law to the people established Jesus' authority.

I thought of all the sermons and books (like this one) that rehash and repackage the Bible, many from very qualified and articulate writers and speakers. Jesus brought new insight, a new way to look at an old truth.

You know Jesus had a lot to communicate when the Gospel writer John says that the Bible could not contain every lesson he ever spoke. So many sermons, stories and parables were heard and never written down. I wonder if we'll be able to hear those lessons in heaven. Maybe we'll have an eternity to catch up and hear Jesus speak live, in person. I can't wait!

Jesus still desires to teach others. Now he speaks through his word, the Holy Spirit and those called to teach.

We all need to sit at his feet and listen more carefully, like we will for eternity, where he'll rivet our attention for years and decades and centuries to come.

TIME TO JOURNEY

1. **Watch "Teacher" from "In His Shoes: The Life of Christ"**

2. **Discussion Questions**

- What teacher in your life made a difference?
- Is teaching easy and for everyone?
- Do you teach the Bible? Why or why not?
- What kind of a teacher do you think Jesus was?
- Why do you think teaching was high on Jesus' list of tasks?
- Have you ever heard a teacher speak with authority? What made the difference?
- What kind of a teacher can make promises from the Bible?
- How important to you are the off-stage actions of a teacher?
- What emotions do you think Jesus used when he taught?
- What kind of a sense of humor did Jesus have?
- Why are stories so effective for a speaker?
- What kind of a response did Jesus want from his listeners?
- How do you think he felt when they rejected his message?
- How do you feel about all the things that Jesus taught that are not written in the Bible? Do you think they are important?
- Do you think we learn in heaven?

Miracles
Bethsaida/Jerusalem

I haven't seen a lot of miracles in my life.

Once while I was a teenager, I stayed home from church after crying all night over a rejection from a girl. The rejections from the opposite sex had been piling up lately in high school and the teenage angst began to pour out in a frustrated night, spilling over into the morning. My parents decided to leave me home. Then, as I floated in a puddle of tears, I suddenly felt a tremendous sense of comfort flow through me. The pain and sorrow disappeared in an instant. I had no insight or mental realization, just peace.

I went to church and my parents were shocked to see me, their faces wondering, "What happened? We left you sobbing like a big baby."

I stored that moment away and went on living my rebellious life. Years later after I became a Christian, I pointed to that emotional recovery as a moment when God miraculously touched my life.

In 2006, during a mission trip to Costa Rica, I visited a home and prayed for a woman in a lot of pain. I've prayed for lots of people on mission trips for healing. This time though, as I opened my eyes, she was healed. The pain was gone, she said. It took some time as the translators communicated what just happened, but it was amazing. Her whole demeanor changed in just a few minutes. The true test of its "miraculousness" came when her husband, a non-believer, professed his amazement too. Even he saw a miracle!

That night, during a service, she walked in with a bag filled with pills, nearly four hundred of them, and dumped them on the dirt. She was done with medications.

I know miracles happen. I hear others talk about them all the time. I just don't see them happening in my life on a weekly, monthly, even yearly basis. But I see them happening all the time in the Gospels, especially when Jesus showed up and confronted an impossible task, like what he did in Bethsaida.

Avner excitedly took me to the ruins of Bethsaida that were unearthed just recently, in archaeological terms. Rami Arav, with the help of the University of Nebraska, began excavating in 1987 and found some spectacular results. The immensity of the find amazed archaeologists. This was a big city and an important one too.

127

We sat amongst the foundational ruins of a once wealthy home with a huge courtyard that even contained a wine cellar, dug into the ground. This was the upper middle class section of town. Avner told me the meaning of the city's name. "Bethsaida is a 'place of fishing with nets.' It was primarily a fishing town because it was so close to the Sea of Galilee."

Bethsaida today sits up high over the Sea of Galilee, but 2,000 years ago, the Sea held more water than it does now.

"So who would have come from this area?" Fishermen, I supposed, answering my own question in my head. But Avner surprised me with his Bible knowledge, pulling out a New Testament and thumbing through it.

"In John Chapter 1 it says 'Now Philip was from Bethsaida, the city of Andrew and Peter,' so three of the apostles were from here."

I looked around. Jesus once walked these streets in front of me.

Avner continued. "This is the traditional location for the feeding of the 5,000."

There's a small church in the area with a big name—The Church of the Multiplication of the Loaves and Fishes—not far from here. The earliest structure that commemorated this spot was constructed in 380 AD, enlarged in 480 AD, destroyed in 614 AD, then excavated in 1932 and rebuilt in 1939, with the original mosaic floors from the 5th Century church depicting fish and bread. Even the Church of Multiplication finds a way to miraculously multiply itself through the centuries.

At the time of the miracle, there was no church here, or gift shop or even a convenience store. No Sam's Club or Costco to buy food in bulk.

I knew the miracle well. "Some believe Jesus fed nearly 15,000, since the Bible only records 5,000 men. What was the population of Bethsaida?"

Avner could see the significance of his next statement. "About 15,000."

My jaw dropped. "Jesus could have fed this whole town?"

"It appears so."

I started to understand the immensity of this miracle. "So he's kind of saying by being right near here, there's enough here of me to feed this entire town and this is one of the largest towns around."

Avner agreed. It would be like Jesus showing up in New York City and feeding over eight million people in Central Park.

Jesus' ability to perform miracles separates him from every other religious figure. Muhammad cannot claim the resume Jesus acquired.

128

Buddha falls way short. Even the modern "prophets" who started twenty-century faiths—Joseph Smith, Charles Taze Russell, L.Ron Hubbard—cannot match the miraculous power of Jesus.

Being present at a miracle had to be a heart-stopping, awe-inspiring moment for the people, especially in a first century culture. Today we see special effects and magic acts that may make us ho-hum the spectacular. "Probably done with mirrors and fishing lines," we shrug.

But some of these miracles, especially walking on water and producing loaves of bread out of thin air, could stir a few "ooos" and "aaahs" from the audience, no matter what century you live in.

I wonder what the miracles were like for Jesus. Remember, for thirty years he quietly walked the earth, doing nothing miraculous. Then, all of a sudden, Jesus burst onto the scene, doing the unimaginable, like a kid waiting to show off his brand new magic set.

"Look what I can do! Shazam!"

The first question to ask about Jesus and the miracles is where did that power come from? Did Jesus have within himself the ability to do the incredible? Dr. Geisler opened my eyes to this question.

Norman Geisler

Jesus' power to heal, there are two views held by perfectly orthodox theologians on that. One is He sometimes used His divine attributes to heal and the other is that He never did, He just submitted to the Father and the Father gave Him the authority to do it. I hold the second view because I think it diminishes the Biblical view of His humanity to say that He was pulling rank. And then what encouragement would that be to me in my temptation if Jesus was tempted in all points like as I am, without sin, if I knew that every time He got in trouble He pulled rank and drew on His divinity rather than submitted to the Father, trusted the Father. The Father gave Him the ability to do what He did as the Father revealed it to Him.

Troy

So using his divine attributes would be like...cheating?

Norman Geisler

Yeah, it would be cheating. It would destroy His example to us who are purely human and don't have any divine attributes to pull over and just have to trust God. He was setting the perfect example for us.

Your attitude should be the same as that of Christ Jesus:
Who, being in very nature God,
did not consider equality with God something to be grasped,
but made himself nothing,
taking the very nature of a servant,
being made in human likeness.
And being found in appearance as a man,
he humbled himself
and became obedient to death—
even death on a cross! Philippians 2:5-8

According to Philippians 2, Jesus walked away from his equality with God and chose to assimilate a less powerful nature—man. He remained obedient to His Father, keeping his title, but surrendering his omniscience (all-knowing), omnipresence (all-present) and omnipotence (all-power).

That means the Holy Spirit empowered him when and where he needed to perform the miracles. The power came from outside himself, just like the other miracle workers in the Bible—Moses, Elijah. It also reveals his dependency on God the entire time.

Paul Young
Therefore this relationship of helpless dependence, 'I don't do anything unless I see the Father do it, I don't say anything unless I hear the Father say it.' To me that helpless dependence is the faith of a human being in a God who indwells Him. I see those miracles; I see this intimacy happening all the time.

And as a result, sometimes, Jesus looks like He's being a little abrupt or He comes across as a liar. I can think of two situations that really manifest this. One is in the wedding at Cana. His mom is there and they've got the friends and the friends are going to be embarrassed. And His mom's a Jewish mom and she says, 'Son, you've got to do something here', you know. And He says 'Woman, what do I have to do with this? My time has not yet come.' And she goes, 'Oh whatever, hey guys whatever He tells you to do, you just do it.'

The other scene is when His brothers come and say, 'Hey Jesus, let's go

130

to the party. We've got this party. It's the biggest party of the year. We'll have a great time.' And He says, 'No, I'm not going to go, you guys go ahead and go, have a good time.' And it makes a real distinct statement that they asked Him repeatedly and He said, 'No I'm not going to go, you go, have a good time.' And then when they're gone, He goes. During that conversation He does say again, 'My time is not yet come', but He goes.

Here's what's going on. At the wedding in Cana, when she says, 'Do something', Father's going, 'Your time's not yet come.' She turns and says 'Whatever He tells you' and Father says, 'Now, your time has come.' That intimacy of that relationship is moment by moment and He's able to walk directly into now, doing something in response to what His mother exhibited in that process.

Same with the brothers, Papa's saying, 'No', and as soon as they leave, now Father says, 'Okay', and He's free to go. And now He stands up and He preaches this sermon about rivers of living water and life in the spirit. He didn't move until He heard the voice of His Father.

Jesus performed a great diversity of miracles—healing leprosy, paralysis, pain, bleeding, fever, calming storms, exorcising demons, curing blindness, muteness even death.

He healed them in a variety of ways too. Sometimes he spoke a word or a rebuke, shouting at the sea, "Calm down!" With those facing physical infirmities, Jesus healed with his words, or by mixing dirt with his spit or by a simple touch. There's no pattern. No formula. There's only one common factor—God.

Paul Young
We see this in His life because you can't put Him in a box. He doesn't seem to have a plan. He just seems to go here and He goes there and He disappoints people's expectations and He makes some people angry and never heals anybody twice the same. I mean, He doesn't even have a book on how to heal people. And, you know, you've got this dynamic, alive, fluid, communication, and relationship that is at the very heart of everything He does.

131

Jesus needed to perform the miracles. What would be the difference between a man claiming to be God and God himself standing before us? Anyone can say the words "I am God." But who can raise the dead?

Norman Geisler

The miracles Jesus did were predicted, number one, so they were necessary to fulfill prophesy. Number two they were necessary to confirm who He was. He often said, ' You know if you don't believe what I say when I say your sins are forgiven you, then I'll tell a man take up your bed and walk, you know, and I'll give that as proof that the Son of man has power on Earth to do this.' This is what He said in Mark Chapter 2 for example. So clearly He connected His miraculous claims with who He was. When John the Baptist went and asked, 'Who are you?' He said through His disciples he said, 'Tell John the blind are seeing, the lame are walking and the dead are being raised. In other words, 'Hey, I'm doing these miracles, do you think I'm the Messiah or not?'

Miracles proved his claims as to his true nature and his relationship with God. Anyone who says they are God better prove so by doing things no man can do.

Miracles like calming the storm, or walking on water or cursing a fig tree showed his power over nature and proved his title as creator of all things.

Old Testament writings proclaimed the ability of the coming Messiah to do miracles. The prophecy of Isaiah 53:4 says he will take up our infirmities, our sickness and struggles. The miracles were the proof that Jesus was who he said he was.

Sometimes the miracles felt like déjà vu.

Didn't Elijah raise a dead person?

Didn't Moses serve bread to thousands?

Jesus' new miracles paralleled those old miracles to show people that he came to fulfill everything they did. He did not just copy the Old Testament prophets, he topped them, showing that he was greater.[7]

Miracles were motivated by faith, or not motivated by a lack of faith or they motivated someone's lack of faith. Jesus applauded the Roman Centurion when he detected the man's faith, then healed his

---

[7] Later at the Mount of Transfiguration, Moses and Elijah show up in a position of submission to Jesus.

servant from a distance with just a word. On the other hand, the Bible says Jesus couldn't heal anyone in Nazareth, while he was standing right there, because he sensed their lack of faith.

Then, in the case of the man born blind, John 9 gave no indication that the man asked for healing or had any faith. Jesus just healed him. The act sparked the faith of the blind man and his family to believe in Jesus after the fact.

The miracles, though, had a dangerous side effect. Crowds. Crowds were good because a large audience experienced Jesus at the same time. However, crowds like to be entertained and they treated Jesus like a magic act, a street performer or a sideshow attraction. "Come see the miraculous healings! Watch him walk on water! Witness the dead rise! Two shows nightly!"

The Pharisees and Sadducees came to Jesus and tested him by asking him to show them a sign from heaven. He replied, "When evening comes, you say, 'It will be fair weather, for the sky is red,' and in the morning, 'Today it will be stormy, for the sky is red and overcast.' You know how to interpret the appearance of the sky, but you cannot interpret the signs of the times. A wicked and adulterous generation looks for a miraculous sign, but none will be given it except the sign of Jonah." Jesus then left them and went away. Matthew 16:1-4

Norman Geisler
Well I don't think Jesus enjoyed miracles in the sense that He liked it as an entertainment exercise because He refused to do a miracle to entertain Herod. He never did a miracle to satisfy anyone's curiosity. He never did a miracle to say, 'Well that guy doesn't recognize who I am, I'll zap him here with a miracle.' He did miracles because it was necessary for His mission. It was predicted and it was necessary. John 12 says, 'In spite of all the miracles He did even the hard hearted Pharisees wouldn't believe in Him anyway.' In Luke 16:31 says, 'Neither will they believe though one were raised from the dead if they hear not Moses and the prophets.' So there are some people who are so hard hearted that even the miracles wouldn't satisfy them. But for the people who are willing to believe and see who He is then the Son of God is confirmed by acts of God. That's what Hebrews 2:4 says, that's what

133

Acts 2: 22, 23 says, that's what 2 Corinthians 12:12 says. Miracles are necessary to confirm a message.

He rebuked a generation that only sought after signs and wonders but did not seek out the one who caused the signs and wonders to occur. How frustrating for Jesus, seeing people only show up to see what he could do for their body instead of what he could do for their soul. Jesus performed the miracles as a means to salvation, as proof that they could put their faith in him. The hard hearted refused his invitation.

I think if I had the power to perform miracles it would shift my perspective from other people to...me. I would begin to enjoy that power and expect more respect. I wouldn't come to serve others. I would want them to serve me. The miracle worker! Step back or you'll face my wrath.

That's a dangerous power to have. But I don't see Jesus losing his perspective.

The feeding of the 5,000 revealed Jesus' real reason for performing such a great miracle. It wasn't just to prove who he was...

Jesus left there and went along the Sea of Galilee. Then he went up on a mountainside and sat down. Great crowds came to him, bringing the lame, the blind, the crippled, the mute and many others, and laid them at his feet; and he healed them. The people were amazed when they saw the mute speaking, the crippled made well, the lame walking and the blind seeing. And they praised the God of Israel. Jesus called his disciples to him and said, "I have compassion for these people; they have already been with me three days and have nothing to eat. I do not want to send them away hungry, or they may collapse on the way." Matthew 15:29-32

The miracles are acts of compassion. Jesus saw their need and wanted to help.

Max Lucado
I think Jesus enjoyed doing good. I don't think He really enjoyed the razzle dazzle of the miracles but I think He enjoyed doing good.

Joel Hunter

I think Jesus enjoyed performing miracles tremendously. First of all, every miracle He performed really helped people out. He just didn't put on a show. It wasn't a magic act, you know, where He goes 'Watch this.' It was always responding to a need and because He loved people, He always wanted to respond to their need. But the other thing that I think He truly enjoyed was that in the miracles that He performed, there wasn't any way that you could attribute them to Him as a man. It was always about the Father's direct intervention in their particular life situation. And so, because Jesus always enjoyed pointing people to the Father, I think He enjoyed those miracles tremendously.

Soon afterward, Jesus went to a town called Nain, and his disciples and a large crowd went along with him. As he approached the town gate, a dead person was being carried out—the only son of his mother, and she was a widow. And a large crowd from the town was with her. When the Lord saw her, his heart went out to her and he said, "Don't cry." Luke 7:11-13

After this passage in Luke, Jesus told the dead boy to get up, reviving him. Sure the story echoed Elijah and his healing of the widow's son (1 Kings 17), however, I don't see Jesus doing it for that reason. It all started with his heart breaking for the woman.

Jesus wanted to help people. Compassion compelled his miracles. It was hard to see a blind person suffer or a bleeding woman in pain or a widow to lose another family member. Jesus had to do something.

Jesus gave life to others through his miracles, but they ultimately caused his death. The Pharisees acknowledged Jesus' miraculous powers, but they didn't accept the way he used that power. Because he healed on the Sabbath, breaking a long standing tradition of non-work on Saturday, the Pharisees organized his arrest. The raising of Lazarus from the dead created a ground swell of buzz that the Pharisees needed to quell.

Jesus risked his life to give others life.

Why would he do that?

135

Jesus could have restrained his power and stayed alive longer, instead he healed out of compassion, challenging the religious leaders for the sake of the suffering soul.

Miracles were an expression of love, not just proof of his Godhood. The miracles proved that He loved us and was willing to risk his life to help us.

Miracles of healing, producing food, walking on water, even his resurrection aren't really that miraculous when you know Jesus the creator.

Naturally he could give sight to the eyes he formed.

Sure he could walk on the water he built out of hydrogen and oxygen molecules.

No problem giving life to the dead. He is life! That's easy stuff when you put it all in perspective.

Today we want miracles to solve our problems or to show proof that God still exists. God never promised us a problem-free life and we don't need any more proof that God exists.

Miracles don't happen as much as some people think. They believe they can command the miraculous with a wave of their hand. God isn't a miracle factory, producing on demand.

Then again, miracles happen more than people think, especially those who believe God has run dry and has a "hands-off" policy when it comes to this earth. Things still happen we can't explain.

I think the true miracle occurs at salvation. When Jesus can break through a heart and create a new person by faith—that's truly unbelievable. It's the reason he performed every miracle then and even today. He wanted people to believe.

However, the miracle of salvation is the one miracle even Jesus cannot control. It's up to the individual to accept or reject God's offer.

Paul Young
He feels the heart of God and He's driven by compassion which is sometimes this combination of anger and grief and love. And to me the healing is not the issue for Him, it's the person. And so I think that's why all healings are different. The scenarios are different but the healings themselves, even at a physical level are all different. He doesn't repeat Himself anytime. And so what's being drawn out of Him in terms of the uniqueness of that process has to be the uniqueness of that individual.

136

He's looking at a creation that He knows He created and yet the creation is so magnificent, so individual. It could be a leper. It could be a blind person. It could be a person with nothing in his eye sockets. It could be a lame person. It could be a person who is spiritually oppressed by the demonic. And He is always seeing His wife, His bride, the one He loves, the one that this is all about. And that uniqueness draws out of Him, the uniqueness of healing that only His Father could transmit through Him.

Have you experienced the miracle of salvation? Jesus sees you, uniquely you, and wants to change the direction of your path from eternal death to eternal life.

The trick is...you have to want this miracle to happen.

TIME TO JOURNEY

1. **Watch "Miracles" from "In His Shoes: The Life of Christ"**

2. **Discussion Questions**

- Have you ever seen a miracle? If so, how did you feel afterwards?

- Which of Jesus' miracles are most "miraculous" for you?

- Why were many of miracles similar to Old Testament figures?

- Do you think miracles in the first century were more miraculous than they would be today?

- If Jesus did not perform any miracles, how would you feel about his claims?

- Are his miracles from 2,000 years ago enough proof today?

- Do we need miracles today?

- What was going on in Jesus' heart when he performed a miracle?

- Why did Jesus perform the miracles?

- What could happen to a person who performed miracles in front of large crowds and received such notoriety?

- How could others try to misuse a miracle worker?

- What miracle would you want to see in your life?

- Do you think miracles still occur?

- Are they to prove God exists or to prove He still loves us or something else?

Satan

Kursi

Every superhero has his arch enemy. Superman has Lex Luthor. Batman has the Joker. The X-Men have Magneto.

Jesus, the ultimate superhero of good, has Satan, the ultimate villain of bad, more frightening than all those other comic book scoundrels combined. As the epitome of everything that is evil, Satan also has access to legions of demons, his henchmen. Satan can tempt and motivate spiritual and physical entities with his arsenal of lies, slander and deceit.

He is the evil behind all evil.

If you believe in God, you must believe in Satan. He is mentioned all throughout the Bible, the Old and New Testament, as a real and active force. Satan has freewill, a personality and a purpose. He wants to undo the things of God, out of spite and selfishness, and crown himself king.

In the Gospels, Jesus believed in the existence of Satan and he should—Jesus created him! According to Colossians 2, all things were made through Jesus, including angels and Satan is an angel.

For reasons not directly mentioned in the Bible, and at some time not clearly stated, Satan rebelled against God.[8] In the process, he managed to convince one third of the angels to follow him[9]. They became known as demons.

As early as Genesis 3, Satan arrived in the Garden of Eden and introduced sin to mankind through the means of temptation, influencing man's freewill to act against God. From that time on, Satan and his demons continued to infiltrate and influence God's people. Much of the Old Testament demonic activity occurred in the form of idols and idol worship, encouraging rebellious worship for physical and sexual pleasure.

Satan worked through armies and nations—such as the Philistines, Amorites, Amalekites, Hittites, Jebusites—to destroy God's people. Satan did whatever he could to stir up hate, create fear and turn people to the pleasures of this world. The only defense against evil then was the sword. Many battles and wars were depicted in the Old Testament pages, fighting Satan's influence in the region.

---

[8] Ezekiel 28
[9] Revelation 12

Then in the New Testament, Jesus arrived and battled evil face-to-face on earth. First Jesus squared off with Satan during the temptation, then in a variety of one-on-one encounters called demonic possessions.

What did Jesus use to battle these demonic forces? Words, whether from scriptures or his own mouth.

Demonic possessions were infestations of human bodies by demons who then manifested themselves in a number of different ways—physically, mentally, spiritually. They caused the people to act in bizarre ways, screaming, twitching, cutting themselves. Scary stuff.

How did Jesus react to these frightening manifestations and how did he feel seeing Satan, his own creation, perform such heinous acts? Could anything make Jesus afraid?

Avner and I traveled to Kursi, off the northeast coast of the Sea of Galilee. From Kursi, we could easily see Capernaum, Bethsaida, other places we had visited in Jesus' localized ministry area. While it felt like we were in the Jewish neighborhood, this area was far from Jewish back in Jesus' time.

Kursi was the other side of the tracks.

Since we were exploring Jesus' encounters with Satan, I couldn't help but notice this was the hottest day on record. Coincidence? It certainly helped to set the mood. Today was hell on earth.

Avner showed me a place half way up the mountain, once tiled with mosaics, that marked a 5th Century Byzantine church. Monks built the monastery here, encasing a cave where they believed the demoniac from Mark Chapter 5 lived.

The mountain in Kursi had a steep, but reachable climax. The heat had sucked all moisture from the ground, making the grass turn to stubble. A fence kept us from climbing the mountain, barring us from the dangerous remnants of land mines of a past war hidden in the ground. Death certainly lurked everywhere in this area, and the theme fit perfectly for our exploration of Satan, who sets land mines all over our lives, trying to get us to detonate our faith.

Tradition holds that Jesus got off the boat with his disciples and was greeted by an explosive demon possessed man here at Kursi. It's the most famous (and lengthy) possession story recorded.

They went across the lake to the region of the Gerasenes. When Jesus got out of the boat, a man with an evil spirit came from the tombs to meet him. This man lived

in the tombs, and no one could bind him anymore, not even with a chain. For he had often been chained hand and foot, but he tore the chains apart and broke the irons on his feet. No one was strong enough to subdue him. Night and day among the tombs and in the hills he would cry out and cut himself with stones.

When he saw Jesus from a distance, he ran and fell on his knees in front of him. He shouted at the top of his voice, "What do you want with me, Jesus, Son of the Most High God? Swear to God that you won't torture me!"

For Jesus had said to him, "Come out of this man, you evil spirit!" Then Jesus asked him, "What is your name?" "My name is Legion," he replied, "for we are many."

And he begged Jesus again and again not to send them out of the area. A large herd of pigs was feeding on the nearby hillside. The demons begged Jesus, "Send us among the pigs; allow us to go into them."

He gave them permission, and the evil spirits came out and went into the pigs. The herd, about two thousand in number, rushed down the steep bank into the lake and were drowned. Those tending the pigs ran off and reported this in the town and countryside, and the people went out to see what had happened.
When they came to Jesus, they saw the man who had been possessed by the legion of demons, sitting there, dressed and in his right mind; and they were afraid. Those who had seen it told the people what had happened to the demon-possessed man—and told about the pigs as well. Then the people began to plead with Jesus to leave their region.

As Jesus was getting into the boat, the man who had been demon-possessed begged to go with him. Jesus did not let him, but said, "Go home to your family and tell them how much the Lord has done for you, and how he has had mercy on you."

So the man went away and began to tell in the Decapolis how much Jesus had done for him. And all the people were amazed. Mark 5:1-20

From this passage we can get some insight into demon possessions:

- The man lived in the tombs, presumably, because no one wanted to be his neighbor. His demonic possession made him a social outcast. His only friends were the dead.
- The man had a superior strength that chains could not contain. Demon possessions might not make you supernaturally stronger, but more persistent in your determination to break things.
- The man cut himself. Either the demons inspired self-loathing or the man wanted to put an end to his misery.
- A demonic possession caused the man to strip himself. We know that since when the man was healed, the Gospel account indicates that he was dressed properly. Either the demons did everything they could to shame the man or they have poor fashion sense.
- The man/demons cried out every night. The constant wailing made him frightful and also indicated the pain he suffered or the pain the demons live with being separated from God.
- The possession was carried out by more than one demon. Demons don't mind sharing a room. The more the merrier?
- The demons recognized Jesus and fell before him in humility. They were in control of the situation until Jesus showed up.
- Instead of being banished somewhere by Jesus' choosing (probably unpleasant), they asked to go live inside some pigs. According to the strict kosher Jewish diet, pigs were unclean. The incident nearly toppled the ham and bacon industry when Jesus granted the demons' wish.
- Apparently the pigs showed some common sense and reacted violently to the possession, preferring to throw themselves off a cliff and drown. Pigs aren't good swimmers, but they desired death over living with demons.
- Sadly, people are just as afraid of good as they are of evil, since the locals asked Jesus to leave their town after he displayed such dramatic power.
- The man, once an adversary of Jesus, now wished to befriend him. The demons kept him from having a relationship with God.
- The man became a witness for God's power.

142

With sweat building on our brows, Avner and I tried to make sense of this demonic scene and what it revealed about Jesus. First of all, I wondered, why did it happen here?

"It is a land considered by many to be out of the Holy Land," Avner said. "It was different not only geographically but also in terms of who lived here. Jews were from the Jordan River and to the west, maybe a little to the east like Bethsaida, but here were others. And for those people, the Jews of the time, including Christ, the others were ones you should avoid getting in touch with, because they're not pure."

I looked out over the coast, trying to put myself in this scene 2,000 years ago. "This is a pretty evil scene because we're talking tombs which are considered unclean, a demoniac who's possessed by the demon. You have herds of pigs. You have Gentiles, and you have the water which is referred to as The Abyss and was something that was feared by them."

Avner squinted in the hot sun, taking its toll on even the most seasoned archaeologist. "For sure it was an evil scene for the common people just to go to the Gentile area was already bad. Accompany it with the tombs and the demoniac and maybe also the water that would be a bad area to go to."

The scene had all the elements and characters for a first century, Jewish horror film. Throw in some rain and lightning and you have *Friday the 13th: The Unkoshered Version*! I could see John cowering behind Peter who was cowering behind Jesus.

Demons were feared by people and rightfully so. They were scary. They made the possessed do unusual and bizarre things.

Yet I notice how calm and cool Jesus reacted around these very disturbing incidents. He did not succumb to the craziness of the situation, showing any panic or loss of control. No teeth grinding. No nail biting.

If anything, I see the demons panicking, not Jesus. Why?

Jesus had the power and the authority. He had nothing to fear. These demons, though feared by humans because of legend and hearsay, became scaredy cats in front of their heavenly boss.

I don't think Jesus was even slightly shocked or overwhelmed with the disturbing behavior he saw exhibited with demon possession. I just wonder if he was just a bit saddened to see his prized creations turn their backs on him after all they knew. Was Jesus disappointed over how Lucifer and his fellow angels turned out?

Jesus created everything – seen and unseen. Satan was once the most beautiful of all creations, as described in the book of Ezekiel

Chapter 28. Now the most beautiful became the most beastly. The God of all truth finds himself the creator of the world's most renowned liar.

I wonder if Jesus had much the same feeling we would have if we invested in our son, giving him the best education, the best training, dressed him in the best clothes, then saw him grow up and declare war on us for the rest of our lives.

Norman Geisler
Jesus knew who Lucifer was, that he was an archangel. He knew the glory he had of the Father at the throne in Heaven and He knew that he fell and He knew that He was going to be tempted by him. Jesus also knew that Lucifer knows that his time is short, as it says in the Book of Revelation. As the demon said, 'Art thou come to torment us before our time?' They knew where they were going. And He knew where they were going. So Jesus knew their ultimate doom and in the sense of the ultimate justice of God. He was satisfied that that was going to happen and certainly He didn't have any revengeful attitude or motive toward them. But He knew they were irredeemable. Because in Hebrews 2 it says, 'That Jesus did not take the nature of angels, He took human nature on Himself, that angels are irredeemable by nature once they make their decision, they're condemned and they're condemned justly.' And so, He didn't have any problem in accepting their ultimate doom.

Max Lucado
I think Jesus, I think God is disappointed anytime anybody settles for second best and tries to strike out on life without God. And again I think that's what sin is, to disobey or disregard God. Sometimes we know what He says and we just defy it, sometimes we just say 'I'm going to lead a life without God' and that's what Satan was, what Lucifer tried do. It's what we try to do, is lead a life without God a Godless life and yeah, obviously yeah, it breaks God's heart.

And Jesus' creations, once angels, now renamed demons, were somehow deceived or convinced to follow Satan in a doomed overthrow of God. How did all that happen? What evidence or case did Satan possibly make that sounded good enough to throw away their eternity?

God's only thinking of himself!
God doesn't want you to have fun!
God wants to bombard you with rules!
It's about God's glory, not yours!

Probably the same excuses he uses today that people still accept.

Many times people desire more convincing proof that God is real before they give their lives to him. They cry out, "If God would only show himself!"

Angels had all the proof they needed. They knew God existed since they saw him with their own spiritual eyes. They surely believed!

You believe that there is one God. Good! Even the demons believe that—and shudder. James 2:19

The demons knew the truth and still they turned their backs on him. They even shudder, acknowledging his awesome power, yet reject that same power. People on earth crave the information demons have. Yet even the demons refuse to bow to the powerful one they see quite clearly.

Interesting to see the reaction of the locals when Jesus displayed his power. When they saw the demoniac healed, they asked Jesus to leave town. They saw a demonstration of his power and refused to accept it. They didn't want someone around who had more power than them.

Jesus' authority over the supernatural made him an outcast, like the outcast he just exorcised.

So obviously seeing is not believing—not for the demons and not for those who saw the demons kicked out. So what is it that keeps people, Satan and demons from fully accepting Jesus' power and succumbing to his authority?

Max Lucado
The only answer is pride. Jealousy, they want to be higher than He is. That was Lucifer's temptation according to the Bible that He most beautiful of the stars was jealous and wanted to be the greatest star. This whole deal of pride and wanting to have the top place on the mountain. Everything traces itself back to that. The core desire I think of every being that has had a conscience...wants to say, 'I matter, I matter.' The greatest fear that we have is that we don't matter. That

145

we come and go and no one knows. That life is nothing more than that little dash between the dates on the tombstone. That's the greatest fear. So we spend all our life trying to justify our place on this place. We wear designer jeans. We set up a foundation. We tell people we know important people. All of that is to say I'm important. And so I think the angels just didn't feel important enough. And so Lucifer who set the pace for the rest would rather be without God than be second place to God.

People reject God today for the same reasons demons rejected him then. We all want to be in control. God isn't so willing to give up his position...for good reason—he's the best one for the job.

Demons caused sickness and pain to people, invading their lives and causing years of suffering. Jesus refused to see the innocent suffer, so he exhibited his power to see his people released. Every exorcism was an act of love, saving the innocent from the guilty.

Paul Young
I think there's anger, again at the damage that that part of creation was inflicting. I think there is grief at the loss because I think that there is relationship between the angels and the God. I don't see any fear in His relationship with to the demonic at all. Because I think He recognizes there's no rivals here. His focus is on the humanity that He has created and the rescuing of them. I see compassion in everything He does.

Here's part of the thing about Lucifer...He's got the most frustrating job in the world. He can come up with any suggestion he wants and God will say, 'You know what, I could use that, that's perfect, that will work for me.' I'm sure he has not come up with one idea that God has said, 'Oh, man we weren't expecting that. Oh boy, what are we going to do?'—you know. This is it, He's not a rival. He's not a rival and so therefore there's nothing that he can bring to the table that God can't weave into the tapestry of His purposes. That's got to be frustrating. I mean, maybe that's why the demonic is so mad?

These stories give me comfort knowing that in the face of evil Jesus firmly and calmly stays in control.

146

People then and today do not treat the demon possessed, the sick, the mentally unstable very well. Avner knew something about the first century treatment of demoniacs.

"It seems for the people then that there is no hope to cure them and since they were really possessed by demons, you'd better not be in touch with them. And many of them would be expelled out of the community and they would find a way to survive on their own."

The world sends the possessed away, to the streets, to the mental hospitals. We don't want to associate with them. They scare us.

Jesus went to them. Unafraid. With open arms. He desired to restore the innocent and to send away the guilty. The ex-demoniac immediately responded to his freedom and wanted to be in the safety of Jesus' presence.

Jesus willingly takes on the role of our spiritual bodyguard and displays all the traits we see in Secret Service agents and even Jack Bauer from "24." He's trained. He's calm. He's cool. He's tough. He has unimaginable skills and knowledge.

Standing here with our view over the Sea of Galilee, the heat trying to conquer us and winning, I asked Avner if he had ever seen evil.

Avner pondered that question for a moment. "Living here in Israel, you see evil all the time. The history, the wars, the attacks are all the essence of evil. I cannot help but to see evil everywhere I go."

Avner's words caused me to re-evaluate my take on evil. The demoniac was an obvious evil. Most evil manifests itself in different people and situations, carefully masking itself behind social, legislative or even religious causes. Evil still lurks in our world, but it constantly shows itself in different forms, redefining its look to match an ever-changing background.

While a screaming man would certainly be scary, I think the other evils Jesus encountered, in the political and religious arenas, were and are far more disturbing.

In movies and books, the human victims fear the demons, believing the spiritual world has all the power. The media portrays evil as relentless and overpowering. Unstoppable. You can stab, shoot, spear, saw away at the killer, but it'll open its eyes as the movie ends.

That's not really the case.   Evil is finite and powerless.

It is Jesus who is infinite and powerful and he has come to set the captives free.

It takes more than just believing—you have to accept Jesus' authority and submit to it too. Once you know who is in control, you have nothing to fear and, like the ex-demoniac, you want to follow him.

TIME TO JOURNEY

1. **Watch "Satan" from "In His Shoes: The Life of Christ"**

2. **Discussion Questions**

- Have you ever been in a scary situation?

- Have you ever experienced a "haunted" or "demonic" situation?

- What did that feel like?

- What is Satan's goal in the Bible?

- Why do we fear evil? Should we?

- How would you react to seeing the demon possessed man?

- How did Jesus react?

- How do the demons react?

- How did the apostles react?

- How do horror movies portray evil?

- What evil do you see going on in your world?

- Why do we feel at times that evil is in control?

- How real and active are demonic forces in the world today?

- Why would demons reject Christ?

- Why do people reject Christ?

- How were Jesus' actions toward the demon possessed different from the world's reaction to evil?

- How should a Christian react to evil today?

JOURNEY 3

Water to Wine

Calm
Sea of Galilee

I don't like turbulence when I fly. Call me crazy. I've felt some pretty rough patches while suspended 40,000 feet in the air.

On one flight, I held the hand of a stranger next to me, an older woman, who I felt needed some comforting as we bounced and heaved through a storm. I tried to be the strong one, smiling gently to her while I saw fear on her face. I placed my hand over hers and told her it would be okay.

She seemed too scared to say much of anything as the turbulence died down and we landed safely on the ground. She appreciated my gesture. I told her I was a Christian and I drew upon God's strength and security during that time.

"We're you afraid?" she asked.

I smiled. "No." I kind of lied, but I didn't want her to panic. I was afraid, but not totally afraid. My body snapped to threat level Red, while my spirit hovered around Yellow.

Could it be possible to calmly live life in the lowest threat level, Green, all the time, no matter what circumstances came my way? I think so.

In Jesus' day, there wasn't much airplane travel, but plenty of boating, especially in the Galilean region. The Sea of Galilee.

Waves in the Sea of Galilee can reach twenty feet high. The body of water sits 680 feet below sea level and the uneven topography of flat plains and high mountains stir up some pretty serious storms. Any local fisherman of the time would know this and immediately panic when a squall crashed into them.

The story in Matthew 8, Mark 4 and Luke 8 tells of the disciples getting on a boat with Jesus and crossing over to the other side. It's easier and faster (and quieter without the crowds) for the men to cut across the sea, instead of walking on land. After a particularly long day, the passage said they were so tired, Jesus decided to take a nap on a nice soft cushion on the boat's stern.

However, a perfect storm struck, interrupting their peaceful outing, and waves swept over the side of the boat. The disciples panicked and woke Jesus. Hold it right here! Let me get this straight…Jesus slept as the boat tossed and turned and water sloshed over the sides and soaked him? In the climax of the crises, Jesus caught some zzzzzz's.

That would be like me sleeping through the turbulence.

That's living life with a threat level Green mentality. How did he do it?

I talked to Menachem Lev, my fishing expert, about the storms at the Sea of Galilee. Menachem's a tough, fire-hydrant sized guy, with a thick neck and steely eyes. Surely he doesn't know fear. When I asked if Galilee ever get scary, Menachem dropped his head, almost ashamed of his fear.

"It is danger. This lake is danger. Without any warning or something, immediately you get wind and sixty-five knots and up."

"Have you been frightened being a fisherman out during a storm on the sea?"

Menachem hesitated, his machismo on the line. "Have I been frightened...yeah. You must pray to God to come back to the shore."

At times like that, a storm's sole purpose is to swallow and destroy anything that tries to conquer it. Seas are temperamental, products of shifting currents, wind patterns and air pressure. Even the moon influences the sea's mood. How can you stop the currents, wind and moon from doing what they're naturally supposed to do?

You're helpless. No one person can stop such an escalating series of catastrophic events, can they?

Seas are portrayed in movies and novels as romantic, but most times they are just dangerous—*The Poseidon Adventure, Titanic, Jaws, Mutiny on the Bounty, Old Man and the Sea.* Back in Jesus' time, as we also see today, the seas meant death.

As the expert fishermen panicked, waking Jesus from his nap, Jesus replied in a tone of disappointment or sleep-interrupted-anger, "You of so little faith. Why are so upset?" I tried to imagine me yelling that at my nervous flight companion.

"Hey lady! What's your problem! Where's your faith!"

Not a very sensitive reaction.

Jesus then did something I could never do. He rebuked the wind and the waves and the sea returned to calm. "Quiet! Be still! Shut up!" His words of rebuke indicate a touch of anger (I know I hate to be woken from a nap), as if the wind and waves did something wrong.

The fishermen, experts on the sea, were amazed at how suddenly the storm stopped. Storms don't do that. It became clear—Jesus had the power to stop violent weather systems.

A storm for a fisherman meant death. For Jesus it meant an opportunity to catch up on some sleep. Quite a contrast.

During a second incident on the Sea of Galilee, written about in Matthew 14, Mark 6 and John 6, Jesus decided to stay on a mountainside to pray and he sent the disciples in a boat to Bethsaida ahead of him. Again, a strong wind stuck and the waters grew rough. Then Jesus finished praying and decided to take a stroll…across the lake…

This storm did not terrify the disciples as much as the other one did, but it created a difficult obstacle to overcome. The more frightening component of this story was the image of a man walking across water.

Then Mark 6:48 uses the phrase, "He was about to pass them…" Really? I almost imagine Jesus whistling as he passed by, giving a casual "Hello" as he happened upon the struggling sailors.

"Some weather we're having," Jesus hummed along calmly while the disciples sweated and strained.

The vision of a man walking on water unnerved them—a Twilight Zone moment for sure, crossing into a realm of the supernatural. Jesus told them to be brave and stop fearing. Peter, now intrigued by Jesus' ability to overcome storms, asked Jesus to join him for a peaceful walk on the Sea of Galilee.

What an odd request. Did Peter look at Jesus and think, "I could do that." Whatever the reason, and I love Peter for asking, Peter took that first step and walked on the water.

Then he saw the storm.

"But when he (Peter) saw the wind, he was afraid and, beginning to sink, cried out, 'Lord, save me!'" (Mark 14:30)

Again, Jesus used those words, "You who have so little faith." Every time I hear those words, I detect a note of disappointment. "After all I taught you guys, showed you and promised you what you will do in the future, you're worrying that you will die right here, right now?"

The disciples faced storms. Jesus experienced calm.

The disciples lacked faith. Jesus had unwavering faith.

Menachem Lev took us out on the sea in one of his fishing boats. This was a substantial size vessel, very solid, loaded with all the modern equipment needed to detect depth and brewing thunderstorms. I didn't feel very vulnerable on board this.

So to capture the feeling of a Jesus-like experience, Menachem lowered me into a traditional fishing boat, about twelve feet long, with room for ten or so. He pulled me through the water behind him.

This small boat felt constricted, defenseless against the elements. A mere dinghy in the palm of disaster. No walls to hide behind. No life raft to escape by.

153

As I took in the loneliness and vulnerability of the small boat in a huge sea, I began to feel a strange desire inside me.

Walk.

I tried to evaluate the voice. God? Satan? Me? Someone wanted to see if I had the faith needed to walk on this water. For some odd reason, I felt I could.

Do it.

I could almost feel that first step. Peter did right here. He felt it and took that first step. Why not me? I have more information and biblical knowledge than Peter had when he took his first step.

Go for it.

I knew I could do it. This was the place where people walked on the water. People with faith. I had faith. Didn't I?

Then, all of sudden, a wave of doubt crashed over my bow. I didn't feel the calm. I felt the panic.

What if you fell in? You would look ridiculous. You would get all wet. You would have to walk around all day in wet clothes. Everyone would think you are stupid. They would laugh at your God. People don't walk on water. You can't.

I backed off. Defeated. Faithless. I saw the "waves" taking me down just as Peter saw.

There appears to be a direct correlation between faith and our reaction to rough waters. Panic only sees the current situation – the wind, the waves. The disciples saw the strength of the storm and remembered how they devastated and killed the innocent in the past. As a result, they visualized their own death, feeling it with certainty. Faith sees the future. Panic recognizes our present lack of strength. Faith trusts the one with all power.

Peter had that faith for a moment then forgot it. He saw the waves, accepting their authority, fearing their ability.

I asked myself a question that I'll ask you.

If you could have one attribute of Jesus, what would it be? The power to heal? To multiply food? To walk on water?

I could answer that question now, standing out here in the seas. I would say if there was one thing about Jesus I would most desire would be the way he calmly faced life. His faith.

I fear that phone call that will shatter my world.

I panic when a distraction interrupts my daily flow.

I worry about a doctor's diagnosis.

I grow an ulcer looking at my bank statements.

154

Like you, I face life's ups and downs all the time. I need calm while I ride the rollercoaster of life. There must be some way to be reminded daily of God's power over this world so we too don't drown in the storms of life.

So where did Jesus find the peace to face the storms? I think he found it in the activity he was engaged in *before* he walked on water.

After leaving them, he went up on a mountainside to pray. Mark 6:46

He prayed. The disciples didn't pray before jumping into the boat. This was routine. "We do this sort of thing all the time. Why should we talk to God? We know how to row."

I make the same mistakes as these apostles do all the time. I wake up and get to work, rowing away through rough emails and turbulent phone calls. I fall to my knees only when I'm knocked to them.

Jesus prayed all the time. When he was alone.

One of those days Jesus went out to a mountainside to pray, and spent the night praying to God. Luke 6:12

With others.

About eight days after Jesus said this, he took Peter, John and James with him and went up onto a mountain to pray. Luke 9:28

Before a long day.

Very early in the morning, while it was still dark, Jesus got up, left the house and went off to a solitary place, where he prayed. Simon and his companions went to look for him, and when they found him, they exclaimed: "Everyone is looking for you!"
Jesus replied, "Let us go somewhere else—to the nearby villages—so I can preach there also. That is why I have come."
So he traveled throughout Galilee, preaching in their synagogues and driving out demons. Mark 1:35-39

Or when facing death.

Then Jesus went with his disciples to a place called Gethsemane, and he said to them, "Sit here while I go over there and pray." Matthew 26:36

Paul Young

Prayer is the conversation of a relationship and this brings us right back to the beauty of the Trinity. We have unity and diversity in the community of the Trinity. That's a Robbie Zacharias phrase, and I love it, it's really what framed the work that I've done on the Trinity. Unity, the oneness, and the diversity, the threeness of the community, the relationship. And prayer is a conversation inside of a relationship and that is so important. This helpless dependence that we experience, the uncertainty of life, Jesus didn't know everything. He wasn't omniscient, He wasn't omnipresent.[10] He wasn't any of those things; He did not draw upon that. He is a human being in helpless dependence upon the presence and the life of the Father who lives and dwells within Him. And so prayer, prayer is like breathing, you know, He's praying all the time.

The disciples recognized something about Jesus that was different. His demeanor. His strength. His calm. They wanted it, so they asked for it.

One day Jesus was praying in a certain place. When he finished, one of his disciples said to him, "Lord, teach us to pray, just as John taught his disciples." Luke 11:1

Prayer reminds us on a daily basis who has that power over storms. Prayer puts us into a position of submission, reminding us of our inadequacies and God's sufficiency. We remember that we do not need to rely on our own strength today.

---

[10] While on the earth, in his earthly skin.

156

Norman Geisler

Jesus needed prayer as a human being like all of us do. He prayed before great events. He prayed after great events. He prayed on the cross several times. He prayed before His temptation. He prayed after His temptation. He needed prayer, we all need prayer because prayer in communion with God. And He had unbroken communion with God like no one else had ever had. He was the perfect pray-er in that He was constantly in prayer, constantly in communication with the Father. So He needed it the way any human being needs prayer and set the perfect example for us. If the son of God needed to pray all those times, all those places and keep constantly in prayer, "a fortiori", 'with the greater force', how much more are we.

The trinity is a unique relationship between God and Himself. There's a connection there that cannot be easily explained. However you shape it, you can't deny that Jesus needed to reaffirm or reconnect his relationship with the other two members of the Godhead through a prayerful conversation.

Maybe his physical body felt the tug away from the spiritual all the time and Jesus needed to center himself, reprioritize, submit this flesh before he faced the day. By coming to earth in flesh, this bodily separation needed a spiritual reconnection at every available opportunity through times of prayer.

Maybe, sometimes, Jesus just needed quiet. Jesus prayed at night, sometimes all night, or early in the morning, before the others woke up. The day had not started. The roosters still slept. The physical body experiences sensory overload and Jesus felt that. To find peace, Jesus found quiet through prayer.

Peace isn't the absence of conflict. Peace is the best means to get you through the conflict. Jesus needed peace because his mission wasn't always peaceful.

"I have come to bring fire on the earth, and how I wish it were already kindled! But I have a baptism to undergo, and how distressed I am until it is completed! Do you think I came to bring peace on earth? No, I tell you, but division. From now on there will be five in one family divided against each other, three against two and two against three. They will be divided, father against son and son against father,

157

mother against daughter and daughter against mother, mother-in-law against daughter-in-law and daughter-in-law against mother-in-law." Luke 12:49-53

While Jesus wanted to pray, I think most of all he wanted to set an example of prayer. By watching him spend so much time in prayer and correlating it to the peaceful way he faced life, the disciples desired that attitude in themselves, asking to be taught. You never see the disciples asking Jesus to teach them how to raise the dead or multiply food. They wanted something else that Jesus had...

Calm, that came through a consistent communication with God.

The best way to calm the waters of life, I see, is to get close to the one who can calm the waters.

If you want peace, install a peacemaker in your heart.

People are attracted to those who find calm during a storm.

No matter how turbulent your life is, hold on to the hand of the one who can control the wind and the waves.

TIME TO JOURNEY

1. **Watch "Calm" from "In His Shoes: The Life of Christ"**

2. **Discussion Questions**

- Have you ever been caught in a storm?

- What did it feel like?

- What great movies or books took place on the ocean? What did they all have in common?

- What common factors do we find in Jesus' two Sea of Galilee experiences?

- What do they say about him?

- When we panic, do we always lose faith?

- What "waves" in your life cause you to panic?

- During what moments in your life have you experienced calm?

- Does it surprise you that Jesus prayed so much? Why or why not?

- Why is prayer so instrumental to finding peace?

- What do you do to "get away"?

- If prayer is so beneficial, why is it so hard to do?

- If you could ask Jesus to teach you something, would it be prayer?

- What's your biggest prayer request right now?

People
Jerusalem

During a recent mission trip to Burundi, Africa, we visited the city of Bujumbura, the capital of this small country. We were part of a mission organization's inaugural visit to the country, by invitation of the President of Burundi himself. The people there were warm and friendly...maybe a little too much.

Burundi is not a big tourist destination so relatively few outsiders stop by. This made our team a novelty. Everywhere I went, all eyes focused on me. Children stared. Many wanted to touch my hairy arms, fascinated with my blonde hair.

When we drove to our location, I could not walk ten feet until a crowd inundated me. We came to evangelize door to door, but the people came to us before we got to their door. Their enthusiasm invaded my personal space. I stood in crowds of fifty to one hundred for hours on end, a lone white man as far as the eye could see, pressed in on all sides. If we went into a house to rest, they lined up at the doors or peeked in through the windows. Once I wanted to grab a quick bite of a power bar, until I found ten sets of eyes staring at me.

People asked me for help, healing and financial assistance. A blind woman pushed through the crowd begging to see. So many demands. I could do nothing but offer spiritual relief. If we handed out a Gospel tract, they mobbed us, fighting each other for a piece of paper. Apparently, no one ever handed anything out to them for free. In America, we get annoyed when someone wants to hand us a menu as we walk down the sidewalk. In Burundi, they would tear your arm off.

This response to us was unusual. I've been on many mission trips and never saw anything quite like it. But the entire time in Burundi I thought, "This is what Jesus experienced."

I learned from that trip that I never wanted to be a superstar on the level of Brad Pitt and Angelina Jolie, who attract attention everywhere they go.

Jesus understood the plight of being a Brad and Angelina. He was watched closely because of his celebrity status, the one everyone had been talking about around the water well.

Jesus was also being examined by others to see him trip up. Lindsay Lohan can relate to Jesus on that level. She can't drive out of a parking garage, without fifty paparazzi swarming her like hornets.

Pharisees were the ancient paparazzi, desiring an unflattering snapshot of Jesus to bring down his reputation and to increase their own status.

As I walked around the streets of Jerusalem, I'm overwhelmed by the variety of people here. Jews, in the Old City, co-exist with Muslims and Christians. Amongst them you have different types of faiths with different levels of customs and dress. Throw into that tourists from every part of the world—English, German, Japanese, African, Brazilian, Australian, Spanish—and Jerusalem is a smoldering melting pot.

How do you reach, I wondered, so many different types of people in such a short time?

Jesus had been a private person for nearly thirty years then sacrificed his privacy for a public persona, throwing himself out there to be studied, swarmed and cross-examined.

Most people, when they reach the cover of People Magazine, turn arrogant and guarded (sometimes for good reason). So how did celebrity Jesus treat people from various social groups and what did he do to make them feel special?

Max Lucado

I think Jesus was easy to be around. I really do. I think that's why people were compelled to be with Him. I don't know how He seemed to have time for so many? I struggle with that every day. You know we wake up with a list of things we think we're supposed to get accomplished and then the list of things we want to get accomplished sometimes takes us away from people we want to be with. But somehow He was able to balance them. You know He didn't have any vain ambition. That to me is, He wasn't out trying to create a reputation. He had one goal and that was to help people.

With so many skin colors, personalities, languages and religious affiliations, could Jesus possibly love them all? Let's see.

People were bringing little children to Jesus to have him touch them, but the disciples rebuked them. When Jesus saw this, he was indignant. He said to them, "Let the little children come to me, and do not hinder them, for the kingdom of God belongs to such as these. I tell you the truth, anyone who will not receive the kingdom of God like a little child will never enter it." And he took the children in his arms, put his hands on them and blessed them. Mark 10:13-16

The apostles pushed the **children** away from Jesus. Kids always get disassociated from adult matters and told to buzz off so the adults can be adults. Jesus pulled the children close, then rebuked others for alienating them. Jesus would probably sit at the Thanksgiving kid's table.

Then they came to Jericho. As Jesus and his disciples, together with a large crowd, were leaving the city, a blind man, Bartimaeus (that is, the Son of Timaeus), was sitting by the roadside begging. When he heard that it was Jesus of Nazareth, he began to shout, "Jesus, Son of David, have mercy on me!" Many rebuked him and told him to be quiet, but he shouted all the more, "Son of David, have mercy on me!" Jesus stopped and said, "Call him." So they called to the blind man, "Cheer up! On your feet! He's calling you." Mark 10:46-49

The apostles rebuked the **sick and the diseased** from getting too close, yet Jesus brought them closer. The culture of the day separated classes – the rich from the poor, the sick from the healthy, the Jews from the Gentiles, the men from the women. Jesus broke down all those walls and associated with everyone.

So he came to a town in Samaria called Sychar, near the plot of ground Jacob had given to his son Joseph. Jacob's well was there, and Jesus, tired as he was from the journey, sat down by the well. It was about the sixth hour. When a Samaritan woman came to draw water, Jesus said to her, "Will you give me a drink?" (His disciples had gone into the town to buy food.) The Samaritan woman said to him, "You are a Jew and I am a Samaritan woman. How can you ask me for a drink?" (For Jews do not associate with Samaritans.) John 4:5-9

Here's a double no-no for a Jewish rabbi—speaking to a **woman** who is a **Samaritan**. Rabbis even today do not address a woman privately. Even worse, back then, to befriend a Samaritan "dog." Jesus had spiritual business to take care of with this woman and would not allow her lineage to keep her from hearing the truth.

As Jesus started on his way, a man ran up to him and fell on his knees before him. "Good teacher," he asked, "what must I do to inherit eternal life?" "Why do you call me good?" Jesus answered. "No one is good—except God alone. You know the commandments: 'Do not murder, do not commit adultery, do not steal, do not give false testimony, do not defraud, honor your father and mother.'" "Teacher," he declared, "all these I have kept since I was a boy."
Jesus looked at him and loved him. "One thing you lack," he said. "Go, sell everything you have and give to the poor, and you will have treasure in heaven. Then come, follow me." At this the man's face fell. He went away sad, because he had great wealth. Mark 10:17-22

Jesus even loved **those who did not follow him**. Great crowds surrounded him at times, the serious students, the casual followers and the lookey-loos. Jesus taught them no matter where they were on the commitment level. Even the rich young man, who put money first in his life, Jesus looked at and loved.

The Son of Man came eating and drinking, and they say, 'Here is a glutton and a drunkard, a friend of tax collectors and "sinners." ' But wisdom is proved right by her actions."
Matthew 11:19

Jesus liked to hang out with the **sinners**, even though his association with them caused damage to his reputation.

I have begun a period of my life when I have been a Christian as long as I haven't been a Christian. Saved at the age of 23, I remember vividly life on both sides of the cross. I know what it means to party and I know what it means to go to church. I understand the mindset of those that get drunk with alcohol on Saturday night and those that "get drunk" with the Holy Spirit on Sunday mornings.

I still feel for those whose lifestyles separate them from God and I always try to build bridges to them. The biggest enemy that prevents

164

me from getting too close to the sinners is always the church. I sometimes feel guilty for having unsaved friends.

I told the story to my church of helping a drunk girl I met in a parking lot get a ride home safely. Another time I witnessed to some drunks in a hot tub in a hotel. Each time I got questionable looks from Christians. How dare I do such a thing. A married man. Someone on church staff hanging out with such people.

Recently I went to a Van Halen concert. While there, I saw people from church. There was a moment of…uh, oh…you caught me. Why did I feel that way, especially since they were there too? Can't I like secular music?

I still hang out with friends who drink, some do drugs right in front of me. I don't do either, but I like hanging out with them. I met a bunch of high school friends for a mini-reunion at a bar. It was fun. They got drunk. I didn't. But I wonder what would happen if members of my church walked in.

Jesus liked to party, but he didn't "party." He risked his reputation to reach the lost.

Those accusations came from another group in Jesus' life—the righteous "saints" of the Jewish religious system—the **Pharisees**.

As Jesus went on from there, he saw a man named Matthew sitting at the tax collector's booth. "Follow me," he told him, and Matthew got up and followed him. While Jesus was having dinner at Matthew's house, many tax collectors and "sinners" came and ate with him and his disciples. When the Pharisees saw this, they asked his disciples, "Why does your teacher eat with tax collectors and 'sinners'?" On hearing this, Jesus said, "It is not the healthy who need a doctor, but the sick. But go and learn what this means: 'I desire mercy, not sacrifice.' For I have not come to call the righteous, but sinners." Matthew 9:9-13

Jesus hung out with both groups—sinners and saints. He accepted invitations to dinner with the Pharisees too. Some of them turned confrontational, especially when a sinner showed up—a young woman too.

Now one of the Pharisees invited Jesus to have dinner with him, so he went to the Pharisee's house and reclined at the

table. When a woman who had lived a sinful life in that town learned that Jesus was eating at the Pharisee's house, she brought an alabaster jar of perfume, and as she stood behind him at his feet weeping, she began to wet his feet with her tears. Then she wiped them with her hair, kissed them and poured perfume on them.
When the Pharisee who had invited him saw this, he said to himself, "If this man were a prophet, he would know who is touching him and what kind of woman she is—that she is a sinner." Luke 7:36-39

Which group did Jesus like more? I think Jesus preferred sinners. Why? I think they were more real, transparent, open about themselves and, doggone it, they liked to have fun! They expressed their joy. They danced. They listened to Van Halen. They didn't hide behind religion, but were probably very honest about their failures. The Pharisees acted one way but lived another.

Sinners can be hypocrites, but they don't use religion to hide behind. That's what frustrated Jesus the most. Pharisees used Jesus' laws as a weapon to attack others.

But, when it comes to the Pharisees, I have to say this…Jesus was downright mean, yes, insulting when he confronted them. The Pharisees called him rude and I would have to agree. My mother never taught me to go to someone's house, accept their food, then attack their reputation.

Max Lucado
Jesus seemed to know when enough was enough with the Pharisees. He seemed to know when it was time to walk away from them. The number of occasions when He said, "Don't have anything to do with them". And His own decision that He would go to the lost sheep of Israel rather than those who considered themselves saved. Seemed that he wanted to go to people who were at least open to the possibility. But the whole idea that there is a population of people around whose hearts were so hard that even Jesus Himself could not soften them is a pretty profound thought and Jesus just watched, He knew their hearts were hard, He knew they would not change. Yeah, he did not pander, you know the cleansing of the temple, He didn't play up to them at all. He did things and you knew were angering them and He

knew was angering them. But again, He didn't come to make them happy.

He called the hearts of the Pharisees' stone. He said they were the blind leading the blind. He used descriptions such as hard-headed, wicked, comparing them to houses without foundations, vipers and tombs. Jesus reserved his harshest words and condemnation for those who were the acting representatives on earth of God in heaven. In Matthew 23, Jesus laid out a number of "woes" for the Pharisees. It's a scathing attack.

In fact, during the times that Jesus talks about hell, it's usually in a conversation with or about Pharisees.

I never read of Jesus getting into debates with sinners over the Sabbath or his statements proclaiming that he was God. Sinners and saints saw the same miracle at times and had completely different reactions. We see this in the raising of Lazarus from the dead:

Therefore many of the Jews who had come to visit Mary, and had seen what Jesus did, put their faith in him. But some of them went to the Pharisees and told them what Jesus had done. Then the chief priests and the Pharisees called a meeting of the Sanhedrin.
"What are we accomplishing?" they asked. "Here is this man performing many miraculous signs. If we let him go on like this, everyone will believe in him, and then the Romans will come and take away both our place and our nation." John 11:45-48

The sinners held revivals. The Pharisees held meetings. The sinners found hope in Jesus. Pharisees looked for reasons to kill him.

Two totally different reactions.

So did Jesus love the Pharisees? Jesus tells us to love our enemies. These were his enemies. Jesus had to love them, but that doesn't mean he had to be nice with them all the time.

Some of the Pharisees and members of the Sanhedrin did believe in Jesus:

Yet at the same time many even among the leaders believed in him. But because of the Pharisees they would not confess

their faith for fear they would be put out of the synagogue; for they loved praise from men more than praise from God. John 12:42-43

Nicodemus, one of two who took Jesus down from the cross and buried him in the tomb, was a Pharisee who met with Jesus at night (John 3), probably out of fear of being associated with Christ. Jesus reserved for Nicodemus the most important statement about salvation in John 3:16.

The religious leaders knew better. Sinners did not. The Pharisees knew the law backwards and forwards. Sinners needed clarification. Pharisees needed conviction. Sinners beat themselves up enough with guilt. Pharisees made others feel guilty with their piousness.

Even though the Pharisees wanted Jesus dead, I don't think he hated them and would have gladly accepted any repentant heart.

Norman Geisler

It's kind of like what Bertrand Russell said, when he wrote his book, "Why I'm Not a Christian," 'Anyone who threatens people with hell is unkind.' And Jesus threatened people with hell therefore Jesus was unkind. Well if there is a hell, anyone who warns people of it, is not unkind, he's loving. If this building is on fire and I know it's on fire and I know you're going to be trapped and I don't warn you do I love you? See the fact of the matter is, He was warning people about their eternal destruction and that's not unkind. That is the kindest thing you can do.

As I read over all the passage in the Bible where Jesus interacted with people, I see an interesting pattern.

He touched them.

Lepers

When he came down from the mountainside, large crowds followed him. A man with leprosy came and knelt before him and said, "Lord, if you are willing, you can make me clean." Jesus reached out his hand and **touched** the man. "I am willing," he said. "Be clean!" Immediately he was cured of his leprosy. Matthew 8:1-3

Women

When Jesus came into Peter's house, he saw Peter's mother-in-law lying in bed with a fever. He **touched** her hand and the fever left her, and she got up and began to wait on him. Matthew 8:14-15

Just then a woman who had been subject to bleeding for twelve years came up behind him and **touched** the edge of his cloak. She said to herself, "If I only touch his cloak, I will be healed." Matthew 9:20-21

The dead

Jesus turned and saw her. "Take heart, daughter," he said, "your faith has healed you." And the woman was healed from that moment. When Jesus entered the ruler's house and saw the flute players and the noisy crowd, he said, "Go away. The girl is not dead but asleep." But they laughed at him. After the crowd had been put outside, he went in and took the girl **by the hand**, and she got up. Matthew 9:22-25

The sick

And when the men of that place recognized Jesus, they sent word to all the surrounding country. People brought all their sick to him and begged him to let the sick just touch the edge of his cloak, and all who **touched** him were healed. Matthew 14:35-36

Because of the crowd he told his disciples to have a small boat ready for him, to keep the people from crowding him. For he had healed many, so that those with diseases were pushing forward to **touch** him. Mark 3:9-10

The handicap

They came to Bethsaida, and some people brought a blind man and begged Jesus to touch him. He took the blind man by the hand and led him outside the village. When he had spit on the man's eyes and **put his hands on him**, Jesus asked, "Do you see anything?" He looked up and said, "I see

169

people; they look like trees walking around." Once more Jesus put his hands on the man's eyes. Then his eyes were opened, his sight was restored, and he saw everything clearly. Jesus sent him home, saying, "Don't go into the village.'" Mark 8:22-26

On a Sabbath Jesus was teaching in one of the synagogues, and a woman was there who had been crippled by a spirit for eighteen years. She was bent over and could not straighten up at all. When Jesus saw her, he called her forward and said to her, "Woman, you are set free from your infirmity." Then he **put his hands on her**, and immediately she straightened up and praised God. Luke 13:10-13

Those with evil spirits
He went down with them and stood on a level place. A large crowd of his disciples was there and a great number of people from all over Judea, from Jerusalem, and from the coast of Tyre and Sidon, who had come to hear him and to be healed of their diseases. Those troubled by evil spirits were cured, and the people all tried to **touch** him, because power was coming from him and healing them all. Luke 6:17-19

Norman Geisler
The lepers were considered untouchable, and I think Jesus deliberately touched the leper that He healed to show that we should come in literal contact with those who have need and literally help them. It would be like Jesus going to an AIDS or HIV ward, you know, today and touching someone or hugging them. He would do that. In terms of touch, He also was touched after His resurrection. The women touched Him. They cling to His feet. He told Thomas,' stick your hand in.' Sometimes the touch was so that they could realize the tangibility of Christ, sometimes so they could realize the compassion of Christ.

Max Lucado
Jesus touched people because of the power of touch. The power of touch says, "I value you enough to get this close to you, nothing

between us any longer." And everything about Jesus said, "I've come to remove the barrier". So He touched the lepers, so He held the children. And so He allowed women to anoint Him and to touch Him. He came to take the distance away. Emmanuel means God with us, not God above us or God somewhere in the same vicinity but God with is.

Jewish laws and custom firmly stated that one could not touch the sick, bleeding or dead or they would need to go through a period of cleansing, separating themselves from the community in case a disease was passed on to them. The law was rightfully hygienic and showed God's concern for a clean environment, protecting people from spreading physical infirmities.

However, the laws became excuses for limiting human contact. These were people in need, suffering, longing for human contact, yet the religious leaders kept their distance. Jesus recognized that humans need touch! Our skin has receptors that need contact. Jesus gave and received contact with all people. He could have spoken the word at times and healed people, but many times he chose human touch.

Paul Young

There is something about touch that connects the heart between people...I don't know if you've seen the Mother Theresa films in which she goes into these hospitals and these kids are just wailing and screaming and all she does is begin to stroke them and touch them and touch them. And she'll do it for an hour, for two hours and you'll find that child begin to calm down.

There's something about the touch, about hugs, about the connection. And I think He loved it and He did it when nobody else would do it. Some of those lepers probably had not been touched by a human being in ten years, in fifteen years. What was that like? You know, what did He communicate because He was willing to touch me? You know, unbelievable. And so there's just this, we like our distance. But touch, the hand shake even. The hand hold, the touch on the shoulder. All of those things communicate life in a way that words cannot. And it's just another expression of the manifest grace and care of God.

The Pharisees would put distance boundaries. They'd say, 'You cannot come within this certain period of space because if you do then you're unclean, you got to go through all the rituals and all that. You've been bad because you've been tainted.' And He's saying, 'No, that's not the way it is at all, I have no boundaries like this.'

Did living as God in spirit form, with flesh and blood, somehow limit his ability to enjoy human contact on our level? Now, all of a sudden, Jesus finds himself in a human body with human touch sensors and he excitedly wants to experience what we experience every time we give or receive a hug?

In some ways, we as humans get to experience things that those on a heavenly level only marvel at—marriage, friendship, high 5's, chest bumps after a touchdown.

Joel Hunter
Physical touch was a very important affirmation. And looking them in the eye and releasing them from the social shame that came with their diseases or their infirmities or their sins. I think that was all a part of setting the captive free, so to speak. Because there is a personal and emotional and a sociological dimension to healing and to redemption and so when He, for example, the woman who had the hemorrhage, touched the hem of His garment, she was healed at that moment. Why did He then turn to her and choose to address her? Because He wanted everyone to see that she was no longer unclean. He wanted to pronounce in her social circles that this woman who had had this issue of blood for this many years, who had been untouchable, literally for that many years. He wanted to lift her up and show everyone that not only was she touchable but she was socially acceptable now and she could have relationships like everybody else. I believe Jesus had a ministry of touching and hugging and a ministry of very personal care that was part of the spiritual redemption of those people.

In addition to touch, I bet Jesus enjoyed human relationship, relishing in it and becoming the supreme example of it.

So with all these different types of people in the world, where would Jesus hang out today if he arrived in our world? The answer got some interesting responses from the experts I talked to.

Max Lucado

Jesus found friends among the partiers, the rabble-rousers and a few of the trouble makers. So where would He find them today, where would we find Him today? I think He would not avoid the pawn shops and the bars and the rough and tumble sections of the city. I think that's where he would work. I think he would however, also find time for those who live in the more successful sections of the city that are just as desperate. You know just because somebody made a good living didn't mean that Jesus would ignore them. They were every bit as desperate as those who were poor. So we tend to say Jesus would never go into country clubs or walk onto a golf course. I think Jesus would go wherever there was somebody who was lonely and open to an honest conversation.

Joel Hunter

I think Jesus would hang out today with a really broad spectrum of people, because everybody needs Him, you know. There's a guy down here who's homeless, who has this cart, everything he owns is in the cart and he sits behind a tree out in front of one of our churches, you know. I think Jesus would just be out there drinking a Nehi with him, you know, and just hanging out with this guy. By the same token I think that He would be in the corporate board room trying to remind those guys what's really important and what they could really do with some of their profits as far as making a difference, you know, in the lives of people. I think He'd be with the mom who is up to her elbows in peanut butter and jelly, and wondering if her life really matters and wondering if, you know, if she's really significant, you know, just paying attention to her kids. I think He'd be with people who are so sanctimonious, you know and so religious and saying not, not so fast, not so much, just as He did with the Pharisees and the Sadducees.

Max Lucado

Would Jesus go into a strip club and a gay bar? I don't know if the places Jesus went were as openly immoral as to create opportunities. I couldn't go into those places I'll be honest with you, I could not. I could stand outside of them and visit with people in the parking lot. But I'm not strong enough to go into those, no. Maybe Jesus was? What's interesting to me and you talk about with Jesus going to abortion clinics and would He be involved in questions like that, one of the fascinating aspects of Jesus life to me is how apolitical He was, that He wasn't going to get pulled into any type of political controversy where that would become the message and people would see Jesus and think "oh yeah, He's politically here". He wouldn't do that. To me that's the point of the question about the coin, "Do we pay taxes to Caesar?" and He says "Render unto Caesar what is Caesar's and to God what is God's." To me Jesus is just saying I'm not going to talk about that, you figure that out. I'm here for some bigger issues. Jesus' apolitical stance troubles some of political evangelicals or Christians because they wish Jesus were more political. But it seems to me that there's a bigger question even than these hot political topics and that's the question of death and sin and that's what He came to deal with.

Joel Hunter
When you consider the spectrum of people that Jesus would hang out with, absolutely, He could go to gay bars. He could go to strip bars. He could go to the worst alleys where junkies shoot up. I think He would go to the people who are the most addicted to the cultures definition of what will bring you happiness. And I think He would go and put His arm around them and say, "You know this will never get you where you want to go". And by the way, I think He would do that with the people who are most repulsive to us. I think He would have found a way to hang out with Hitler. I do, I think He would have gone and sat in a cave with Osama Bin Laden, you know. I think He would have, those villains that all of us have, I believe that Jesus would have and could have loved them like none of us have quiet discovered how to do.

Norman Geisler
Jesus was not at all averse to hanging around with publicans and sinners. He was called a wine bibber not because He was a drunkard but because He hung around with people. He went to the parties where they were. When the Pharisee invited Him over to his house He didn't turn him down. He went over to the Pharisee's house. With Zacchaeus, the same thing, in Luke chapter 19. Jesus went where there were people who wanted His message. Who wanted to hear who He was and who were willing to believe. He said to the Syrophenician woman He hadn't even come except to the lost house of Israel, you know. He said to her when she said well just give us some crumbs that come from the

174

table, you know; He commended her for her faith. So I believe Jesus would be in the ghetto, He would be with the poor and oppressed in our society. He would not be with the up and outers He'd be with the down and outers.

Paul Young

He would hang out with sinners and get in trouble, you know. They're not going to contaminate Him; He's going to contaminate them with the life that is inside of Him. Who would He be with? He would be, the worst, with the worst. He would be with me. He would be with the worst of us, He would be with me. And I would love it. You know, we're not any different from each other. We are, apart from Him, we're lost. And there's no core difference between me and somebody who gets caught. And if it's not for Him, the healing in my life and the healing in your life, it's just not a possibility. But He does, He comes to us. We find Him in the middle of our lives. He enters into this soul that is still so damaged by history and by what people have done to us and all this stuff. And He's not ashamed to be called my brother and He knows everything there is to know about me. Is that beautiful? Yeah I want some of that, you bet.

Jesus hung out with sinners, not to get drunk and pick up chicks, but just to associate with them and give them access to his grace. It wasn't the place that contaminated him. Jesus brought forgiveness and life wherever he went.

Many people that Jesus hung out with were acceptable, good, God-fearing Jews. Some though, lived independently of the religious establishment. Jesus didn't seem to care.

As I tried to imagine seeing Jesus on the streets of Jerusalem, he had to be friendly, kind, smiling, with eyes that looked at you, unthreatening. He probably shook hands, gave hugs, kissed cheeks. When you met him, you wanted to see him again.

It became very clear to me. People were the most important reason of why Jesus came to earth.

Max Lucado

Here's the deal when it comes to Jesus and his charismatic nature. He was sinless. I've tried to imagine what it would be like to stand next to somebody who had no vain ambition, had all genuine interest in my

175

well-being, who never said a single self-promoting word, who never mislead me. Even as I'm talking right now I'm a little concerned, how I'm coming across am I using the right word. Jesus had none of that, absolutely genuine. Totally transparent. Really committed to your well-being over His own. Would shoot straight with you. Never play games with you and thoroughly loved you. Really loved you. He was crazy about you, thought you were the most fascinating person He'd ever met because He made you. So I think all of that comes together to create a remarkably compelling and magnetic personality.

TIME TO JOURNEY

1. **Watch "People" from "In His Shoes: The Life of Christ"**

2. **Discussion Questions**

- Do you love people, like people, tolerate people or hate people?

- What is God's relationship DNA? Why is it so important to him?

- What do you think Jesus was like if you first met him?

- How would you describe the people you hang out with?

- What can we tell about someone by the people they hang out with? What can't we tell?

- How has God "touched" you?

- How would you feel being a celebrity, constantly bothered by people?

- What kind of people do you have a problem with?

- Where do you think Jesus would hang out today?

- Do you think Jesus needed to get away from people at times?

- What is one place you go to see people?

- Where do you go to avoid people?

- What keeps you from loving people more like Jesus?

Rejected
Nazareth

While we were shooting documentary footage at Nazareth Village, the twentieth century tourist stop for first century living, I started to notice that things were not going well. Maybe it was the heat. Maybe the schedule. Maybe it was Nazareth.

I could tell the locals were not cooperating. I used that location before and was pleased at the hospitality and work ethic. Not today.

We received attitude and huge sighs every time we asked them to do something. One time we set up this complicated shot, but once the food arrived, they ran to eat, leaving us hanging. They refused to do what we asked them to do. They made the day very difficult by their passive rejection of our project.

It turned out they felt we were not paying them enough so they only gave us only a portion of their energy. I expected a representative from the Israeli equivalent of the Screen Actors Guild to show up and call a strike.

I began to understand the rejection Jesus encountered here in Nazareth, from his family to his neighbors. How difficult that must have been for God to so love the world that he sent his son, yet even Jesus' own hometown rejected him.

Jesus grew up for over twenty years in Nazareth, then one day, around the age of 30, went to the Jordan River to get baptized, disappeared into the wilderness, emerged after 40 days and focused his ministry in the area around the city of Capernaum (Galilee). As his reputation and following grew, he returned to Nazareth but did not get a home town hero's welcome.

Jesus stopped off at the local synagogue on the Sabbath, grabbed the scroll and opened to the book of Isaiah.

"The Spirit of the Lord is on me,
because he has anointed me
to preach good news to the poor.
He has sent me to proclaim freedom for the prisoners
and recovery of sight for the blind,
to release the oppressed,
to proclaim the year of the Lord's favor."

Then he rolled up the scroll, gave it back to the attendant and sat down. The eyes of everyone in the synagogue were fastened on him, and he began by saying to them, "Today this scripture is fulfilled in your hearing." Luke 4:18-21

Cue the crickets.
Dumbfounded looks.
A couple chuckles and throat clears.
What did he just say to the crowd that made them pause?

- "God has anointed me."
- "I am going to preach good news."
- "I am going to free prisoners."
- "I am going to give sight to the blind."
- "I am going to release those who are oppressed."
- "I am going to declare God's favor upon the land during this time."
- "Scripture has been fulfilled right before your eyes and you're looking at him."

It's a rather bold approach Jesus took. He didn't ease them into the topic or start with the introduction, "Remember that time when my mom suddenly got pregnant and you thought it was promiscuity...?" or "You know I've been away for a while at the Jordan and the wilderness, then at a wedding in Cana, doing some things, maybe you've heard of...?"

Nope. Jesus just spilled it out, a dramatic *da-da-duuuummmm* moment.

"I'M THE ONE PROPHETS SPOKE OF A THOUSAND YEARS AGO!"

Now if they rejected Jesus' announcement, that means that all the childhood miracles mentioned in other writings—claiming that Jesus spoke in complete sentences as a baby, made a bird out of dirt, saved his little brother from a snake bite and raised his playmates from the dead—could not be true. If that were true, why did this happen?

Coming to his hometown, he began teaching the people in their synagogue, and they were amazed. "Where did this man get this wisdom and these miraculous powers?" they asked. "Isn't this the carpenter's son? Isn't his mother's name Mary, and aren't his brothers James, Joseph, Simon and Judas? Aren't all his sisters with us? Where then did this man get all these things?" And they took offense at him. Matthew 13:54-57

They responded by saying:

"Sure we know him. It's Mary son. James' brother. Now he thinks he's so smart, making all these cuckoo claims about miracles and prophetic fulfillment. What a disgrace to his mother!"

Wouldn't their response be:

"Of course, he did all those fabulous miracles when he was a baby! We remember him well! He's back! Such a good boy!"

Some believe Jesus traveled to Tibet to hang out with Buddhist monks or wandered around Stonehenge to connect with the Earth's energy. If that were the case, then the locals would probably have accepted his announcement more readily, since Jesus would have gained the reputation as a traveling mystic or psychic seer. That was not the case.

They knew him only by his trade—the handy man—and his family that lived around the corner.

This proves that Jesus lived as an average human being, a normal son in a normal family, for nearly thirty years. Time passed and few indications were revealed to them that Jesus was anything other than just another working class guy from Nazareth. The only "super-human" moment of his childhood and early adulthood that was even worth mentioning occurred at the age of twelve. If someone wrote a biography about me, I have more noteworthy highlights in my life by the age of thirty. Jesus kept a low profile, nestled securely in his Nazareth address, a boring home body.

This is why they rejected him.

God is used to rejection—people have rejected the love of God since Adam and Eve—but what was it like for Jesus to see if firsthand, face-to-face, from those closest to your heart.

That subtle smirk from a next door neighbor.

181

A disappointed shake of the head from his little brother.

A waving off of the hand from his teacher.

Rejection from two groups must have hurt the most, starting with Jesus' family, who rejected his claims of being anything other than any ordinary older brother.

In one scene, before a holiday in Jerusalem, his younger brothers mocked him. The tone of this scene was one of cynicism and sarcasm.

After this, Jesus went around in Galilee, purposely staying away from Judea because the Jews there were waiting to take his life. But when the Jewish Feast of Tabernacles was near, Jesus' brothers said to him, "You ought to leave here and go to Judea, so that your disciples may see the miracles you do. No one who wants to become a public figure acts in secret. Since you are doing these things, show yourself to the world." For even his own brothers did not believe in him. John 7:1-5

"If you're so important, go show them some miracles in the big city, Mr. Miracle-Man!"[11]

That's cruel, but families can be.

The siblings had a hard time shifting gears from Jesus the human to Jesus the God. That's understandable, isn't it? Imagine if your brother or sister declared their deity...the insane asylum, right?

Families know us better than anyone else on earth. They see us behind closed doors. So many tell-all books written by children have come out revealing sides of their celebrity parents we thought were so perfect.

Families should be supportive. They help us find our dreams and guide us to them. Jesus' family called him crazy, out of his mind. That seems a little harsh.

Norman Geisler
James didn't believe Him until after the resurrection, according to 1 Corinthians 15. And in Mark it says, 'His relatives thought He was crazy and they came to carry Him away.' So, I mean, there's a sign of true

---

[11] If Jesus' brothers had no idea who he was, that proves Joseph and Mary could keep a secret about his miraculous birth announcement.

authenticity of the text. If you're writing a text to build up Jesus and make Him something He wasn't you would have never said, 'One, His brothers didn't believe in Him and two, His relatives thought He was nuts.'

How difficult it must have been for Jesus to have this side of him, this wonderful, amazing, mind-boggling aspect of his nature and be unable to share it with those closest to him. Many Christians who have non-believing families understand this. They've given their lives to Christ, yet their own family does not understand their zeal. Jesus lived that way for years, yet loved those in his family who did not believe.

Jesus also faced rejection from another group close to him—those in his hometown, who knew him as well as his own family.

Neighbors know us second best after our families. They see us outside, dealing with the problems of life. They hear us complain in the garage, kicking the car that doesn't start, yelling at the kids and the dog when they can't be found.

Luke 4 says the town was so furious at Jesus for his blasphemy that they wanted to toss him off a cliff. I visited the cliff traditionally associated with his rejection. In fact, it was just outside our Nazareth hotel, about a hundred yards down the road. I looked at this steep mountain, with a sheer rock face—perfect for tossing heretics off of—and the first thing that came to mind was the determination required to scale that mountain to reach the top.

You have to be pretty ticked off to make that climb. This was not a spontaneous moment, a flare up of unreasonable anger. This was a deep rooted commitment to kill. They understood clearly what Jesus said in Isaiah and would have none of that in these parts.

That's quite a hometown welcome. A parade to the mountain cliff.

Paul Young

Somebody who can hear the voice of the Spirit is always going to rock the world of the religious. And here you've got a situation in which He seems to have this intimacy in His relationship with God. What are they going to argue with, that He's mean and He's abusive...No. They've got to find something else and it's going to come from a religious slant. But there's something about the way He thinks that's dangerous. You know, and so the people who know you or think they know you tend to be the ones who build agendas around who you are. How He deals with it? I'm sure it grieved His heart. I'm sure it did. I'm sure there's a sadness to it. He obviously doesn't have a chip on His shoulder about it. He doesn't attack and so He absorbs it and He understands that this is part of a loss. But I'm sure that grievousness was there from the very beginning.

Many from my hometown or my high school or college, as they read this book, are having a hard time believing that the same Troy Schmidt who partied every weekend in high school wrote a book about his experiences with Christ. I hope they won't toss me off a cliff (thankfully I didn't grow up in Colorado).

Hometowns use their last available information of you to determine your identity. If you were the quarterback on the high school football team, you're always the quarterback. If you were the slacker, you're always the slacker. If you were a nerd, always a nerd, even if you become the head of Microsoft.

It's a difficult adjustment for people to see beyond your past. My wife knew Tom Hanks' wife, Rita Wilson, when they grew up in a church in Los Angeles. Now she sees Rita walking the red carpet and starring in movies and my wife only remembers her as that girl from Youth Group. That's an extreme shift in identity. It's hard to see people any other way, from the kid who threw paper airplanes or cracked jokes in Biology class, to throwing touchdowns in the Super Bowl or doing stand-up on Letterman.

Joel Hunter
When it says, "He came to His own and His own received Him not," that must have been crushing...On the one hand He was not surprised because He knows people by this time. He has seen betrayal all the way along. He has seen friends that would be, that would do anything to advance themselves or be afraid of anybody who would get them into trouble or push against the status quo. So on the one hand He's not surprised. But, on the other hand, knowing what He had to offer them and knowing that He was the only one that could offer it; He was hurt for them, not for Him. He was hurt for them and what they were passing up. That was really His grief. When He was looking over Jerusalem and He's weeping, you know, He's not weeping for Himself, He's weeping for them. "Jerusalem, how often would I have gathered you but you would not". So that's where His hurt comes from.

184

The rejection Jesus felt from those closest, his family and his neighbors, had to hurt the most. These were the ones Jesus grew up with, prayed for, spent the most time with. Now they turned their backs on him. Jesus could do so much for them, yet they wouldn't allow him too.

Jesus said to them, "Only in his hometown, among his relatives and in his own house is a prophet without honor." He could not do any miracles there, except lay his hands on a few sick people and heal them. And he was amazed at their lack of faith. Mark 6:4-6

Their unbelief was so deep Jesus did not perform any miracles there. He couldn't. They refused to believe him and they suffered because of it. While his hometown had more difficult hurdles of belief to overcome than other towns, in a way it should have been easier to accept Jesus on his claims.

He did nothing sinful to make them suspicious. He lived more godly than anyone else. If they had a contest for the Mr. Most Righteous in Nazareth, Jesus probably would have won every year. Yet his normalcy created the biggest obstacle.

Mark 6:6 said Jesus was amazed by their lack of faith. How could Jesus be amazed? Did it catch him by surprise? Certainly he expected some opposition, understanding that the claims he made were difficult to believe. What probably surprised Jesus was the intensity of that rejection. Jesus did nothing to deserve such an ice cold shoulder.

Yet the preconceived notions of him were so strong, they created barriers of acceptance. This still happens today. People reject Jesus because he didn't turn out the way they expected. They think Jesus will bring them success and take care of all their problems and when Jesus doesn't, people reject him.

Jesus is used to rejection. It doesn't mean he has to like it.

Eventually Jesus' family would come around. Jesus' brother James became a pillar in the church. Paul met with James, the writer of the epistle of the same name.

Then after three years, I went up to Jerusalem to get acquainted with Peter and stayed with him fifteen days. I saw none of the other apostles—only James, the Lord's

brother. I assure you before God that what I am writing you is no lie. Galatians 1:18-20

Over time and because of the resurrection, we can only hope that many from Nazareth and others from Jesus family accepted him as God.

He was one hometown boy who certainly made good. Very, very good.

Norman Geisler

'Jesus was in the world, the world was made by Him and the world knew Him not', John says. That had to be really hard to take. You're the creator of the universe, you come in and your creatures don't even recognize you. You come unto your own, your own people, the Jewish people and they crucify you. That's got to be really tough to take. I've been through enough in my life, I've been stabbed in the back enough by friend and foe to know that it's hard to take it from a foe but it's a lot harder to take it from a friend. And Jesus was literally stabbed in the back. He was crucified by the people who should have known who He was, who should have accepted Him. His own people, in His own place, who saw the miracles.

TIME TO JOURNEY

1. **Watch "Rejected" from "In His Shoes: The Life of Christ"**

2. **Discussion Questions**

- How would you describe your relationship with your family?

- Have they supported you always?

- Families should be there for us. Where else would you go if your family turned you down?

- What would you think if one of your brothers said he was God?

- How do you think Jesus acted as a family member for 30 years?

- Why would Jesus' family be so hard to convince? Shouldn't they be the easiest?

- What did your neighbors think of you when you were a child?

- What do they think of you now?

- Have you been back to your hometown recently? What was it like?

- How do you think Jesus acted as a neighbor for 30 years?

- Was his normalcy growing up a benefit or a detriment to his claim as God?

- Why was the town's reaction so harsh?

- Why couldn't Jesus do any miracles in his hometown?

- Do you think you would have reacted differently? Would do miracles if your hometown rejected you?

Identity

Caesarea Philippi/Mount of Transfiguration

I have an ID that I carry with me everywhere I go. My ID has some important information on it. My name, address, height, weight (I wish that weight was my current weight), eye and hair color, my organ donor status (someone can have whatever organs I have left). Sometimes we carry IDs that give our blood type, home country, allergies, work status and our voting affiliation.

Interesting how a little card can define us.

If we lose our ID, we're in trouble. If a cop stops us and we have no ID, we're considered suspicious. He cannot accept our verbal word with proper, verifiable, seeable identification. Walking around without an ID may mean we don't want people to know who we are.

Even worse, what happens if someone steals our ID and tries to pass themselves off as us? Identity theft is a growing problem as we trend toward reducing mankind to binary numbers and magnetic strips.

But do IDs completely and totally identify us? The security trolls at the airport need pacification with my ID, allowing me to pass. The grocery store worker looks at my ID, then at me, then at my ID, verifying my identity, then allowing me to purchase hundreds of dollars' worth of food. My ID seems to work for them.

Sure, identification cards give us privileges, but they do not express my past hurts, my culinary preferences, my dreams, my relational style, my worries. My passport shapes my identity, but does not define me as a person. People make assumptions about me based on my Starbucks Gold Card, my AAA card and Star Wars Fan Club membership ID.[12]

I am more than just a sequence of 16 numbers, a credit score or a driver's license picture (again, I wish I was 35 years old again). Those are parts of a whole to understanding who I am.

When people misidentify me, I find myself hurt. If they described me as a brown eyed, black haired jockey from Canada, I would be like…hey, that's not me! If people had preconceived notions about me just because I'm 6 foot 6 inches tall, or a writer or a Christian or that I like video games, that would hurt.

What if someone said about me: "That guy's a jerk. He drives a Jeep."

---

[12] I'm kidding, but you made an assumption about me, didn't you?

189

You base your entire assumption of me on one little fact? My car? Definitely not fair.

Jesus wondered what others thought of him when he came to a region called Caesarea Philippi. As his time on earth began to wind down, Jesus took a poll and asked what people thought about him. The passage in Matthew 16 reads:

When Jesus came to the region of Caesarea Philippi, he asked his disciples, "Who do people say the Son of Man is?" They replied, "Some say John the Baptist; others say Elijah; and still others, Jeremiah or one of the prophets." Matthew 16:13-14

Now when I'm concerned about what others are saying about me, it could be misconstrued that I'm facing an identity crises. Like a politician running for office, I'm worried that people don't like me. It comes from an unhealthy need to be accepted. That's not the case with Jesus. He knew who he was.

The reason Jesus asked this question was wrapped around the location where Jesus and his disciples stood.

Caesarea Philippi. Of all the locations Avner and I visited, this one connected with me the most. For the first time in all the places we visit, Jesus incorporated the surroundings into his speech.

I saw what Jesus was saying.

This possible location for Jesus' Identity Challenge is in a steep, rocky area of reddish hued bedrock, north of the Sea of Galilee on the southwestern base of Mount Hermon, where sacrifices occurred to the gods Zeus, Pan and Nemesis.

Two altars have been uncovered, plus a third area, believed to be a goat pen, where the sacrifices sat on deck, awaiting their turn. These sacrifices happened here, identifying it as a very pagan place.

As we walked through the very well preserved area, I asked Avner the significance of the name Caesarea Philippi.

"Well, the city honored the emperors, or Caesars. So it was called Caesarea. But there is much bigger and more important Caesarea on the Mediterranean coast, a place that King Herod built and become the main harbor of the whole region. A place where the tanner Cornelius lived and Paul used as a place to launch to his missionary trips. So, to defer the two Caesareas this was named after the son of Herod, who become the ruler for this region and his name was Philip so Caesarea Philippi."

We descended the numerous, uneven steps down the mountain. "But, locally they know it as Banias," I asked. "What is the significance of Banias?"

"Banias refer to what we can see here, the remains of a cult place where they worshipped the pagan god Pan, the god of nature. That is because here there is a huge spring." Avner pointed to the rushing stream, pouring out of the mouth of a cave, looking quite refreshing on this hot day. "It's one of the main sources of the Jordan River. Because it produces an abundance of water, it stands for the power of nature. And in the pagan world the god that's associated with power of nature was Pan. So the place was named after him, Panias. Yet in Arabic it's hard to pronounce 'P' and it was corrupted to 'B' so the name became Banias."

I studied the tourist map showing the distinct outline of the altars that once stood here. "So this area has always been associated with the gods and the god worship that went on here?"

"It was centerpiece of a lot of pagan worship here and that is because of a few reasons. Because of the great power of nature that can be seen here. The green which is not common in this region, the water, and the big spring. It's also beyond the area of the Jews."

I couldn't imagine a good Jewish boy's reaction to this cultural practice of sacrificing to gods. "What is the significance of these three gods?"

"Zeus is the head of the Pantheon and you'd better have a temple to him everywhere. Pan represents the wild part of nature. And as for Nemesis, we're not sure but because of the main road passing through here, a lot of army campaigns came through. So, that might be the association with Nemesis as the goddess of victory and revenge and power of war."

I sat down at the foot of a well preserved pillar. "Now, Jerusalem would have been the main place where the Jewish people would have gone to offer sacrifices and worship God. Would this be comparable to a pagan temple, similar to the Jewish temple in Jerusalem?"

"Banias can be compared to the temple in Jerusalem. Not in everything. There was only one Jewish temple and here were many pagan temples. Even in this country there were very many of them. So there is nothing to compare to the centralization of Jerusalem as it was."

I understood the significance of what Avner meant. Pagan religions franchised, while the Jewish religion centralized. If the faith spread out too far and in too many directions, it could be corrupted and adjusted to fit personal needs. Over time, those gods would be identified with whatever people wanted them to. By keeping the Jewish religion in one place, the faith and practices can be preserved and monitored much more easily.

I pointed to the altars, visible through the rubble. "So, there were animal sacrifices that occurred here?"

"Yeah, animal sacrifices occurred here in front of each place of each one of the gods. Probably mainly goats but it could be any other animal. But only animal sacrifices, there were no human sacrifices here for sure. They slaughtered the animal and then divided the parts to burn for the gods and parts that were kept for the people and the priest. That was one of the sources for the priest to make some living."

"What did they do with the blood?"

"There were times when the blood was collected and used in the sacrificial ceremony and sometimes it was used for food. "

I could not see this as the sort of place a Jewish tourist in Jesus' day would put on their itinerary. Why didn't Jesus ask "who do you say I am" on the Mount of Olives, overlooking the temple, or by the Sea of Galilee where he did great miracles?

Instead, Jesus chose the most vile location to ask a hard question. It's like having a Bible study at a Wicca meeting.

But maybe that reveals why Jesus asked the question here. In Caesarea, they didn't know Jesus. He could have shown his ID and they would have shrugged. "So what? Get in line with the other gods." Jerusalem, Bethlehem and Nazareth had the prophets and scripture to understand his identity. This place was a blank slate, so they filled in their spiritual void with some pagan practices.

Caesarea Philippi was avoided by Jews for the most part, yet the locals here needed to hear the truth about the one true God more than anywhere. The world will have many opinions about religion, yet there is only one truth. How are they going to know unless someone comes here and tells them?

The responses to Jesus' question were varied. Some thought John the Baptist had resurrected or maybe his spirit infiltrated another man. Others thought Elijah returned in bodily form or Jeremiah, Jonah, Moses, Ezekiel, or any of the top five prophets, take your pick.

While I would love to be compared to any great prophet, for Jesus that was an insult. Jesus exceeded all of them added together and multiplied by seventy. In fact, he performed many of the miracles these prophets performed and more!

Today the world does the same thing, reducing Jesus to a prophet, a soothsayer, a great magician, a teacher, a historical figure, a ghost. Only one description sufficed then as it does today.

"But what about you?" he asked. "Who do you say I am?" Simon Peter answered, "You are the Christ, the Son of the living God." Matthew 16:15-16

The depth of this answer in light of the mixed messages being sent from their environment pleased Jesus. The Jewish world looked for resurrected prophets. The Pagan world worshipped legends and idols.

Only Peter got it right.

Norman Geisler

Thou are Christ, the Son of God. Thou are the Messiah, Christ means Messiah. Thou art the Messiah, bingo, you're the one who came to fulfill prophesy. And you're the Son of God. That's an incredible thing for any Jew to say. Any human being to say. You're the Messiah is one thing, but you are the Son of God is another thing. If they had known the Old Testament well, they would have known the Messiah was going to be the Son of God because Psalm 2 talks about Him as being a son and it talks about Him in Proverbs about what is His name and what is His son's name. So it talks about Him being a son. So if they'd known the Old Testament very well they could have figured this out. And it talks about Him in Psalm 45, quoting Hebrews 1:8,'Unto the Son he said thy thrown O God is forever and ever.' They could have figured it out from there or, 'The Lord said to my Lord', Psalm 110:1 which He quotes in Matthew 22. But, that showed that Peter had insight that showed that Peter was getting the point. That He is not only the Messiah but the Messiah is also God.

Jesus is the Christ, the promised Messiah from scripture.

Jesus is the Son, one member of the Trinity.

Jesus is God, the eternal creator and giver of life.

Any other description missed his true identity. Just one of the three paled in comparison. To understand Jesus' true identity, the disciples had to accept all three claims.

So what's the big deal? Why are all three important?

If Jesus is not the Christ, then scripture lied about the promised one. There must be another savior to come from the line of David to die for our sins.

If Jesus is not the Son of God, then his relationship with God was misstated and God was not his Father. This meant Jesus lied and so did the voice from heaven that called out during the baptism.

If Jesus is not God, then he is a creation of God and not eternal, not greater than a goat or your Uncle Seymour. His sacrifice would not be an eternal sacrifice for all people, for all time. His blood would be no more pure than mine and therefore meaningless.

Jesus wanted to separate himself clearly from the other gods that populated the worship centers around the area. Jesus made himself distinct from false gods, wooden idols and lifeless sacrifices that remained dead on bloody pagan altars.

Jesus replied, "Blessed are you, Simon son of Jonah, for this was not revealed to you by man, but by my Father in heaven. And I tell you that you are Peter, and on this rock I will build my church, and the gates of Hades will not overcome it. I will give you the keys of the kingdom of heaven; whatever you bind on earth will be bound in heaven, and whatever you loose on earth will be loosed in heaven." Then he warned his disciples not to tell anyone that he was the Christ.   Matthew 16:13-20

Norman Geisler

I think what Peter said in Caesarea Philippi, that made Jesus happy was that he came to the self-discovery without Jesus banging him over the head, of who Jesus really was. Because Jesus wasn't flashing His credentials, as I said He wasn't pulling back His shirt and showing the big G on His chest. He was just making covert claims. Trying to draw them out. Get them to see, get them to believe. And so He asked them, 'Whom do men say that I am?' Well, you know, John the Baptist, the prophet, someone like that. Well who do you say I am, so He's getting around to the real question and then of course Peter, 'Thou art the Christ, the son of the living God.' That made Him very pleased and since Peter said that He answers Peter and says, you know, 'This is the rock like foundation I'm going to build my church on.'

As I looked at the towering walls of bedrock surrounding this location in Caesarea Philippi, I can see how Jesus incorporated the natural resources into his proclamation.

"...and on this rock..."

"The rock" at Caesarea Philippi is immense, unmovable, solid. The altars are built into the rock and from that massive rock comes the mouth of the underwater stream. It's breathtaking, surrounding you on all sides. It can be chiseled and chipped away, but you'll never move that rock.

Jesus' identity is rock solid, a firm confirmation of truth, strong enough to build a foundation, the platform of our mission into the world. The church can only operate effectively if it never forgets Jesus' identity – the Christ, the Son of God, God Himself.

But Jesus was not finished.

Running out of this rock, from an underground origin, is a stream emerging from an opening that many called the Gate or Entry way into Hades.

Avner explained why. "The cave seems as if it is the mouth of the underworld. Once the cave was a source of water, supplying one of the main tributaries of the Jordan River, people relate to it as a passage to the underworld—the gate to Hades—and most probably the reference in the scripture refers to this place as the mouth of hell because of that and because it is the center of evil, the pagan practice here so much stands against their believe in God."

Jesus chose Caesarea Philippi to say to his followers that those gods, devils and demons won't destroy his identity. God's church still exists, solid as a rock. I don't see any Zeus Temples in my area today. The Church of Pan has faded away.

That watery stream can erode away the rock over time, but it'll never completely decimate that area. Jesus' identity will stand the test and the attacks over time.

Jesus showed them a symbol of hell to remind them of the reality of hell. He stood before them as the one who would overcome death and hell and could help others do the same if they just got his identity correct.

I have been crucified with Christ and I no longer live, but Christ lives in me. The life I live in the body, I live by faith in the Son of God, who loved me and gave himself for me. Galatians 2:20

One day, as we stand at the gates of heaven, all we need to show is Jesus' ID, our new identification. Our old ID is gone. Our new ID has come. We throw out our old identity and take on Jesus' new one to get passed the gatekeepers, to receive eternal life.

Without that proper ID, we must show our own, our life and what it has to show for itself. The Bible says our lives amount to nothing, compared to what Christ has done. Our good works can't pay the admission fee, so we are directed to another place. The mouth of hell.

Eight days after this incident in Caesarea Philippi, to further solidify his identity, Jesus took Peter, James and John up to a high mountain, today called the Mount of Transfiguration.

After six days Jesus took with him Peter, James and John the brother of James, and led them up a high mountain by themselves. There he was transfigured before them. His face shone like the sun, and his clothes became as white as the light.
Just then there appeared before them Moses and Elijah, talking with Jesus. Peter said to Jesus, "Lord, it is good for us to be here. If you wish, I will put up three shelters—one for you, one for Moses and one for Elijah."
While he was still speaking, a bright cloud enveloped them, and a voice from the cloud said, "This is my Son, whom I love; with him I am well pleased. Listen to him!"
When the disciples heard this, they fell facedown to the ground, terrified. But Jesus came and touched them. "Get up," he said. "Don't be afraid." When they looked up, they saw no one except Jesus.
As they were coming down the mountain, Jesus instructed them, "Don't tell anyone what you have seen, until the Son of Man has been raised from the dead." Matthew 17:1-9

Our identity is shaped by who we know. By having Moses and Elijah appear with him, Jesus identified himself with the greatest prophets, miracle workers and heroes of the Old Testament. Since they appeared together, Jesus could not be Moses or Elijah. They are separate and distinct. Even their alignment made a statement. By appearing at his right and his left, Moses and Elijah positioned themselves in submission to the one in the middle. Jesus was the authority, the highest ranking official.

At this moment Jesus showed his true identity, tearing off his human mask, and showing his true nature. Jesus glowed brightly, his Godly righteousness shining through. I wonder how long Jesus had waited for such a moment, his flesh covering that inner light of his that burned so brightly inside, aching to illuminate the world.

Joel Hunter

I'm trying to picture Jesus, and I've been doing this for a long time, on the Mount of Transfiguration, and what all of that must have felt like for Him. On the one hand it must have been like "SEE", you know "This is my posse, you know, this is who I am." That was one of those mixed moments for Him—He was always straddling heaven and earth.

It also helped to have God himself show up and approve Jesus' identification. God's words proclaimed so much.

- Jesus is God's son.
- God loves Jesus.
- God was pleased with everything Jesus had been doing.
- We should listen to what Jesus says.

How wonderful it must have felt for Jesus to have his identity correctly revealed by the one, His Father, who knew him best.

In Caesarea Philippi and on the Mount of Transfiguration, Jesus made the same proclamation to them – don't tell anyone my identity. Why did he do that when our mission is to tell the world?

Jesus wanted to make sure the disciples got his identity right before they went out and told others. Not until his resurrection would they completely understand who Jesus was – his power over death, the fulfillment of prophecy, the meaning of his sacrifice. Anything stated before that (and done without the Holy Spirit guiding them at Pentecost) would not be a full, complete, correct identification.

Today we have all the information to correctly identify Jesus Christ.

I found myself faced with that question for years and years. I identified Jesus a number of ways – a legend, a historical figure, a metaphor, as apathetic, a holiday tradition. Then finally God showed me clearly who he was by reading scripture, Matthew chapters 1 and 2. In a moment, inside my apartment in Van Nuys, California, I read two chapters and realized Jesus' true identity—not the one I perceived from the world's information, but the one Jesus wanted me to know.

Jesus is the Christ, the Son of the living God.

I accepted Jesus' identity and everything changed for me.

I received a rock solid foundation to build my life upon.

I received eternal life.

Jesus' question at Caesarea Philippi is the most important question anyone can answer.

"Who do you say that I am?"

Jesus wants to make sure we get his identity correct.

So…who do you say Jesus is?

TIME TO JOURNEY

1. **Watch "Identity" from "In His Shoes: The Life of Christ"**

2. **Discussion Questions**

- What forms of identification are vital to getting by on this earth?
- Do you like the picture on your ID?
- Who do people say that you are?
- How do you identify yourself to others?
- Where could people go to discover who you are?
- Of all places, why would Jesus pick Caesarea Philippi to ask them about his identity?
- Who do people say Jesus is today? Why do people want to re-identify Jesus?
- Why is this question from Jesus the most important question in the world: "Who do you say that I am?"
- Why is understanding Jesus' identity so important?
- Why have so many different religions/cults come and gone?
- Why was Peter's confession the right answer?
- What was the "rock" upon which God was going to build his church?
- Why was it important to point out the gates of hell?
- What power does hell have?
- If we were to meet your friends, what would that say about you?
- What do we learn about Jesus on the Mount of Transfiguration?
- How does correctly identifying Jesus transform us?

Emotions
The Temple Mount/Mount of Olives

I know it's weird to imagine that God has emotions, but where do we think we get our emotions from? We are created in his image, his likeness, so like him we laugh, we cry, we get disappointed, we get excited and we get angry.

Emotions aren't wrong. Mr. Spock from "Star Trek" came from a race that found emotions to be illogical. Life with emotions isn't illogical…it's boring.

Emotions give depth to our monotone lives. They bond us with others at football games and funerals. Emotions drive the rollercoaster and tissue industries.

As the hours ticked closer to the cross, Jesus showed two very profound emotions—anger and sadness—as his three year ministry began to wind down.

Little things get me angry. Okay, mechanical things get me angry.

Computers that lock up.

Videos that take too long to load.

Screws that get stripped.

Light switches that short circuit.

Cars that won't start.

Phones that lose their charge.

When I get angry at these things, my first thought is always to throw, punch or kick the device. Somehow my mind quickly rationalizes that by further destroying the mechanical demon it will somehow teach it to mess with me.

Only the guy at Home Depot gets the last laugh. "Back again, Mr. Schmidt?"

Is my anger like God's?

When I get angry, it's because I don't get my way. God always gets his way, so that's not why he gets angry.

When I get angry, I lose control, flying off the handle, like a frustrated coach or a crazy dictator. God is in control, so that's not why he gets angry.

God's anger isn't like human anger. While each Gospel records at least one incident where Jesus cleared the temple, scholars believe he did it twice. One occurred at the beginning of his ministry, as recorded early in John 2, and the other occurred after his triumphal entry (during the week of his crucifixion), recorded later in Matthew 21, Mark 11 and Luke 19.

That means Jesus walked into the temple, saw what was going on, then proceeded to trash the place…two times.

In the temple courts he found men selling cattle, sheep and doves, and others sitting at tables exchanging money. So he made a whip out of cords, and drove all from the temple area, both sheep and cattle; he scattered the coins of the money changers and overturned their tables. To those who sold doves he said, "Get these out of here! How dare you turn my Father's house into a market!" His disciples remembered that it is written: "Zeal for your house will consume me." John 2:14-17

When I get angry, I don't think. I react. I burst.

Jesus' anger burned slowly, a culmination of witnessing spiritual abuse over years of time, maybe from his childhood at the age of twelve. Maybe he had been planning on clearing the temple for a long time.

The best indication that Jesus did not lose control can be found in his whip making. Do you know how long it takes to make a whip out of cords? You have to find the cords first, then weave them in such a way that they work properly. By that time, I've forgotten what I was angry at and I would probably transfer my anger to the cords that won't whip properly!

"Stupid cords! They never work the way I want them to work!"

Jesus reacted to what he saw by pausing and calmly making a whip.

When I get angry, I don't really have a good reason. My anger never makes a bold statement or causes people to reconsider their ways. It just makes me look bad.

Jesus' anger had scriptural basis.

Jesus entered the temple area and drove out all who were buying and selling there. He overturned the tables of the money changers and the benches of those selling doves. "It is written," he said to them, "'My house will be called a house of prayer,' but you are making it a 'den of robbers.'" Matthew 21:12-13

202

Did Jesus get angry because people were buying and selling animals and exchanging money? No, what they were doing was fine. It was not feasible for a person to carry animals on long journeys to Jerusalem as a sacrifice. They would probably die or get injured, making them unworthy for sacrifice.

Not everyone had sacrifices that were unblemished. Merchants in Jerusalem offered a service of providing a sacrificial animal to anyone willing to pay. The "sacrifice" was the expense of buying a sacrifice.

Since people traveled from all parts of the region, they had different currencies. The money changers provided a service that kept the currency—the shekel—consistent in town. Our airports and banks provide the same service to travelers from all over the world.

There's two possible reasons Jesus got angry and called them robbers.

One, Jesus got upset at the animal sellers and money changers for charging extraordinary rates. Jesus witnessed greed as entrepreneurs capitalized off of holy holidays. It's okay to charge a fee for their time and energy, but don't rip people off.

The second reason for Jesus' anger focused on their location. They turned the religious center into an un-worship-ful marketplace. According to the specifications of the temple, God did not design a foyer for such transactions. That should be occurring just outside the temple. Because of overcrowding in the streets, they moved their tables into the outer court of the temple, a prime spot, but right where the Jews and Gentiles were invited to worship.

Leen Ritmeyer[13]

The buying and selling of the sacrificial elements usually took place in the royal stoa or massive hallway at the Southern end of the temple mount. But during the high holidays, for example the feast of Passover,

---

[13] I had a chance to talk to Leen Ritmeyer, a Dutch-born archaeological architect who spent 22 years in Jerusalem from 1967-1989. He holds the M.A. in Conservation Studies from the Institute of Advanced Architectural Studies, University of York, England, and the Ph.D. from the University of Manchester, England. Ritmeyer is known for the research he has done on the archaeology and architecture of the Temple Mount in Jerusalem. Ritmeyer is well known for his architectural models of the buildings of ancient Jerusalem. His models of the historical Jewish Temples have been exhibited at museums.

and the Feast of Tabernacles, there were so many pilgrims that the royal stoa was inadequate. Some of the sons of the high priest set up stalls inside the holy temple mount, the original temple mount. It's most likely Christ drove those people out and that's why the priests got so angry, because they were run by the sons of the high priest. So they upset the authorities as well.

The Jewish businessmen cared little about interrupting the Passover celebration, so they so interrupted worship with distracting and disturbing sights, sounds and smells.

The quiet, reflective holy place turned into a loud, obnoxious marketplace. How can you pray with a goat bleating in your ear? Or while two people argued over the best price? Or while a cow relieved himself?

Greed prevented true worship. Not only were the merchants robbing people of their hard earned money, but they were robbing followers of the opportunity to pray to his Father.

So Jesus' anger was justified. This was his Father's house…and his house too. If robbers entered my house, I would get angry and it would be justified. In fact, the laws state I have the right to kill a thief in my house if I feel threatened. I can take any measures possible to rid myself of this dubious threat.

Jesus used violence to make his point since a three point sermon would not have worked. But he made that point in control of his emotions, sticking up for the underdog and defending the sanctity of his own house.

The Bible talks about the wrath of God in many places and I begin to see a pattern all those times.

God gets angry at wickedness and sinfulness.

God gets angry at injustice, abuse and innocent suffering.

God gets angry at idol worship, as people focused on other religions that pulled them away from his love.

God gets angry at people who misrepresented him, especially religious leaders who worked for themselves.

If God didn't get angry, we would call him heartless and uncaring, maybe even approving of injustice.

Norman Geisler

There's nothing wrong with being angry there's just something wrong with sinning when you get angry and He didn't sin when He got angry. In fact, if you don't get angry at sin you aren't sinless. So, part of Jesus' sinlessness was to be angry at sin and part of our problem is that we don't get angry at sin. So I think that was important to show His humanity. It was important as a manifestation of His divine justice otherwise He wouldn't be God if He couldn't get angry at sin.

At the Church of the Nativity, Dr. Shumali told me an interesting story about the door into the church.

"In the 18th century, the fight over the keys of the door, of this small door, led to a very well-known war, which is the Cremian War between France, England and Turkey from one side and Russia from another side."

As a result, the church was divided between the Armenians, the Greek Orthodox and the Franciscans. And they still have their disagreements to this day.

"The stairs leading to the grotto of the Nativity, the first section of the stairs has to be cleaned by the Greek Orthodox. The second section has to be cleaned by the Franciscans. If by accident, a Greek Orthodox monk sees the Franciscan cleaning more stairs on his side, there will be a fight."

But that was not the only time religious groups bickered over petty things.

The Holy Sepulchre in the old city of Jerusalem marks the spot where people believe Jesus died then rose again from the dead, offering all who believe eternal life. The original landscape has all been cleared away to make room for a giant structure that houses nearly six churches. Infighting between the denominations goes all the way to back to 1192, when the Arab leader in charge of the Holy Land, Saladin, tired of the bickering between the churches and came up with a solution.

A Muslim family was given the keys to the door of Holy Sepulchre.

I met with Wajeeh Nuseibeh, the member of that family in charge of the door of the Holy Sepulchre. I had seen him before during my trip here years ago and it appeared that he hadn't left his post since. He proudly told me his story.

"Yes, I am the door keeper of the Church of the Holy Sepulchre. And you see just our family is allowed to open and close the church of the Holy Sepulchre. And it should be a Muslim family."

"How long have you been doing this?" I asked.

"Thirty years I've been here," Wajeeh replied. "I'm always in charge of opening and closing the church."

"So do you consider this an honor?"

"Sure, it is very honor to be neutral between all the Christian groups because it's a part of the history of this church and part of the status quo of the church."

Status quo, I thought…it sounds so clinical and non-spiritual. "What do you think of the fact that the Christian churches couldn't get along?"

"Having different groups here, we have Greek, Catholic, Armenian, everybody, and everybody would like to have a piece of the church, would like having more power, more part of the church."

"What would you think if the Christians held the keys to the Dome of the Rock?"

Wajeeh, standing professionally at the door, his eyes on the surroundings, glanced at me for a moment ruffled by the thought. I don't think he had ever been asked that question. "You see, Muslims are different. We have one team of Muslims. But the Christians are divided, we have five groups here in the church."

Wajeeh saw nothing but division in his time there at the Holy Sepulchre. As a Muslim, he should have been drawn to Christ by the churches' love and compassion. Their unity should be their witness to the world. Yet, they failed miserably, for over a thousand years!

Leen Ritmeyer
When you go to Jerusalem and you go inside the Holy Sepulchre where the different religious groups fight amongst each other. And there is documentation of many, many fights over the cleaning of one step, between people that are very much antagonistic and all supposed to believe in Christ.

Other denominations mock Christianity because of their division. No wonder God gets angry.

The other emotion Jesus expressed in his final moments before the cross was sadness. It's stated very simply and succinctly in the shortest verse of the Bible and the easiest to memorize:

Jesus wept. John 11:35

I can understand Jesus getting angry because I've read of the wrath of God before, but I've never read of God bawling out his eyes while talking to Moses, or asking for a hanky when visiting Elijah, or getting choked up talking to the weeping prophet Jeremiah.

I have read that God lamented and mourned throughout the Old Testament, but now I see through Jesus the manifestation of that sadness in the form of tears. God has tear ducts?

I'm struck by the transparency Jesus showed by crying. Today, society tells boys not to cry and to act like a man. I can't imagine first century Israel was any different. Jesus felt emotional over the situation and decided to let it all out.

So what made Jesus cry? Two situations. We pick up the scene after his friend Lazarus died, the brother of Mary and Martha.

When Mary reached the place where Jesus was and saw him, she fell at his feet and said, "Lord, if you had been here, my brother would not have died." When Jesus saw her weeping, and the Jews who had come along with her also weeping, he was deeply moved in spirit and troubled.
 "Where have you laid him?" he asked.
"Come and see, Lord," they replied.
Jesus wept.
Then the Jews said, "See how he loved him!" But some of them said, "Could not he who opened the eyes of the blind man have kept this man from dying?" John 11:32-37

I guess what strikes me is the statement "he was deeply moved in spirit and touched." What moved and touched Jesus so deeply he began to cry?

Norman Geisler
A human being consists of three things: intellect, emotion and will. Androids have a will and intellect but no feeling. Jesus was truly human, and part of being truly human is having feeling. Actually the Greek there, in John chapter 11, when He was at Lazarus' tomb and when He was seeing the people around crying, it said, 'He convulsed with emotion.' We've all felt a burst of emotion and we couldn't hold back

and then suddenly it says, 'He wept', you know, He released it and let it out. So I can't think of any more beautiful, touching picture of His humanity than that in John 11.

It's hard not to cry at a funeral. A funeral is so final. The ultimate goodbye. The separation of lives. I've heard men wail for their wives. Children cry for their fathers. Mothers sob for their sons. I've done funerals and find myself getting choked up over people I didn't even know.

Jesus was not immune to the emotional swell created by the scene of mourning, especially since it involved Lazarus, Mary and Martha, his close friends.

Joel Hunter
First of all, He was human and so even though He knew He'd see Lazarus again, He missed him for the moment, you know. It's like us at a funeral. We are absolutely confident that we know we're going to see believers again but we're going to miss them until we see them again. And there's just this human reaction. And it would be a very short time before He would see Lazarus again but yet there is this moment of intermission where you miss them, you know, and everybody else misses them. When people you love hurt, you hurt too when their empty, you're empty too. It's just part of being in the human condition. It's part of the price of relationships.

Jesus knew in just a few moments that he would raise Lazarus from the dead so he was not crying out of hopelessness, those dead-end tears when someone has no assurance of a reunion in heaven. Maybe Jesus wept over seeing their hopelessness, their feelings of finality when standing before them was the giver of life. Jesus cried because they missed his message of eternal life.

Paul Young
He even knows what He's going to do and He's overcome by the emotions of it. Because here is the epitome of loss. Here is what sin has done. Here is the destruction. And it is someone He has a tender place for—it is His friend. And He sees how sin is killing. And the grief of it, I mean, it is just overwhelming.

The second emotional event happened as Jesus overlooked Jerusalem from the Mount of Olives, as he approached the city before his triumphal entry.

As he approached Jerusalem and saw the city, he wept over it and said, "If you, even you, had only known on this day what would bring you peace—but now it is hidden from your eyes. The days will come upon you when your enemies will build an embankment against you and encircle you and hem you in on every side. They will dash you to the ground, you and the children within your walls. They will not leave one stone on another, because you did not recognize the time of God's coming to you." Luke 19:41-44

As he approached Jerusalem, he wept because he knew in forty years, 70 AD, Roman armies would destroy Jerusalem completely desolating the city, slaughtering its inhabitants and preventing it from ever functioning as the primary Jewish religious center.

I was talking to Avner about the devastation of 70 AD as we looked over the temple from a stone walkway leading to the Wailing Wall. As we talked, a Jewish regiment received a blessing before heading out to defend their country. I could tell the scene was emotional. Avner explained why.

"During the '67 war I was not far from Jerusalem. And like everybody, I just heard in the news that the Israelis entered the old city and the first thing that everybody did was run here to the Wailing Wall. And I burst in tears when I heard the soldiers were here and the guards, the commanders and ministers who just came to the place. And many of you must remember this wonderful picture on the cover of the Life magazine with this guy standing here and raising his eyes to see the flag that was here on top, with such big eyes was a solder, nineteen years old, twenty years old now he is a famous surgeon in the hospital in Jerusalem. But that picture really expressed the feeling, the very deep emotions that everybody, the Jews had, when the Jews were allowed back in."

Jesus understood how many tears would be shed for nearly 2,000 years over the loss of this place.

Jesus also cried because Jerusalem could not see what he offered them. Jesus offered peace between people, countries and God with man. Many in Jerusalem missed it, just like they missed the prophecy of his coming next door in Bethlehem.

And riding into town was what they were all looking for, but refused to accept.

Jesus came to a city on the Mount of Olives called Bethpage, overlooking Jerusalem. The story picks up in Matthew:

As they approached Jerusalem and came to Bethphage on the Mount of Olives, Jesus sent two disciples, saying to them, "Go to the village ahead of you, and at once you will find a donkey tied there, with her colt by her. Untie them and bring them to me. If anyone says anything to you, tell him that the Lord needs them, and he will send them right away." This took place to fulfill what was spoken through the prophet:

"Say to the Daughter of Zion,
'See, your king comes to you,
gentle and riding on a donkey,
on a colt, the foal of a donkey.' "

The disciples went and did as Jesus had instructed them. They brought the donkey and the colt, placed their cloaks on them, and Jesus sat on them. A very large crowd spread their cloaks on the road, while others cut branches from the trees and spread them on the road. The crowds that went ahead of him and those that followed shouted,

"Hosanna to the Son of David!"
"Blessed is he who comes in the name of the Lord!"
"Hosanna in the highest!"

When Jesus entered Jerusalem, the whole city was stirred and asked, "Who is this?" The crowds answered, "This is Jesus, the prophet from Nazareth in Galilee." Matthew 21:1-11

Jesus certainly fit the image of a Messiah. Messiah means "anointed one" and describes a person sent by God to save and rule over people. Moses, Joshua and David fit those qualifications. They delivered their people from the enemy and brought freedom for the Jews.

Jesus chose the donkey and foal to fulfill the prophecy of Zechariah 9:9. When you read the passage, you understand why the people mistook him for a nationalistic hero.

Rejoice greatly, O Daughter of Zion!
Shout, Daughter of Jerusalem!
See, your king comes to you,
righteous and having salvation,
gentle and riding on a donkey,
on a colt, the foal of a donkey.
I will take away the chariots from Ephraim
and the war-horses from Jerusalem,
and the battle bow will be broken.
He will proclaim peace to the nations.
His rule will extend from sea to sea
and from the River to the ends of the earth.
As for you, because of the blood of my covenant with you,
I will free your prisoners from the waterless pit.
Return to your fortress, O prisoners of hope;
even now I announce that I will restore twice as much to you.
Zechariah 9:9-12

They wanted Jesus to take away the chariots and war-horses and break the bows and arrows of their enemies. The people wanted peace from sea to sea. The people wanted a political-Zechariah 9-messiah. But Jesus came as a spiritual messiah, offering peace in a different realm.

Jesus did not arrive to save them from the tyranny of Rome, but the tyranny of death. Caesar was not about to be overthrown, Satan was. The people were about to be freed from their slavery to sin and from the prison of a waterless pit. Jesus promised twice as much as they wanted—freedom from this world and the world to come.

I guess the main thing that makes God weep is when people refuse to accept him. They missed him at the funeral and they missed him in Jerusalem. He stood right there, in the flesh, and nobody remembered his words or accepted his promises.

That's truly sad.

I wonder if God still cries in heaven.

211

Max Lucado

I think there's a sadness in heaven about the rejection of God   This gets us into the topic of heaven but, can there be sadness in heaven and there still be joy? I think so. The days that I'm joyful I'm not completely void of tragedy but there's a deep and abiding trust and knowledge that it's going to all work out okay, that it's all in good hands, in the right hands. So I believe that Jesus does carry a burden for people right now obviously yeah, He does. And there's a sense of sadness of the number of people who disregard and disobey Him.

Joel Hunter

I'm not sure I've ever considered that question...Does He still cry? If you love, and if those you love hurt then you have a great empathy. He's always interceding for us at the throne, that's what He does. And the high priest is still our priest. And the priest is always one who takes on the burdens of his congregation, you know, his children, so in a way I think He does. He knows ultimately this is all a part of God's perfect plan but life has many dimensions and just because you know something is going to work out alright doesn't mean you're not immersed in the hurts of the moment. And so it very possible yes, He could cry.

Paul Young

Oh, yeah. Absolutely. You know, emotional life comes out of the very character and nature of God. We're created in His image. That's, you know, that' why we're relational. God's never done anything by Himself, you know. Why would we think we can do stuff by ourselves? Emotional life, it's a reflection of that very nature and character of God. And yeah, I think He cries, you bet. He weeps with those who weep and He rejoices with those who rejoice. That's why He keeps saying, 'Write it into scripture', and say, 'This is the way I want you to relate to each other. Don't be surprised when all of the sudden, as I heal your emotions, you begin to weep with the ones who weep and you begin to have joy with the ones who rejoice.'

These two emotions Jesus expressed point to the same cause.
Jesus felt angry when people were kept away from experiencing the relationship of God.

212

Jesus felt sad knowing people were not accepting a relationship with God.

Both emotions dealt with a separation of relationship. Both emotions show God's deep love for his people. Both emotions reveal his hatred of sin and his disappointment that we would choose sin.

As long as there's a break in the relationship between God and man, God will continue to get very angry and quite sad.

TIME TO JOURNEY

1. **Watch "Anger" from "In His Shoes: The Life of Christ"**

2. **Discussion Questions**

- What gets you angry?
- How do you express your anger?
- How is your anger different from God's?
- Why do people get upset at God at times when he expresses his wrath?
- How would you react if robbers entered your house?
- What did Jesus do in the temple that you should do when you feel anger?
- What is the difference between passion and anger?
- What are you passionate about?
- How do you feel about churches fighting amongst themselves?
- Is there any way you could be contributing to something that makes God angry?

3. **Watch "Wept" from "In His Shoes: The Life of Christ"**

4. **Discussion Questions**

- What movie/commercials made you cry?
- What funeral made you cry?
- Is crying always a sign of hopelessness?
- What surprises you about Jesus' tears?
- How would you feel differently if these moments of Jesus' crying were not in the Bible?
- Why are tears considered a sign of weakness, especially for a man?
- Thinking of the news today, what is God crying about?

Communion
Upper Room

What would I want for my last meal?

Probably pizza, not frozen, hand tossed. All meat. Extra cheese, ooo, with cheese in the crust. Finally, I can trash this diet, not having to worry about my cholesterol and calories since I'll be dead before it digests.

While I ate this disgustingly greasy pizza, I would remember all the good times I had around a dinner table with family and friends, talking about school, church, the future and God.

Maybe I could choose as my last meal a Thanksgiving feast and make it symbolic as an expression of thanks for the wonderful life I had.

Or, we could go out to eat. Somewhere we always went to as a family or somewhere expensive since we'd be saving money in the future with one less mouth to feed. Mine!

I wonder if I would be able to eat in those circumstances. Would my stomach turn as I thought about my impending death? Would I lose my appetite as I thought about my wife being all alone and all the things she counted on me to do? Would I drop my fork and cry that I would be missing graduations and weddings and grandkids?

Not much of a final meal when the only thing on your mind is death. Every bite I take would be one bite closer to death. Every sip is one sip closer to death.

Death. Death. Death. I'm going to die. Die. Dead. Not a very pleasant meal. Is this how criminals feel facing the death penalty on Death Row?

So how did Jesus feel at his last supper?

Jesus chose to eat with his disciples, his closest friends for the past three years. He gave the menu for his final meal.

On the first day of the Feast of Unleavened Bread, when it was customary to sacrifice the Passover lamb, Jesus' disciples asked him, "Where do you want us to go and make preparations for you to eat the Passover?" So he sent two of his disciples, telling them, "Go into the city, and a man carrying a jar of water[14] will meet you. Follow him. Say to the

---

[14] Men didn't carry water jugs. That was women's work, so miraculously Jesus predicted this man's appearance and set up the exact accommodations he was

owner of the house he enters, 'The Teacher asks: Where is my guest room, where I may eat the Passover with my disciples?' He will show you a large upper room, furnished and ready. Make preparations for us there." The disciples left, went into the city and found things just as Jesus had told them. So they prepared the Passover. Mark 14:12-16

Leen Ritmeyer
In the morning he sent Peter and John to prepare the Passover. They would have gone to the market. They would have selected a lamb. It would have been inspected by the priest, so it was a perfect lamb without a broken ear or a broken leg. They would have gone into the temple courts, through the court of the women, into the court of the Israelites. The lamb would have been killed by the priest. The blood would have been caught in silver and gold vessels and brought to the ram of the altar and splashed against the bottom of the altar. The animal would have been flayed, the skin taken off, the inside taken off. And then Peter and John would have taken that lamb where Christ was going to eat the Passover.

To understand the setting of this Last Supper, Avner and I traveled to a private residence on the outskirts of Jerusalem where a Christian family has decorated a room for an accurate portrayal of the scene. The tables were low, about a foot off the ground, surrounded by pillows. Three tables were arranged in a U-shape, disagreeing with Da Vinci's famous rendition. The food arrived in bowls, encouraging dipping, passing and lots of reaching across your neighbor's plate. My mom would have yelled at Peter at the Last Supper. "Don't reach!"

It was such a communal, inviting scene where joy and happiness would be expressed—a time when friends could relax and laugh. However, Jesus had a packed agenda, a list of items he wanted to communicate at this meal.

Humility. First he washed their feet. This was the most humbling task any person could do. When I went to Egypt, I was told not to show the bottom of my feet when I sat and crossed my legs. This would be considered an insult. When Saddam Hussein's statue came down in Baghdad, the people beat it with their shoes.

---

looking for.

By washing their feet, Jesus wanted his apostles to remember to serve.

It was just before the Passover Feast. Jesus knew that the time had come for him to leave this world and go to the Father. Having loved his own who were in the world, he now showed them the full extent of his love. John 13:1

The best way Jesus could show the *full extent of his love* was by serving them through the washing of their feet. He wanted serving to be their theme in life.

"You call me 'Teacher' and 'Lord,' and rightly so, for that is what I am. Now that I, your Lord and Teacher, have washed your feet, you also should wash one another's feet. I have set you an example that you should do as I have done for you. I tell you the truth, no servant is greater than his master, nor is a messenger greater than the one who sent him. John 13:13-16

Urgency. The opposite of serving is self-serving and one disciple at the table served only his own interests. Jesus wanted to "out" Judas because the clock was ticking.

"I am not referring to all of you; I know those I have chosen. But this is to fulfill the scripture: 'He who shares my bread has lifted up his heel against me.'
"I am telling you now before it happens, so that when it does happen you will believe that I am He. I tell you the truth, whoever accepts anyone I send accepts me; and whoever accepts me accepts the one who sent me."
After he had said this, Jesus was troubled in spirit and testified, "I tell you the truth, one of you is going to betray me." His disciples stared at one another, at a loss to know which of them he meant.
One of them, the disciple whom Jesus loved, was reclining next to him. Simon Peter motioned to this disciple and said, "Ask him which one he means."

Leaning back against Jesus, he asked him, "Lord, who is it?" Jesus answered, "It is the one to whom I will give this piece of bread when I have dipped it in the dish." Then, dipping the piece of bread, he gave it to Judas Iscariot, son of Simon. As soon as Judas took the bread, Satan entered into him. "What you are about to do, do quickly," Jesus told him, but no one at the meal understood why Jesus said this to him. Since Judas had charge of the money, some thought Jesus was telling him to buy what was needed for the Feast, or to give something to the poor. As soon as Judas had taken the bread, he went out. And it was night. John 13:18-30

Jesus knew his betrayer dined at the table with him. I would have a hard time swallowing my food knowing someone within a butter knife's distance wanted to kill me. Jesus removed Judas not because he was afraid, but to speed up the process.

"Go do what you're going to do!" I would tell my betrayer to have seconds, thirds and how about coffee with your dessert. Jesus wanted to get down to business. He wanted to save the world, but Judas was leaning back and picking his teeth. The crucifixion needed to coincide with Passover and time ticked away. Jesus was ready to die.

This moment coincided with the Feast of the Unleavened Bread, which marked a night of urgent preparation for the Jewish people. In the Book of Exodus, the Israelites had to quickly make unleavened bread and could not wait for it to rise. The theme of the festival was all about urgency and it was Jesus' feeling too. It was time to get to the cross.

Unity. Jesus emphasized unity at the Last Supper. The bread represented his body broken for everyone. The wine represented his blood, shed for everyone.

Everyone—the faithful apostles and the betrayer. Everyone.

This moment not only united the group around the table, but believers for centuries who would carry out the same ritual with they practiced communion. It has united followers across two thousand years of time.

Communion encourages group self-examination. As believers, we come together to remember what Jesus did for us personally and for us corporately. It levels the playing field. No one gets more salvation or shown any favoritism. Jesus died as one for all.

Joel Hunter

I think the atmosphere and I think His attitude at that time is one of ultimate love, ultimate sobriety. And I think that He is more deeply in love with these disciples for what's about to happen. Because He knows how much they need Him and He knows what He's about to do for them.

Death. Washing feet was unselfish, but it was nothing compared to the unselfish act of crucifixion that was about to happen. Jesus wanted to prepare them for his death.

And he said to them, "I have eagerly desired to eat this Passover with you before I suffer.   Luke 22:15

Who eagerly can't wait to suffer? Only someone passionately willing to lay his life down for others.

The event also coincided with the Feast of Passover, the Old Testament holy days marking the Israelites' salvation from Egypt. Avner knew well of the emotions surrounding this, having lived in Israel.

"For a Jewish person, Passover stands for, above all, being sure there is a salvation. Even being in a very bad situation like Egypt for instance and when Jews celebrate Passover they are going through a lot of events along the history that God saved us from other troubles. So the idea of salvation by God that's a very strong part of it."

Passover marks God's miraculous intervention to free the Jews from oppression. Now, in the next twenty-four hours, God's miraculous intervention through the crucifixion of Jesus Christ would help the Jews and all people to be free from the oppression of sin.

It would not be a lamb's blood sprinkled on a doorway that would cause death to pass over our lives, but the blood from the Lamb of God, who takes away the sin of the world, sprinkled over our death certificate paying the debt in full. The next few hours marked a new beginning in God's plan for his people.

Avner explained more about this idea. "Leaving Egypt was born of being Jews. Getting the Ten Commandments in the desert that's the beginning, that's the beginning of the faith not for one people, Abraham and the few descendants of him, but for a nation. The last supper stands for the same thing. A new beginning."

219

The smell of death truly permeated the air around this table, not only with the symbolism of the Passover meal, but with the betrayer in their midst and the trials about to happen.

Leen Ritmeyer
I can just imagine Christ, sitting now at the table with all his disciples and that dead lamb on the table knowing that the next day he was going to be as dead as that lamb is. If I were Christ I would not be able to eat of that lamb. But he did for our sake. He knew he was the Passover lamb, he was going to fulfill it and it was graphically portrayed in front of him in the shape of that lamb on the table.

Jesus refused to allow the mood turn towards despair, so he established a new practice to occur routinely in Christianity. He even, get this, allowed the new ritual to supersede the old ritual. This would be like changing the meaning of Christmas or Easter for Christians today. Communion now marked the ultimate Passover—not just for those Jews in Egypt thousands of years ago, but for everyone, thousands of years to come, for eternity.

While they were eating, Jesus took bread, gave thanks and broke it, and gave it to his disciples, saying, "Take and eat; this is my body." Then he took the cup, gave thanks and offered it to them, saying, "Drink from it, all of you. This is my blood of the covenant, which is poured out for many for the forgiveness of sins. I tell you, I will not drink of this fruit of the vine from now on until that day when I drink it anew with you in my Father's kingdom." When they had sung a hymn, they went out to the Mount of Olives. Matthew 26:26-30

Every crises can be viewed as either grave or great. We can focus on the loss or the gain. Jesus marked this grave moment with a great celebration, doing three things to keep the moment positive.

- *One, he gave thanks.* Jesus gave thanks for his broken body and shed blood. He accepted the torture and death to come because it would give hope and life to those that believed.
- *Two, he looked forward to eternity.* Jesus didn't dwell on the bloody chaos of the next few hours, but he focused on the future,

when all believers, gathered at a table in heaven, would raise their wine glasses in celebration of salvation.

- *Third, he sang a hymn.* I sing when I'm happy. It's hard to sing when you're sad. Even blues songs are kind of catchy. Jesus found joy in the sorrow through song.

I guess from this last supper I learn how to face difficult times. I admire Jesus' courage to face his death, even to the extent of hurrying it along, without any fear. I marvel that Jesus took time to serve others, when he could have shifted into a "woe is me" mindset, "I'm about to die!"

He wanted to make this moment memorable, instead of forgettable. I want to forget my crises moments. Jesus wanted people to learn from it.

All throughout, Jesus gave thanks, focused positively and singing songs. Only a man so consumed by God's will for his life and a sacrificial spirit could react this way.

The communion supper seemed to relax Avner and I felt him opening up as we concluded with some very emotional thoughts.

"What would you want to do if you had your final moment and you had all your loved ones around? What would you want to do or say during those times?"

Avner looked away, the impact of that moment hitting him very quickly. "I think I would express my love and how thankful I am for their love to me. And also to hope there would be a continuity of my ideologies that I tried to deliver to them all along. And something would be continued, not personally, but to the level of what should be done and how the world should be in my eyes."

For the first time, I noticed tears welling in his eyes. "That would be a hard moment."

"Very hard. For sure."

TIME TO JOURNEY

1. **Watch "Communion" from "In His Shoes: The Life of Christ"**

2. **Discussion Questions**

- Where would you go to eat for your last meal?

- What would you want to eat for your last meal?

- Who would you want to join you for your last meal?

- What would the topic of conversation be at that dinner?

- Would you be thinking of serving others or being served?

- Why did Jesus tell Judas to hurry up?

- Would you be in a hurry to die?

- What would you do to delay the meal?

- What did the Passover represent?

- What does communion represent?

- What is Communion like for you? Is it special or routine?

- What new insights have you gained by Jesus at the Last Supper?

- What song would you sing before you died?

- What would keep you from becoming negative during this time?

JOURNEY 4

Olive Trees to the Mount of Olives

Crushed
Gethsemane

During our time in Nazareth, at the first century village, we visited a real working olive oil press. The olives were collected and placed inside of a circular trough that housed a huge round millstone, weighing easily 200 pounds. The stone sat inside a wooden axle tied to a donkey that walked around the circle, then rolled over the olives, crushing them.

The scene was powerful and dangerous as the workers shifted the olives in the trough to make sure they were crushed evenly, quickly moving their fingers out of the way as the stone rolled by. Then the freshly crushed olives were put inside a basket and mounted inside a press. The press was a complicated Rube Goldberg contraption where weights were added to increase the pressure on the basket of olives as precious olive oil flowed from the crushed olives.

It was a violent scene, especially if you were an olive. The Olive Defamation League would be in an uproar over the mistreatment of its own kind. Olives would be horrified at the brutality shown to its fellow fruits, rolled over by a stone, tossed by human hands then smashed inside a press. All of that just for olive oil.

As I watched the brutality against those olives, I understood how Jesus felt *crushed* before his crucifixion. He was about to have something in common with an olive.

They went to a place called Gethsemane, and Jesus said to his disciples, "Sit here while I pray." Mark 14:32

As our walk in the shoes of Jesus began to wind down, we visited Gethsemane, on the side of the Mount of Olives. In Jesus' day, this was a garden of olive trees. Today, you can still find remnants of olive trees nearly 1000-1500 years old. Not the original ones Jesus saw or touched, but a close son or grandson of the ones from Jesus' time.

The tourists visit a church on the mountain surrounded by a beautifully landscaped Garden of Gethsemane. The place was packed with busloads of tourists, disturbing the quiet reflection Jesus sought on this mountain two thousand years ago.

So we stopped first at a place on the Mount of Olives, just a few hundred yards away from the church, untouched by tourism. Jesus didn't pray in a well-manicured garden, but in a natural setting of olive trees. I

225

could feel my spirit relax here, away from the faces and crowds. It's what I needed and what, I'm sure, Jesus needed.

The ground was rocky and full of roots from the ancient olive trees. We were there in the day, but at night I imagined these twisted olive trees cast a scary, haunted shadow on the scene. If you studied the trunk long enough you could see the outline of laughing faces and the branches of the tree reaching out with gnarled fingers, ready to snatch you away.

Here's the scene: Jesus left the last supper with his disciples and needed to retreat for a time of prayer before things got hectic. Maybe you have a place where you like to get away. Maybe it's driving in your car or a day at the beach. Maybe it's in your room listening to music or on the back porch listening to nature.

Jesus chose an olive tree garden on a mountain (hence the name Mount of Olives) to get away and pray. Jesus took in his last moments of freedom in human flesh before he transformed into a resurrected body. An overwhelming line up of pain was coming his way and he knew it.

The location was ideal, not only because it was a quiet patch of olive trees, but it overlooked the temple where sacrifices for sin occurred. Where Jesus knelt to pray, he could see the place where animals were massacred and their blood spilled out for the sins of the world. The foreshadowing was blatantly obvious. Soon Jesus would become a sacrifice, the perfect, ideal, eternal sacrifice. This location acted as a visual reminder for his purpose for coming to earth.

He took Peter, James and John along with him, and he began to be deeply distressed and troubled. "My soul is overwhelmed with sorrow to the point of death," he said to them. "Stay here and keep watch." Mark 14:33-34

The word Gethsemane in Aramaic means olive press. The olives that fell from the trees around him reminded Jesus of how crushed his body was going to be, all for the purpose of squeezing his precious, sinless blood out for the world. As Jesus knelt over to pray, maybe he took those olives in his hand, crushing them in his hand.

"This will be me in just a few hours…"

The pressure was so great that Jesus, the God/man, confessed that his soul was overwhelmed to death. The vise began to tighten around his chest. While his spirit understood the purpose of the imminent events and his mind knew preciously the agenda, Jesus still felt the pressure.

In fact, Jesus suggested to God that if there was any change in the plans or optional way to go about this, he was willing to follow it.

Going a little farther, he fell to the ground and prayed that if possible the hour might pass from him. *"Abba*, Father," he said, "everything is possible for you. Take this cup from me. Yet not what I will, but what you will." Mark 14:35-36

This was not a cry of a quitter, but a committed follower, making absolutely sure he was on the path he needed to be on.

Are these the words of a worrier? Worry focuses about something that may or may not happen. Jesus did not have unrealistic expectations nor was he overcome by the possibilities. Jesus' reaction was not pessimistic or hopeless.

Jesus could definitely be stressed. Stress is a natural reaction to what you know will happen. It is a real response to real difficulties about to come. There's nothing wrong with stress. It's how you handle it.

"I really want this hour to pass," Jesus prayed, "But I'll do whatever you want." Jesus communicated his submission in the midst of his stress.

The "cup" he speaks of represents the cup of wrath of God and its imagery appeared in the Old Testament.

Awake, awake!
Rise up, O Jerusalem,
you who have drunk from the hand of the LORD
the cup of his wrath,
you who have drained to its dregs
the goblet that makes men stagger. Isaiah 51:17

This is what your Sovereign LORD says,
your God, who defends his people:
"See, I have taken out of your hand
the cup that made you stagger;
from that cup, the goblet of my wrath,
you will never drink again. Isaiah 51:22

This is what the LORD, the God of Israel, said to me: "Take from my hand this cup filled with the wine of my wrath and make all the nations to whom I send you drink it. Jeremiah 25:15

Starbucks coffee comes in three sizes: Large, Grande, and Venti. God's cupful of wrath always came in the Large Grande Venti size, a combination of all three. Like a Super Big Gulp of Wrath.

God was about to pour out his anger against sin, drenching whoever stood in his way. This was not a mouthful or a thimble full, but a big, tall goblet of wrath. Jesus knew this was not going to be good. God poured out his wrath on Sodom and Gomorrah and on many armies in the Bible that stood in his way. Jesus trembled at the thought of that kind of wrath.

Someone unfamiliar with God's wrath and who didn't know what he was about to face would not be so upset. Jesus' reaction was justified.

Max Lucado
Look at Him pleading for help. Look at how afraid He is. He says, "My soul is overwhelmed unto the point of death." I don't think I've ever been to the point where I've said that.   I mean, I've been overwhelmed but I've never thought I literally was going to die.   And Jesus was afraid. The language there suggests the picture of a man who is afraid. And look at His reaction, He falls on His face.   He's not calmly, serenely praying. He falls on the face. I can see grass stains and mud stains on His face in conjunction with the blood that's coming down that's breaking through His skin from the blood veins. Here's a God struggling to fulfill His work that He came to fulfill in the flesh. And when He prayed, "Lord if you could take this cup away from me," He meant it. He really meant it. I don't think He's said, "We'll let's just go through this routine so it will appear in the Gospels". He really thought if there's another plan B, if there's a way out of this, I would like to hear it. There wasn't, and He stood up to it.

I can't help but wonder on this lonely, scary mountain, staring at the temple where Jesus saw lambs killed, if his words really communicated fear. I find myself having a problem with God being afraid.

There's a fear that's drowns in the unknown, many times creating unrealistic scenarios. That can't be the fear Jesus was experiencing. There's a fear where the body prepares for the inevitable, when the senses go to high alert. That could certainly describe Jesus' physical state of readiness, a characteristic that comes with being in a human body. There's also a fear that communicates respect for God and the moment. Jesus respected the wrath of His Father.

Jesus did not have the kind of fear that turns men into cowards, like his disciples would display at the end of the encounter with the palace guards and Judas. They would run away afraid for their lives.

Instead of running away, Jesus stayed put on this mountain and prayed. He continued to feel the squeeze, so much so that an angel showed up to strengthen him (Luke 22:43). The only other time an angel showed up to comfort Jesus occurred in the wilderness, days without food or companionship. Jesus, then, felt the physical pressure after forty days in the desert. He had only been in the garden for forty minutes or so.

Like Jesus, we've all faced those traumatic moments in our lives when we feel overwhelmed, at the end of our rope. We know what's coming—a phone call from the bank, a conversation with your boss, a note from your spouse—and we can't escape it.

And being in anguish, he prayed more earnestly, and his sweat was like drops of blood falling to the ground. Luke 22:44

The medical condition is called hematidrosis, a medical fact so rare, few know about it or have seen it. It only occurs when someone is so...so...so overwhelmed with grief and sorrow that the blood vessels under the surface of the skin burst and bleed through the pores.

Jesus experienced the kind of pain a mother would feel after losing a child, or a person on death row about to face an uncertain eternity, or a business leader feeling the threat of bankruptcy.

If I were in the garden with Jesus, I'm sure I would say to him, "It's going to be okay" or "It'll all work out" or "You just need to have faith."

Somehow I think these would all fall short with Jesus. Of course everything God does works out. Of course Jesus has faith—he knows all that. My words cannot take away the pain.

229

Jesus was about to be brutalized beyond belief, on every level, and he knew it and he wasn't looking forward to it. I could say to Jesus, if I knew what I know now, "It'll be over soon" or "You'll resurrect after three days," but Jesus knew that too.

Norman Geisler

I think Jesus was upset in Gethsemane about some of the same things He was upset at Lazarus' tomb. He looked at the unbelief around Him. He looked at death before Him; He's tasting death of a friend for the first time. He gets in Gethsemane, He knows what's going to happen, He knows He's going to taste death and He prayed, 'Father if it's possible, let this cup pass from me but, nevertheless thy will not mine be done.' He always submitted to the Father. So, It's one of those things like, I know I have to do this. I know I've chosen to do this because no one takes my life from me. I lay it down freely , John chapter 10, but it's going to hurt . It's going to hurt badly, and yet he endured the cross despising the shame, sat down the right hand of the throne of God, Hebrews tells us. So, He saw the end too.

Jesus did not want to experience pain and his soul was crushed. I looked down on the ground and picked up one of the thousands of rocks on this mountain and was reminded of the rocks added to that olive press to increase the pressure on the olives. Here in this place, Jesus felt more pressure added to his spirit. Like an olive spilling oil under duress, Jesus oozed blood from his pores.

I wonder how I would have acted sitting in that boat, approaching the shores of Normandy, knowing full well my chances of life were less than 50-50. I'm sure I would have let forth a few bodily fluids, from blood to vomit. While the cause to defeat the Nazis was good and right, it still would not minimize the pain.

Jesus' reaction to the impending pain gives us permission, at times, to be a little nervous before surgery or to cry when we break our arm. Responding to physical pain with tears is not a sign of weakness or a lack of faith in any way.

The Garden of Gethsemane shows me a side of Jesus I did not expect – one that hated pain. As I read scripture, I find God's laws as warning signs to keep his people from experiencing pain. His laws are preventative measures for us to live a pain-free life. God doesn't want his creation to experience pain. It was never his intention for this world.

We want a life without pain, but even God sees it necessary—
while we are here on earth—to experience pain to get to a greater good.
I have no right to ask for a pain-free life if Jesus himself willingly
allowed himself to experience torture and abuse.

Joel Hunter
He knows the method of death. Suffocation is a horrible, excruciating
kind of death and nobody wants to physically suffer like that. Nobody
but a delusional person would bounce happily toward that end and say,
"this is what I've been waiting for, oh boy, you know, now they're going
to see". And so I think, again, He's human here and He is, He's just
asking one more time. "I don't want to do this, I don't want to suffer
like this, I don't want to go through this kind of pain but what I want is
not as important as what you want". I think simply knowing how things
are going to turn out does not necessarily make suffering any less
painful, I think it makes it more purposeful but I don't think it makes it
any less painful.

Jesus wanted to soothe the pain, so he came here to pray to his
Father, seeking spiritual comfort from his relationship with God.
However, Jesus desired companionship from his friends too in his
greatest time of need.

Then Jesus went with his disciples to a place called
Gethsemane, and he said to them, "Sit here while I go over
there and pray."
He took Peter and the two sons of Zebedee along with him,
and he began to be sorrowful and troubled. Then he said to
them, "My soul is overwhelmed with sorrow to the point of
death. Stay here and keep watch with me."
Going a little farther, he fell with his face to the ground and
prayed, "My Father, if it is possible, may this cup be taken
from me. Yet not as I will, but as you will." Then he returned
to his disciples and found them sleeping. "Could you men
not keep watch with me for one hour?" he asked Peter.
"Watch and pray so that you will not fall into temptation. The
spirit is willing, but the body is weak."
He went away a second time and prayed, "My Father, if it is
not possible for this cup to be taken away unless I drink it,

231

may your will be done." When he came back, he again found them sleeping, because their eyes were heavy.
So he left them and went away once more and prayed the third time, saying the same thing. Then he returned to the disciples and said to them, "Are you still sleeping and resting? Look, the hour is near, and the Son of Man is betrayed into the hands of sinners. Matthew 26:36-45

Jesus just wanted a friend. Three times he found his closest friends sound asleep, tired after a full day of activities, lethargic after a big Passover meal and maybe a bit depressed after the sorrowful words spoken by Jesus at the Last Supper. Jesus only asked for an hour of their time. So many times over the last three years he was there for them, now he asked them to be there for him.

Through this I understand the antidote my friends require when they are distressed. They just want a friend too. No sermons. No empty words of encouragement. Just be near and available. That's all Jesus wanted.

The rejection by his friends added another stone to his soul, crushing his spirit even further. Jesus sought the comfort of relationship—both spiritual and physical—in his time of greatest pain.

I know God empathizes with my pain because he knows pain. This is not a God who sits on his throne and shrugs when I mess up, thinking "I wish he was a little braver. Doesn't he know it will all be over soon? He needs more faith."

The author of Hebrews suggests that Jesus cried other times, his soul crushed over and over by the pain he witnessed in his lifetime.

During the days of Jesus' life on earth, he offered up prayers and petitions with loud cries and tears to the one who could save him from death, and he was heard because of his reverent submission. Hebrews 5:7

It was in a garden that pain entered the world when Adam and Eve chose their own desires over those of the world. In the Garden of Eden, man severed his relationship with God through disobedience. Selfishness brought a flood of pain onto the Earth that not only troubled mankind, but God himself.

And now, in this garden, like a perfect book end to the story, Jesus began the process of paying for the penalty of that disobedience, restoring man's relationship with God, and offering a pain-free, worry-free, stress-free eternity in heaven to those who believed.

He will wipe every tear from their eyes. There will be no more death or mourning or crying or pain, for the old order of things has passed away." Revelation 21:4

I was also reminded of another use of olive oil and why Jesus chose the Mount of Olives and the Garden named "Olive Press." Olive oil was used to anoint a new king.

So Samuel took the horn of oil and anointed him in the presence of his brothers, and from that day on the Spirit of the LORD came upon David in power. 1 Samuel 16:13

Samuel anointed David as the future king of Israel and Jesus came to this mountain as the anointed King of Kings. Just as David faced battles to protect his kingdom, Jesus prepared for a battle to protect his people, for now and all eternity.

We left the desolate area and decided to enter the traditional location for the Garden of Gethsemane. A huge church, the Church of All Nations, sat surrounded by a beautiful garden that is more aesthetic than a real first century depiction and currently more crowded with nearly three hundred pilgrims milling about this sacred place.

I talked to one of the Roman Catholic monks[15] who worked there. He looked like a kindly old grandfather and seemed very approachable. At the moment, though, he looked stressed, a theme, it seemed, consistent on this mountain.

I asked the monk in this place of prayer what he needed prayer for. He at first seemed surprised someone would ask him for his prayer request. Then he got over his shock and quickly answered:

"Patience."

After seeing him in action, dealing with busloads of people, I knew why. The sign at the door asks for silence and the man's job was to fire off a "SHHH!" every five minutes.

"Let me guess. Tourists."

He sighed. "That's right."

"What do they do?"

---

[15] Who asked to remain nameless.

The poor guy acted like he didn't want to commit any more to the conversation, revealing to me more than he should. After a pause, he went on.

"They come here and they don't treat this place as a place of prayer. It's all about pictures. It's lost its holiness."

I felt bad since I had a camera crew with me, but he was right. We had been looking for more photo opportunities on this trip, than spiritual opportunities to connect to God.

Prayer is our connection to God. When we're feeling crushed, stressed and in pain, we need the reassurance of that relationship. That's where Jesus went in his time of need. Why can't I?

I encouraged the monk, then took his advice and decided to quietly go off and pray at a rock in the center of the church believed to be the rock Jesus knelt before. I prayed for the monk and for the people around me, lost and busy. In the craziness of this holy shrine, people missed the point of this Garden and failed to connect with God.

And the keeper of this area, the holy man, just wanted to talk to a friend.

TIME TO JOURNEY

1. **Watch "Crushed" from "In His Shoes: The Life of Christ"**

2. **Discussion Questions**

- What is one moment in your life that you felt crushed?

- What did you do to get you through that difficult time?

- Where is one place you go to get away and reflect?

- Why did Jesus pick a place in front of the temple?

- Why did Jesus pick a place in an olive garden?

- Why did Jesus pick a place with so much symbolism?

- What will you think now when you see olive oil?

- Why was Jesus under so much pressure? Wasn't he God?

- What's the difference between worry and stress?

- When you are stressed, what do you seek for relief?

- Is it okay with you that Jesus was afraid?

- How does his reaction give you comfort?

- When you're afraid, what do you seek after?

- Why is companionship so important during these difficult times?

- Why would God need a friend?

- Why is prayer so important too?

- In light of Adam and Eve, why did Jesus choose a garden?

- Does Jesus' response in the garden surprise you? Why?

- What lessons can you learn from Jesus' time in the garden when you face stress?

Betrayed
Palatial Mansion/David's Citadel

I've been trying to think of a time someone betrayed me and I really can't think of it. I can think of times people disappointed me, but an outright act of turning their back on me or accusing me of things I just did not do…I don't know if that has ever happened.

I imagine divorced people feel that way, especially if one acted unfaithfully. That must feel like betrayal.

Or a business partner who realizes a longtime co-worker has been stealing thousands of dollars.

Or a celebrity who walks into the grocery store and sees a tabloid headline that reads about their Love Child with Bigfoot! "Who told?"

Betrayal must happen among criminals, as people tattle on others for a reduced sentence. You expect betrayal among thieves.

But to have a good person betrayed by a bad person…that's unjust. That's just wrong. You just don't see that happen. Especially when their crime is righteousness.

As if Jesus was not already facing enough struggle emotionally during the countdown to crucifixion, his body reacting physically to the stress, Jesus faced relational turmoil between himself and, what seemed like, everyone around him.

Let's look at all the people who betrayed Jesus in less than a day.

But the hand of him who is going to betray me is with mine on the table. The Son of Man will go as it has been decreed, but woe to that man who betrays him."
They began to question among themselves which of them it might be who would do this. Luke 22:21-23

Judas. In the Upper Room, during the Last Supper, Jesus knew the first act of betrayal would begin with Judas Iscariot, a long time traveling companion, hand-picked to be an apostle. Jesus gave Judas responsibility for the money. He trusted him. This was not an act of rebellion from a longtime foe, but a stabbing in the back by a disciple, a sidekick, a friend who slept side-by-side with Jesus many nights by the campfire.

237

Judas' betrayal directly led to the death of Christ. He turned Jesus over by leading the authorities to him in the garden and uncovering their hangout.

Judas knew he messed up and his post-betrayal actions revealed his despair. He tried to return the bribe he received for the insider information. He hung himself later, unable to live with himself (or knowing someone would probably have killed him anyway).

Peter. At that same table, Jesus predicted the second act of betrayal from an even closer friend. Peter.

"Simon, Simon, Satan has asked to sift you as wheat. But I have prayed for you, Simon, that your faith may not fail. And when you have turned back, strengthen your brothers."
But he replied, "Lord, I am ready to go with you to prison and to death."
Jesus answered, "I tell you, Peter, before the rooster crows today, you will deny three times that you know me." Luke 22:31-34

The denial of a friend…how sharp is that dagger in your back? To have a friend deny any involvement with you, to reduce you to a non-person, to strand you all alone without assistance, had to hurt. Jesus invited Peter to the inner-inner circle. Jesus stayed in Peter's house in Capernaum. Peter confessed the true identity of Jesus as the Messiah, the Son of the Living God. Peter witnessed the transfiguration.

Simon Peter and another disciple were following Jesus. Because this disciple was known to the high priest, he went with Jesus into the high priest's courtyard, but Peter had to wait outside at the door. The other disciple, who was known to the high priest, came back, spoke to the girl on duty there and brought Peter in. John 18:15-16

The location of this betrayal occurred in the high priest's courtyard, near a place known as the Palatial Mansion in Jerusalem.[16]

---

[16] There are other locations where this courtyard may be. The Church of St. Peter of Gillacantu is one such location and so could be the place of an Armenian Church, St. Saviour, in Mount Zion, the supposed home of Caiaphas. Avner took me to the spot he felt best matched up to the courtyard and so I took

The Palatial Mansion was the Beverly Hills of Jerusalem where, oddly enough, the high priests and members of the Sanhedrin lived. Archaeologists uncovered a courtyard area and you can stand in the place today. The dig was so massive, nearly an entire block, the city authorities enclosed it and put a street over it. You travel underground to see this museum even though you are really on ground level.

Avner took me this amazing find, unearthed in the Jewish Quarter of the Old City between 1969 and 1982. He pointed out a number of clues that indicated two characteristics of the people who lived here—they were rich and they were religious.

The remnants of plaster on the walls, mosaics on the floors and furniture in the homes all point to a home of the rich and famous.

The discovery of mikvahs (Jewish purification baths) and stone jars (filled with water for the purification rites) tells archaeologists that Pharisees and high priests lived here.

Leen Ritmeyer

I believe the Palatial Mansion was the home of the high priest because there were four mikvahs. Every high priest had to purify himself before he could serve in the temple. That's number one. Number two is the enormous size of the building. It's not just a living room. It's a reception room. Also the location is very important. It was right next to where the Hasmonean palace would have been, so he would have had an easy route straight into the temple.

Now if this were the home of high priest, Caiaphas, that means at the time of Jesus' trial, Jesus was brought there. There's also a reception hall connected to the home. Inside that reception hall they would hold meetings like the trail of Jesus. Connected to that reception hall is a courtyard where Peter sat and waited to hear the outcome of the trial.

Now Peter was sitting out in the courtyard, and a servant girl came to him. "You also were with Jesus of Galilee," she said.
But he denied it before them all. "I don't know what you're talking about," he said.

---

his expert advice. Leen Ritmeyer confirmed this also.

Then he went out to the gateway, where another girl saw him and said to the people there, "This fellow was with Jesus of Nazareth."
He denied it again, with an oath: "I don't know the man!"
After a little while, those standing there went up to Peter and said, "Surely you are one of them, for your accent gives you away."
Then he began to call down curses on himself and he swore to them, "I don't know the man!"
Immediately a rooster crowed.
Then Peter remembered the word Jesus had spoken: "Before the rooster crows, you will disown me three times." And he went outside and wept bitterly. Matthew 26:69-75

Leen Ritmeyer
I can imagine Peter being there and being in the light of the fire. He then moved away. There's one place in that courtyard where you can look through one doorway into the entrance hall through another doorway to the very center of the large reception room where Christ would have stood in front of the high priest.

Peter's denial was an amazing twist to the line of betrayal that was happening. Peter certainly ranked in the least-likely-to-betray-Jesus category. Such a bold, in-your-face guy. Peter even drew a sword to fight off Jesus' arresters! Then, moments later, Peter forcefully denied any relationship with Jesus. Even though Jesus predicted it, the sting of Peter's betrayal still had to hurt.

Joel Hunter
The betrayal must have hurt more than the nails.

Disciples. Jesus' disciples also betrayed him in the garden of Gethsemane.

Then all the disciples deserted him and fled. Matthew 26:56b

That's a harsh word. Deserted. The minute a little trouble brewed, Jesus' friends ran for cover. Friends are supposed to stand up for you and be willing to die for you. Especially your closest friends.

But Peter declared, "Even if I have to die with you, I will never disown you." And all the other disciples said the same. Matthew 26:35

They all gave their word at one time to Jesus. Their devotion. Words are certainly cheap when the enemy turns the heat up.

Then all of sudden: "What's that...a sword? I'm out of here..." Jesus lost all his friends in a matter of hours.

Judas and Peter represented two of the twelve apostles. Think of it: 1 out of 6 apostles betrayed Jesus publicly. The other ten betrayed him passively, by running and hiding and not sticking up for Jesus when he needed them most. Those are terrible odds.

The religious. Jesus was also betrayed by the Pharisees, Sadducees, chief priests, elders and scribes, those religious leaders in charge of the Jewish faith.

While he was still speaking, Judas, one of the Twelve, arrived. With him was a large crowd armed with swords and clubs, sent from the chief priests and the elders of the people. Matthew 26:47

The religious community today is supposed to send deacons to the hospital to pray, ministers to prisons to lead the lost or servants to homeless shelters to feed the poor. I have never seen one organize an army to arrest people.

The First Baptist Church Armed Services Division.

The Community of Faith Goon Squad.

The Holy Family Enforcement Ministry.

When did churches begin arming themselves and hiring hit men? The Sanhedrin organized a group of soldiers and officials with swords and clubs to bring Jesus in on charges of healing on the Sabbath and blasphemy. "How dare Jesus call himself God then prove it through his actions by performing miracles on such a high, holy day! Arrest that man!"

The very group who knew the scriptures and the prophecies of Isaiah, Micah, Psalms and Zechariah describing the coming Messiah refused to believe the facts and turned their back on the one they were waiting for. The very group who knew the commandment "You should not kill," found justification for killing an innocent man. They had to bend the rules to get their way.

Annas the former high priest and Caiaphas the current high priest (and son-in-law to Annas) both failed to support Jesus. Shouldn't the religious system have given him all their support? Jesus came to free them from the very system that consumed them. However, if the people were freed from the religious duties in the temple, they would lose their jobs and their palatial homes.

The political. Rome prided themselves on their civilized political structure based on truth, justice, trials and law. The goal of Rome was to conquer then peacefully rule over a number of different societies. Yet on this day, they failed to uphold justice and betrayed a citizen of their domain.

Avner took me to David's Citadel, once a fortress for King David. The area has been beautifully restored, but it could have been the location for a very ugly scene.

"The palace is probably the location for the trial of Jesus because after King Herod's death, the Romans took over and the Roman governor used to use the palace whenever he made it from Caesarea to here and he did at this Passover in 30 A.D. when Jesus was caught and brought here."

Pilate represented the Roman government and he listened to the charges brought against Jesus. Since blasphemy was not a crime in the Roman system (Romans worshipped a bunch of gods), the religious system trumped up the crimes against Jesus, charging him with insurrection, tax evasion and attempted overthrow of Rome.

"Pilate was interested in keeping things quiet," Avner said. "He didn't want to get into trouble. The Romans whenever they conquered a place they respected the local law including the local faith of the area and let the people that led the religious activities, the religious authority, to continue to have the power."

No credible witnesses supported these charges making them nothing but hearsay. Pilate heard the case, asked some questions, then let it drop. All Pilate wanted to do was to get this case off his agenda and move on. It had become a thorn in his agenda, so early in the morning.

Eventually, tired of the interruptions, Pilate just let the people have their way, never using any wisdom or discernment, but succumbing to the popular opinion polls.

Pilate called together the chief priests, the rulers and the people, and said to them, "You brought me this man as one who was inciting the people to rebellion. I have examined him in your presence and have found no basis for your charges against him. Neither has Herod, for he sent him back to us; as you can see, he has done nothing to deserve death. Therefore, I will punish him and then release him.'"
With one voice they cried out, "Away with this man! Release Barabbas to us!"
(Barabbas had been thrown into prison for an insurrection in the city, and for murder.)
Wanting to release Jesus, Pilate appealed to them again. But they kept shouting, "Crucify him! Crucify him!"
For the third time he spoke to them: "Why? What crime has this man committed? I have found in him no grounds for the death penalty. Therefore I will have him punished and then release him."
But with loud shouts they insistently demanded that he be crucified, and their shouts prevailed. So Pilate decided to grant their demand. He released the man who had been thrown into prison for insurrection and murder, the one they asked for, and surrendered Jesus to their will. Luke 23:13-25

The city. Whether it was by bribery or fear of the Pharisees, an entire city that once accepted the miracles Jesus gave out for free turned on Jesus and refused to vote for his release. They reduced Jesus' status lower than that of a traitor and a killer by accepting Barabbas' release over his. Jesus was the Anti-Barabbas, one who always told the truth, hurt nobody and even brought people back from the dead.

How painful for Jesus to then hear a group shouting "with one voice":

"Crucify him! Crucify him!"

Quite a change from the shouts Jesus heard just days before:

"Hosanna to the Son of David!"
"Blessed is he who comes in the name of the Lord!"
"Hosanna in the highest!"

What happened? How quickly the city turned on him.

Today, many of these institutions—religious, political and secular—would love it if Jesus, the Bible and the church would just disappear or die. They are just reacting defensively against something they don't understand. They are scared of the unknown qualities of the Christian life and the quantity of God's love for them. These are natural responses opposed to God.

People who are betrayed usually deserve it. Drug dealers and dictators get stabbed in the back all the time, as well they should. They probably betrayed someone to get where they are at and then surrounded themselves with betrayers in the process. This was not the case with Jesus.

Betrayed by Judas, Peter, his disciples, the religious system, the government and an entire city, Jesus—well versed in the Bible and well trained in defense of the truth, with the power to speak and cause people to fall backwards, literally—responded to all the allegations by saying…

Nothing.

I would be screaming for truth, justice, my rights and my lawyer. Show me the evidence! Where are your witnesses! Using my miracles, I would cause all the Pharisees to go blind and the accusers to become mutes. I would darken the sun then run for cover. I would send out my hosts of angels who over thirty years announced my birth in the sky and command them to sing the Doxology.

I would ask my Father to show up with one his "This is my son with whom I am well pleased" moments and amaze everyone with a voice from the sky.

Jesus, though, allowed the betrayals to happen one-by-one. He did not fight back or defend himself.

He knew what he needed to do. He needed to die.

Norman Geisler
First of all, you have to have betrayal in the story in order to get Him crucified. I think the reason there was so much betrayal is to show us that He did it alone. He wasn't getting any support from the people you normally can expect support from. Peter is denying Him three times, this is the rock, you know, this is the guy He's counting on with his

testimony. And it's tough. It's tough to suffer. It's tougher to suffer alone and it's tougher yet to suffer when your friends are betraying you at the same time. Anybody who has experienced any of that, which I have some in my lifetime, knows exactly what He was going through.

Jesus did not need to defend himself. Time would proclaim his innocence.

Lies caused Jesus to be nailed to the cross. That should come as no surprise. A lie caused sin. Deception turned friends of God into betrayers of God. Adam and Eve turned their backs on God in the garden and now the world turned its collective backs on Jesus.

It's happened before and once again Satan, the father of all lies, led the smear campaign, turning longtime enemies (Roman government vs. the Jewish religion, Pharisees vs. Sadducees) into friends, united against a common foe.

Jesus next faced brutal physical punishment, but I wonder what hurt more—the whip of an enemy or the betrayal of a friend?

Betrayal is completely foreign to the nature of God. God kept his promise to save Noah and his family from the flood. God kept his promise to create a nation through Abraham, Isaac and Jacob. God stayed with the Israelites in the desert for forty years. God promised to send a Messiah to save his people, a king that would sit on the throne forever. He never left his people.

Just because a new opportunity arises or a situation gets uncomfortable or events become too difficult are never reasons for God to turn his back on us. He can't do it. If God says he'll be there, he'll be there.

Max Lucado

The theme of betrayal is built into the story because it's a reality of human nature. We all betray God, we all betray Jesus. We all betray each other to one degree or another. And the great redemption of the Gospel is the redemption of people who betray.

Paul Young

Because it is such a key part of how we relate to each other. We're all about betrayal. We're all about damaged relationships. What hurts in your life hasn't happened through relationships? Well the healing is going to happen through relationship. This is part of being human in a world that is like this. I mean, He experiences it.

How painful for God who would has never betrayed to be betrayed.

The reasons for betrayal haven't changed and still today those that call Jesus their friend turn their back on him.

Even me?

I had to wonder, have my actions ever betrayed my love for God?

Like Judas, did I seek financial gain over Christ's gain?

Like Peter, did I turn into a coward under peer pressure and deny my relationship with Christ?

Like the disciples, did I run away from defending the Lord, hiding my faith in some back room?

Like the religious, have I acted all "holy" yet secretly I have other motives?

Like politics, do I say I want justice, yet I show none to those around me?

Like the city, am I swayed by unpredictable tides of popular opinion instead of the love of Christ?

Betrayal has many causes - greed, power, self-preservation, peer pressure. All of them fall under one category - selfishness. A person's own needs outweigh the needs of others, even a friend, so they run, turn their backs, deny or point fingers.

I don't know where I would have been during those crucial hours before Jesus headed to the cross, but something tells me I'm just as much as a betrayer as the others.

TIME TO JOURNEY

1. **Watch "Betrayed" from "In His Shoes: The Life of Christ"**

2. **Discussion Questions**

- Have you ever been betrayed? How did that feel?

- What causes people to betray others?

- What caused Judas to betray Jesus?

- What caused Peter to betray Jesus?

- Do either of their betrayals surprise you?

- What was the purpose of the religious system?

- When you think about the homes in the Palatial Mansion, what motivated the Pharisees to betray Jesus?

- What was the purpose of the political system?

- What motivated the Roman government to betray Jesus?

- What causes us today to betray Jesus?

- What has God ever done to betray us?

- How do you think Jesus felt seeing everyone betray him?

- How do you think he feels today when he is betrayed?

- Why is betrayal a necessary theme to the story?

248

Sacrifice
Temple Mount

The most iconic image of Jerusalem, the one that stands out in most pictures of the Old City, is not a Jewish symbol, but a Muslim mosque.

The Dome of the Rock has a fascinating history and explains a lot about Jerusalem since the time of Jesus. After the second Jewish temple, the one built by Herod that Jesus frequented, was destroyed by Roman armies in 70 A.D. and the Roman Empire finally toppled, the Muslims conquered the Byzantine Empire in the area known then as The Levant (Israel, Egypt, Jordan, Iraq) and took over Jerusalem in 637 A.D. Between 685 and 691 A.D., the dome was constructed to rival another dome structure, the Holy Sepulchre.

When the Crusaders defeated the Muslims during the siege of Jerusalem (1095-1099), they gave the Dome of the Rock to the Augustinians (monks that lived after the Rule of Saint Augustine, 354-430 AD). They turned the location into a church. The Knights Templar, made famous by The Da Vinci Code, converted the nearby mosque, the Al-Aqsa, into their headquarters.

Then came Saladin, the brilliant and charismatic Muslim leader, who took back Jerusalem in 1187. The cross on the dome was removed and a crescent put in its place. Besides renovations and surviving an earthquake, the Dome has survived intact and remained in Muslim control for nearly 800 years.

On May 14, 1947, the United Nations declared Israel as its own country. The event prompted an attack by seven Arab states. Jordan took over Jerusalem and the West Bank from 1948-1967 and refused to allow Jews to enter the Old City.

Jewish forces responded on June 5, 1967 and took back the area in an event that has become known as the Six Day War. Soldiers hoisted the Israeli flag over the Dome and some Jews wanted the Dome to be blown to bits. Israeli military commander Moshe Dayan, the cool looking guy with an eye patch, had the flag taken down and gave the spot back to the Muslims to keep religious peace. And so it stands today.

The area has always been a three-way tug of war between Muslims, Christians and Jews, all of them claiming it as their own. Outsiders, especially non-Muslims like ourselves, are rarely allowed a peek inside this sacred dome. Visitors frequent the courtyard, but few are allowed inside the mosque, considered sacred by Muslims and which could be defiled by "non-believers" who step foot on the ground.

In fact, during my last visit there in 2003, we could not enter the courtyard area, thanks to Ariel Sharon's September 28, 2002 visit to the Dome with an escort of Israeli police officers to make a political statement of power. The move caused riots, bus bombings and ill-ease between the factions.

Needless to say, we were nervous entering the site, wondering if our visit would set off the next intifada or revolt. We were told by our guides not to say the wrong thing or step into the wrong designated area or accidentally fart inside the temple (considered sacrilegious).

The entire time we filmed inside the mosque and the courtyard, a Muslim representative stood within ear shot, listening to every word we said, making sure we did not say anything counter to Muslim belief. At times, we turned the camera on, then the cameraman pretended not to be filming while I talked indirectly to the camera, in order to capture my commentary at the location.

Despite a few setbacks, the Muslim operators of the Dome turned out to be quite accommodating. They allowed us into the mosque early in the morning, around 8:00 a.m., before prayer time at 11:00 a.m. and gave us full reign of the facility. Sadly the Dome was undergoing a facelift and a maze of scaffolding blocked our view of the beautiful marble and mosaic interior that had survived hundreds of years.

We removed our shoes before entering the rotunda area, carpeted in red, that surrounded the centerpiece of the Dome and the whole reason it was built here.

The Rock.

Muslim tradition says that Muhammad visited this rock on his night journey in 621 AD, called the Isra and Mi'raq, a two part trip that began with Gabriel bringing Muhammad a winged white horse named Buraq. As legend states, Muhammad rode the steed to a mosque far away, never explicitly stated as being in Jerusalem, only presumed to be. In the second part of the journey, Muhammad climbed a ladder to heaven and met with all the prophets throughout time, including Moses and Jesus, and lead them in prayer. He even got some face time with Allah.

I stood before this rock realizing how important it was to all three of the religions because of one man—Abraham. This is the location, all three say, where Abraham agreed to sacrifice his son.[17]

---

[17] Once I was given the chance, I placed my hands on the rock just so I could say I did. An opportunity not many are given.

However, this is also where the Muslims disagree greatly with the Jews and Christians. The Muslims say Abraham brought Ishmael, his "firstborn" through the handmaiden Hagar. The Jews and Christians say Abraham brought Isaac, the promised firstborn from his wife Sarah.

The Koran never states it was Ishmael, only referring to the boy as "son." The Bible very clearly states it was Isaac.

Genesis 22 tells the story of God asking Abraham to sacrifice Isaac in the region of Moriah as a burnt offering. God promised Abraham and Sarah their own child even while they were in their great-grandparent years. Now he was asking Abraham to kill him?

The story goes that Isaac wondered where the sacrifice was as he carried the wood up the mountain. "God will provide," Abraham responded.

As Abraham lifted the knife over Isaac, an angel stopped his hand and told Abraham he passed the faith test. He was willing to give to God the one thing that meant the most to him. His one and only son. This example became the foreshadowing of God providing his one and only son as the ultimate sacrifice.

Then God provided a ram, conveniently stuck in some branches. This too foreshadowed God providing a sacrifice, later, through Jesus Christ, the lamb of who takes away the sin of world, according to John the Baptist.

Abraham's willingness to sacrifice even his own son was the primary reason for the temple being here. This location marked a place of extreme, sacrificial faith. While Abraham did not have to sacrifice his son, God only wanted to test his obedience and trust. Abraham loved his son, but God wanted to see who he loved more.

Thousands of years later, God was about to show the world who he loved more.

Avner, because he was Jewish, could not join us as we entered the Dome of the Rock. But I talked to him right outside the temple gates about the significance of Abraham's action from a Jewish perspective.

"The sacrifice by Abraham, the sacrifice of Isaac, is very significant because it was indeed the ultimate test of the faith of Abraham. Abraham, sick [longing] for a child so long, was ninety-five or more when the boy was born. And it was all of his hope. And when God told him take your son, your only son and sacrifice him, he didn't ask any question. All of the events before, when God told him to go forth and leave Haran and come to here, there was a promise beside it…you'll have a nation coming out of you…you'll have the land. And when he was told to sacrifice Isaac there was no promise. He just was saying go and do. And the obeying was the way that is quite unbelievable to say 'I do believe in God.' And it became the symbol of believing. In Judaism of course it stands as it is. In Christianity it's also a perfect version of the sacrifice of Jesus, real sacrifice of Himself, for humanity, as what was not done by Abraham and Isaac."

"I know there is a belief that it occurred there but has it been proven?" I asked. "Has it been archeologically proven that that incident occurred right there?"

"The beliefs say, the traditions say, that the binding was done here on top of the mountain. The Bible talks about Abraham walking three days from Beersheba which is to the south of us to the mountains of Moriah. Then, in the Book of Psalms, it says that the Temple Mount is Mount Moriah so that even at the Bible itself we have a link saying that it is the place. And since the temple is the ultimate place of faith it is going very well to be identified with the mount of Moriah."

I looked up at the temple courtyard walls above us. Suddenly I felt all the historical impact of all the Old Testament commands, all the work of David and Solomon, all the Old Testament prophecies, coming together in a location just one hundred yards from me. "God always seems to have a unifying effect in everything He does. And He wants it all to, sort of, line up nicely. It seems like this would be the place where it all lines up nicely."

Avner nodded. "True, true."

Norman Geisler

Well the Abraham/Isaac story is a preview, as it were of what Christ is going to do. God is going to take His own Son, the Son whom He loved and He's going to offer Him on the altar for us. There's going to be a substitution there because at the last minute, of course, because God didn't really want him to kill his son, he wanted to test his faith. There is going to be a substitution of the ram because Christ is the ram who died for us. The place is going to be the later place of the temple, the very temple in the very place in Jerusalem He is going to die for the sins of the world. There's so much in that story, Abraham believed that God would raise him from the dead, you know. In Hebrews chapter 11 tells us he said 'He had no hesitation of going through with it because if he killed him God was going to raise him from the dead'. And Christ was going to be raised from the dead.

252

Following the pattern of Abraham and Isaac, Jesus himself was about to walk to his death, sacrificing himself for our sins. Isaac carried his wood for his own sacrifice and Jesus labored to the place of his sacrifice carrying his own cross. While that death needed to occur outside the city limits, according to Jewish law, the parallels between the two types of sacrifices were clearly established.

So what would motivate Jesus to sacrifice his life? What encouraged him to move on despite the pain he was about to experience? Why didn't Jesus turn and run from his impending death? He did nothing wrong. Sacrificial lambs don't go to the altar quietly. They bleat and struggle under forced submission. Why should he?

Jesus realized that everything—all of history and all of eternity—was riding on this moment. Finally, it was all coming together.

The term "atonement" means a reconciliation between two parties once at odds with one another. Here's how the Old Testament atonement sacrifice occurred:

Then Moses said, "This is what the LORD has commanded you to do, so that the glory of the LORD may appear to you." Moses said to Aaron, "Come to the altar and sacrifice your sin offering and your burnt offering and make atonement for yourself and the people; sacrifice the offering that is for the people and make atonement for them, as the LORD has commanded." Leviticus 9:6-7

In order for atonement to happen, blood would have to spill.

The elders of the community are to lay their hands on the bull's head before the LORD, and the bull shall be slaughtered before the LORD. Then the anointed priest is to take some of the bull's blood into the Tent of Meeting. He shall dip his finger into the blood and sprinkle it before the LORD seven times in front of the curtain. He is to put some of the blood on the horns of the altar that is before the LORD in the Tent of Meeting. The rest of the blood he shall pour out at the base of the altar of burnt offering at the entrance to the Tent of Meeting. Leviticus 4:15-18

253

Not only does the sacrifice have to die, but its blood must spill. Blood is life while inside the body. Outside the body it dies. No one can live without blood.

Blood signifies life and death. The priests sprinkle the blood on the altar to show that a death has occurred, while giving life to the one who offered the sacrifice. How?

"'When a leader sins unintentionally and does what is forbidden in any of the commands of the LORD his God, he is guilty. When he is made aware of the sin he committed, he must bring as his offering a male goat without defect. He is to lay his hand on the goat's head and slaughter it at the place where the burnt offering is slaughtered before the LORD. It is a sin offering.   Leviticus 4:22-24

The laying on of hands transferred the person's sins into the sacrifice. He had to admit his sins, then pass the guilt to the animal that was killed right in front of them. It would be hard to watch an innocent creature die for your sins, but God wanted them to see it with their own eyes.

Every sin brought a death penalty to the sinner, but God allowed a substitution to occur through the sacrificial system. The shedding of blood brought death to the substitute, but life to the one offering the sacrifice. The sacrifice paid the price for the sinner. However, the sacrificial system was only a temporary fix to a lifelong problem.

God made it clear that death was a consequence of sin in the garden with Adam and Eve, so death became the payment for sin. To pay for man's sin, something needed to die. It showed the gravity of man's actions and the extent he needed to go to pay for that sin.

Jesus' death would offer atonement between God and man. As Jesus headed to the cross, he knew that his blood needed to spill since the sacrifices bled to death. His death had to be final and complete.

Jesus did everything he could, sacrificed everything he could, to pay for our sins, but the rest is up to us.

We have to acknowledge our sin and "lay our hands" on Jesus, placing our sins on the cross. How do we do that? By faith…believing that he died for our sins, just as Moses and Aaron believed that a lamb, bull or goat would pay for their sins.

Nothing could be more innocent that a lamb. That lamb did not lie or sleep with his neighbor's wife. The lamb did not fail to recognize

254

the Sabbath or worship that idol. The lamb did nothing wrong, yet once that innocent lamb died, the sinner was forgiven. Jesus died for all kinds of despicable sinners, even though he never committed one sin.

For the wages of sin is death, but the gift of God is eternal life in Christ Jesus our Lord. Romans 6:23

As a result, we do not receive temporary forgiveness for our sins, but eternal forgiveness. One death, Jesus, for all sinners. Since the sacrifice was the eternal God, the reward is eternal life.

The Old Testament priests worked at the temple once located at the Dome of the Rock. However, priests are not needed any longer. Jesus became our new High Priest.

When Christ came as high priest of the good things that are already here, he went through the greater and more perfect tabernacle that is not man-made, that is to say, not a part of this creation.
He did not enter by means of the blood of goats and calves; but he entered the Most Holy Place once for all by his own blood, having obtained eternal redemption.
The blood of goats and bulls and the ashes of a heifer sprinkled on those who are ceremonially unclean sanctify them so that they are outwardly clean.
How much more, then, will the blood of Christ, who through the eternal Spirit offered himself unblemished to God, cleanse our consciences from acts that lead to death, so that we may serve the living God!
For this reason Christ is the mediator of a new covenant, that those who are called may receive the promised eternal inheritance—now that he has died as a ransom to set them free from the sins committed under the first covenant.
Hebrews 9:11-15

In the Old Covenant, priests used animals and a sacrificial system to routinely pay for man's sin. In the New Covenant, Jesus died for our sins. His blood cleanses our consciousness of guilt. We now have an eternal inheritance, freeing us of all sins.

255

In fact, the law requires that nearly everything be cleansed with blood, and without the shedding of blood there is no forgiveness. Hebrews 9:22

In order for God to forgive, the debt must be paid. Jesus made our relationship with God right and cleaned up our mess by dying for our sins.

Nor did he enter heaven to offer himself again and again, the way the high priest enters the Most Holy Place every year with blood that is not his own. Then Christ would have had to suffer many times since the creation of the world. But now he has appeared once for all at the end of the ages to do away with sin by the sacrifice of himself.
Just as man is destined to die once, and after that to face judgment, so Christ was sacrificed once to take away the sins of many people; and he will appear a second time, not to bear sin, but to bring salvation to those who are waiting for him. Hebrews 9:25-29

Jesus' death would be sufficient. He'll only have to die once. That surely comforted him at this time. He won't have to come back for every generation and do this over and over again.

All of this information Jesus understood very clearly as he walked to his own sacrifice. He knew the rules and responsibilities of both sides of the covenant. Jesus knew the consequences and the historical meaning behind this moment. He understood and accepted the task, no matter what it cost.

Jesus did not struggle or protest with the immense responsibility he was given at great personal cost. In fact he kept silent.

Jesus willingly gave up his life as a sacrifice. He predicted his death three times, so he knew what he was getting into. Jesus did not want to save his life. He wanted to lose it for others.

And he said, "The Son of Man must suffer many things and be rejected by the elders, chief priests and teachers of the law, and he must be killed and on the third day be raised to life."

Then he said to them all: "If anyone would come after me, he must deny himself and take up his cross daily and follow me. For whoever wants to save his life will lose it, but whoever loses his life for me will save it. What good is it for a man to gain the whole world, and yet lose or forfeit his very self? If anyone is ashamed of me and my words, the Son of Man will be ashamed of him when he comes in his glory and in the glory of the Father and of the holy angels. I tell you the truth, some who are standing here will not taste death before they see the kingdom of God." Luke 9:22-27

Max Lucado

I'd die today for my kids, for my family, I would. That to me is a no brainer. If it came down to me living or them living I'd say "gosh let them live" you know. Would I give up my life for the poor, and for the insignificant, for the marginalized like Jesus did? I think the answer to that question is by looking at my life and not as much as I'd like to say I would. I don't give up enough of my life. It's easy for me to give up my life for some neat people. But what do I do on behalf of those that no one wants to help. For me to be like Jesus that's going to be measured in my concern for people who can do nothing for me.

As I stood there by that rock encircled by its controversial and historic dome, I thought of the Holy of Holies, the inner sanctum of the temple where God's presence dwelled, that sat right on this spot. So much division and hate has emanated from this one spot that God once called his earthly address. So much death and blood were spilled on this location, from this location and because of this location. Some people deserved those deaths. Others did not.

I tried to imagine what I would have seen 2,000 years ago if I went directly back in time. Priests slicing the throats of goats. Sheep screaming for release. The presence of God just a few steps away behind thick curtains.

This is where God connected with his people. We looked at so many places where Jesus walked, but this was the only one where God the Father personally touched down. I could understand the fear and awe others may have felt being in this place.

This was also the place where God established the pattern of sacrifice that Jesus himself fulfilled just minutes from here as he marched to Calvary to die for me and to take away my sins. I can't imagine anything more beautiful and touching…or painful.

Jesus' effect on civilization is seen even today in the Muslim world, where he is recognized, in all places, on the Dome of the Rock.

Yusef Natsheh, Director of Antiquities for the Dome of the Rock, gave us a very detailed (and biased) tour of the Dome when we visited. He was a quiet, gentle man – quite opposite from your jihad screaming fanatics that stereotype his faith. He pointed out to us text written along the walls, arches and ceiling of the Dome.

"Mostly these are citations and chapters from the Koran, praising Allah, mentioning the prophet Muhammad, a commemoration of the building and showing some beliefs of Islam. One of the most significant of these texts we can see along the inner face of the arcade which really mentions Jesus Christ and his mother Mary. These are one of earliest scripts of Islam, with green background, written in gold. This is part of a long script that extends more than 240 meters that runs along the octagon of the Dome of the Rock. It admits that Jesus Christ is a true prophet and all of his miracles are supported by God."

As I peered closely, I could see the text though I did not know Arabic. Translated, it read: "Bless your envoy and your servant Jesus son of Mary and peace upon him…"

The power of Christ even exists in a most unlikely place. Even Muslims cannot hide that Jesus has done something wonderful here.

As Jesus pushed on through the streets of Jerusalem, growing closer to his death, surely he caught glimpses of the temple through his blood soaked eyes, a motivation for him to take one more step…one more step…

Only love could motivate such dedication to die and sacrifice one's own life for others. God so loved the world that he showed the world that he loved it more than his own son, who he willfully allowed to die in our place.

We should be so indebted to Christ, so smitten by his sacrifice, that we follow him obediently and completely for eternity.

TIME TO JOURNEY

1. **Watch "Sacrifice" from "In His Shoes: The Life of Christ"**

2. **Discussion Questions**

- Have you ever sacrificed your life for someone?

- Why would anyone sacrifice their life for someone?

- What would you do if you knew today you were going to sacrifice your life for someone?

- Do you find the Muslim inscription on the Dome of the Rock honoring Jesus surprising? Why or why not?

- What similarities do we see between Abraham and Jesus on this mountain?

- Why would Abraham and Isaac follow through with the sacrifice to the last possible minute? Would you?

- Why was the sacrificial system effective? Ineffective?

- How does blood cleanse the person offering the sacrifice?

- How would you feel sacrificing an animal and knowing it died for your sins?

- Why would Jesus sacrifice his life for us?

- If Jesus was willing to die for our sins, how does that make you feel about your sins?

- How should we respond to such an act of sacrifice?

Crucifixion
Holy Sepulchre/Golgotha

Probably the most excruciating pain I've ever felt was when my appendix decided to call it quits. I was watching Entertainment Tonight, alone in our apartment, while my wife shopped with the kids. I remember Mary Hart making some announcement and then it hit. A news item had once come to light about a man who went into an epileptic seizure every time he heard Mary Hart's voice and I wondered, was this happening to me?

I hit the floor as the pain twisted inside of me, refusing to let go. I crawled to the phone and called our neighbors upstairs. They thought I was joking (a side effect of trying to be funny all the time) and hung up on me. I called my in-laws who thankfully believed me, obviously not appreciating my sense of humor, and rushed over to take me to the hospital.

For one month, twenty-one days in the hospital, I dealt with the pain and side effects of a nearly burst appendix. I remember praying that it would end…somehow…some way.

That's the best frame of reference I have for what Jesus went through at the crucifixion. It's a weak comparison and many people have more excruciating stories from car accidents to cancer, but it's the best I can do. We all have our pain stories. None of us has one like Jesus Christ.

The difference? He chose his pain for others. How many of us can say we wanted our appendix to burst or that bullet to hit our spine or our car to speed out of control causing years of painful therapy for the sake of another person to have life? Not me. I'm a big cry baby when it comes to pain. I don't think I'm alone on this one, but I try to avoid it. Jesus wanted the crucifixion and all the extras thrown in.

Jesus chose this time in history when Romans had perfected the execution of prisoners. A biblical sacrifice for sin required the spilling of blood. Crucifixion spilled a lot of blood. But, couldn't Jesus, after he was declared guilty by Pilate, simply have been stabbed by a Roman guard with a spear? Quick, easy, simple, blindsided. One wound, sufficing cleanly as an outlet for blood, and it's all over. Instead, Jesus chose to enter time with a government that approved a brutal means of torture.

Jesus not only chose the pain, he chose a lengthy, excruciating pain. Jesus chose a death that lasted nearly twelve to eighteen hours. He didn't want a death that was quick, merciful and relatively painless.

Why didn't Jesus choose to die during a time with a better judicial system? If he came now, he would get caught up in lengthy trials and appeals which add another twelve years to life. Even the ACLU would probably have backed him. Jesus chose a corrupt government that cared little about human rights.

Jesus allowed himself to come at this time, with this government, with these people and turned himself over to every imaginable painful experience when all he had to do was shed some blood and die.

Max Lucado
Jesus wanted us to know that He knows how we feel. Jesus wanted us to know how far He would go to reach us.

Then the governor's soldiers took Jesus into the Praetorium and gathered the whole company of soldiers around him. They stripped him and put a scarlet robe on him, and then twisted together a crown of thorns and set it on his head. They put a staff in his right hand and knelt in front of him and mocked him. "Hail, king of the Jews!" they said. They spit on him, and took the staff and struck him on the head again and again. After they had mocked him, they took off the robe and put his own clothes on him. Then they led him away to crucify him. Matthew 27:27-30

This doesn't feel necessary. In fact today, if our prison guards were caught doing this, human rights organizations would be all over them. The guards at Abu Ghraib seem like wimps in light of this kind of abuse. This was and is senseless. Jesus' lawyers would have a field day of appeals. But Jesus allowed it.

- Stripped naked.
- Thorns thrust into this scalp.
- Mocked with words and actions.
- Spat upon.
- Beaten on the head…again and again.

I was stabbed by a thorn gardening one day. A one inch needle went half way into my palm. At that moment, pain rippled throughout my body. I grabbed my hand and wanted to declare myself unfit to do any more chores for the rest of the day…or week. When it happened, I immediately thought of the crown of thorns. One thorn hurt like heck and Jesus had nearly ten or fifteen jammed into his scalp.

And that was the easy part of Jesus' day of pain. Jesus even predicted it.

He (the Son of Man) will be handed over to the Gentiles. They will mock him, insult him, spit on him, flog him and kill him. Luke 18:32

Flogging in the first century consisted of twenty lashings with a leather whip, since they believed twenty-one led to death. The whip had pieces of metal embedded into the end, which tore and shredded the skin. An expert at whipping took over during this part, which meant Jesus was in good hands, so to speak.

Max Lucado
When I read of the descriptions of the beating that He took, how severe that was. How a soldier was assigned to the simple task of making sure He was alive. That it was in such likelihood that He could have died that they had to have somebody watching to see if He was alive. His back was really turned into raw meat. The chunks of muscle had already been yanked out. He could have died at any point. Just being nailed to a cross, you know, is sufficient enough.

God created our bodies with pain receptors. These nerve endings are sensitive detectors designed to alert our minds to trouble spots on our body. If you get cut, the alarms go off and you immediately reach down to that area and take care of the problem. It's a brilliant warning system of personal health care.

Except when you are beaten to a pulp. The very nerve endings Jesus created began firing off over every inch of his body, for hours and hours.

Verbal abuse hurts in a different way. I think God takes enough abuse every day. I can't imagine the number of mockings, punches and spittings that occur in conversations from billions of people. Someone calls me a jerk and my world falls apart all day, only because I wonder if

I am a jerk and public opinion matters to me. God gets called every name in the book every day, all the time.

But how did the abuse feel in the flesh, stripped naked, feeling a shame that Adam and Eve felt with their nakedness, his privates exposed, his manliness demeaned? How low can a person go?

I cannot imagine Jesus, God himself, allowing his people, who he created, to mock, beat and spit on him.

Chuck Norris, Jackie Chan or even Bruce Willis would eventually throw some punches and get themselves out of this one. Jesus had the power to stop it. Remember back in the garden of Gethsemane, when the guards, led by Judas, came to get Jesus:

Jesus, knowing all that was going to happen to him, went out and asked them, "Who is it you want?"
"Jesus of Nazareth," they replied.
"I am he," Jesus said. (And Judas the traitor was standing there with them.)
When Jesus said, "I am he," they drew back and fell to the ground. John 18:4-6

Jesus had a voice that could serve as a roundhouse kick. Three words, "I am he" and they are flat on their gluteus maximuses. Jesus, though, chose to say nothing. He withheld his verbal punches.

All of this abuse was meant to speed up the death of the prisoner. Jesus needed his death to happen in one day so he chose the best and most efficient torturers in the history of torturers. There needed to be no mistake that Jesus was dead. The Romans were the best at what they did, so Jesus awarded them the "honor" of being his executors.

Jesus walked into a pain factory and took everything they had. The works, with all the toppings. The guards even made stuff up. The part about dressing Jesus in the purple robe and mocking him…the guards improvised that one just for him. It's not every day people come into the shop claiming to be king.

The pre-crucifixion was enough to kill an ordinary man. This appetizer of torture would have satisfied all the requirements needed for a sacrifice. Jesus' blood certainly spilled by now. But again, Jesus wanted it all.

As they headed to the crucifixion, they forced Jesus to carry his cross, which was probably the cross bar which attached to a stake in the ground. Why should a healthy Roman guard do all the work? Make the prisoner carry his own cross.

I'm moved by the fact that he carried his own instrument of death. I would drop it and run. Or beat them with it. Or swing it like in the final scene of "The Graduate." "Back off, Roman scum!" Jesus held on to it as long as it could.

It appears, like, he almost wanted to die.

Joel Hunter

He didn't deserve it. He didn't sin at all to deserve it. It wasn't just an accident that happened to Him. Jesus' suffering was intentional and it was for us. It was for the redemption of the world and so the choice of the suffering, the length of the suffering, the choice of the method, the exhibition of the extent to which He would linger just to be in a world of suffering that much longer and not escape when He could have escaped.

This is why when Jesus told his disciples to carry their own cross and follow him, they immediately knew what he meant. They had seen this happen before. Jesus showed them the literal of what they thought was a figurative.

The Via Dolorosa (or the Way of Grief/Sorrow) is a path marked out in the Old City of Jerusalem with nine stations on the street and five inside the Holy Sepulchre. The path begins at the location of Antonio's Fortress (instead of the alternate location of David's Citadel which is where scholars believe Pilate slept when he came to town) then meanders through tight streets to the other stations that are rooted deep in tradition, with little historical fact, having become over time more legendary than anything.[18]

Walking the Via Dolorosa with Avner, I noticed spiritual pilgrims from all over the world, including Germans, Brazilians and Koreans when I was there. They carried their measly six foot crosses through the streets. It hardly felt sacrificial. For starters, they all got a good night's sleep and a nice breakfast at the hotel in the morning, where nobody beat them or betrayed them.

---

[18] Such as the story about Veronica and the indentation on the wall created by Jesus' when he stumbled. These Stations of the Cross are marked in all the Catholic churches in Jerusalem.

Yet here they were feeling like Jesus when they were light years away from his torture. And yet, I noticed a few things about the death walk – nobody smiles as they carry a cross. It forces a sort of sadness upon you. They all looked despondent, yet it hardly looked painful at all.

The walk worked its way up hill. Man, those Romans were cruel by making a bloody prisoner carry their cross in a cardio-vascular nightmare. I was winded with my overstuffed backpack and a tripod. Here I was, a healthy man with no visible wounds, carrying a ten pound load up the stairs and the only annoyance I endured were shop keepers trying to entice me into their store.

I'm sure Jesus did not have to endure the greedy taunts from businessmen. Jesus had no need for a *Guns and Moses* T-shirt or a paperweight with his mom's image on it.

One of the stations that is very biblical on the Via Dolorosa caused me to pause and ponder. Simon of Cyrene.

A certain man from Cyrene, Simon, the father of Alexander and Rufus, was passing by on his way in from the country, and they forced him to carry the cross.   Mark 15:21

Here's a guy passing by from the countryside and all of a sudden he's chosen at random to carry the cross for Jesus.[19]

For some reason, when I read about Simon of Cyrene, I think Jesus took a short cut on his path to the crucifixion. Ridiculous thought, huh? I thought he was supposed to die for my sins, not get some help from an out of town tourist.

Simon's cross-carrying was highlighted, I believe, to indicate how close to death Jesus was. The guards, seeing Jesus' condition, wanted him to live long enough to die on the cross, so they called in Simon. In the eyes of those sadistic guards, dying on the cross was the best part, the main attraction in their eyes! Simon made sure Jesus made it to his destination before expiring along the way.

As I finished my walk on the Via Dolorosa, a tourist woman labored in front of me struggling with her suitcase up the rocky steps of the Old City streets. I just wanted to get home to the hotel after a long day and here was a woman and her suitcase standing in my way. I

---

[19] The Bible provides plenty of information for those at that time who wanted to confirm the reality of this guy. Go to Cyrene, the Gospel writer Mark says, look up Simon or his sons Alexander and Rufus, since by the time the book of Mark was written Simon may have died.

immediately thought of Simon. He too wanted to get home to Cyrene, a guy on his way somewhere else, when all of a sudden here comes the crucifixion parade. So in the spirit of Simon, I grabbed her suitcase, which had to weigh the airline legal limit of fifty pounds, and pulled it up the streets.

"No, no, no, you don't have to do that," she told me in a Slavic/English accent.

"It's no problem." It was. I did it anyway. She wanted to tip me at the end and I refused. She thanked me for my help. I simply appreciated the experience of carrying someone else's cross. Hardly a worthy comparison.

Through all his pain, Jesus appreciated a little help getting up the hill to the site of the crucifixion. He still appreciates a little help as we take his message of his cross to the world.

In prisons, when someone on Death Row heads to their execution, someone shouts "Dead man walking!" It's an odd statement. Dead men don't walk. However, condemned men do. They are not dead. They are as good as dead. Death is inevitable.

That applied to Jesus. That applies to us. We all have a death sentence and a day when we will die. The question is what are we carrying to our graves?

Carrying his own cross, he went out to the place of the Skull (which in Aramaic is called Golgotha). John 19:17

Golgotha (or Calvary in the Latin) could be one of two places. One possible location is at the Holy Sepulchre, a volatile piece of land that has seen four different buildings constructed in the same place.

Emperor Hadrian ruled Rome from 117-138 and he did the Christian community a great favor. He constructed pagan temples on top of holy sites venerated by Christians less than a hundred years after the actual events. To deter pilgrims, he built the first structure, a temple to Jupiter[20] on top of the site the locals marked as the place for the death and resurrection of Jesus Christ. Through his sacrilegious methods, Hadrian marked the spot on which the Holy Sepulchre was built, much as he did with the Church of the Nativity.

When Constantine, the first Christian Roman emperor, took power in 306-312 AD he allowed the worship of Christianity and sent his mom on a building mission – find the holy sites of the life of Christ and

---

[20] Some believe it may have been constructed to worship Venus or Aphrodite.

turn them into tourist attractions, I mean, places of worship. His mother, Helena of Constantinople, took a road trip and began the process that has changed Israel into a pilgrimage for people today.

Constantine's construction crews leveled the entire area, keeping only two original rocks exposed – the heel of Golgotha and the tomb of Christ, which you can still see today. The tomb is covered by a marble slab to keep people from chipping pieces away.

Radical Muslims destroyed that church in 1009 and the Byzantines performed a reconstruction in 1042

The modern Holy Sepulchre was constructed by the Crusaders and opened on July 15, 1149.

In the meantime, another location for the death and resurrection of Jesus has popped up. It's in an area known as the Garden Tomb.

In 1882-83, a British Army officer named Charles George Gordon saw the area and believed it to be the true location and so it became an alternative to the Holy Sepulchre. While the grave aesthetically appears more tomb-like, with its traditional bedrock carved room, the rock in the back gives the area some credence. "Skull Hill." It's the meaning of the name Golgotha…the place of the skull. Standing at Gordon's Calvary, I could see that skull.

The thirty foot tall jagged rock is a spooky sight. The face in the stone appears and disappears as you move left and right. While the "skull" is not always clear, it makes itself clear when it wants to. As we shot a sequence in front of the rock, a photographer snapped my picture. In his photos, the skull looked over my shoulder, staring down at me…a face of death.

The contrast between the two locations could not be more evident. The Holy Sepulchre is considered sacred and holy today, visited by thousands from a variety of denominations, including Eastern Orthodox, Armenian Apostolic, Roman Catholic, Greek Orthodox, Coptic Orthodox, the Ethiopian Orthodox and the Syriac Orthodox churches, all sharing in a piece of the pie.

Yet something about Gordon's Calvary that struck me. The rock with the spooky face looked out over a parking lot for a bus terminal. When we visited there in 2002, the terminal was not paved or developed. Today, lines of buses fill the entire foot of the possible cross location.

The bus stop was filled with youths who were engaged in activities behind the buses. Many boys ran around talking smack, flirting with girls, butting heads, you know, boy stuff. However, two of the guys got a little too personal and a fight broke out, engaging a mob of twenty or so who surrounded the two in an awkward skirmish dance around the lot.

As I watched them, I thought, wow, this could be the place where Jesus died, yet fights and "sin" occurred right at the foot of the rock. No one seemed to pay attention to the face of death looking over them or the hope of Jesus' sacrifice that could bring peace. It stood right in front of them and yet it meant nothing to them.

I also noticed a satellite tower on the top of the rock, which is a sacred, off-limits Muslim cemetery. The combination of transmitters and buses made this a hub that took people and messages out to the world. And here was the place where the ultimate message of salvation began, however, I don't think that was the message currently being spread. For the most part, the significance of this place was missed.

The message needed to get out, I pondered. Who was going to deliver that message to the world?

Jesus knew his death would either be hailed as the most extraordinary event of all mankind or ignored like an advertisement at a bus stop.

But that did not stop him.

The gospel accounts of his crucifixion say nothing about nails being driven into his body in order to hang him on the cross, but Jesus mentions this when he appeared to Thomas.

Now Thomas (called Didymus), one of the Twelve, was not with the disciples when Jesus came. So the other disciples told him, "We have seen the Lord!"
But he said to them, "Unless I see the nail marks in his hands and put my finger where the nails were, and put my hand into his side, I will not believe it."
A week later his disciples were in the house again, and Thomas was with them. Though the doors were locked, Jesus came and stood among them and said, "Peace be with you!" Then he said to Thomas, "Put your finger here; see my hands. Reach out your hand and put it into my side. Stop doubting and believe." John 20:24-27

The Roman guards would nail their victims to the wooden cross beams – one in each hand and one through both feet. Avner showed me a cast of a Roman nail punctured through bone found in a grave site, proving that crucifixions occurred in the area.

I wondered if Jesus, while being attached to the cross, thought about all the wood working he did as a carpenter. He knew full well the impact and pain associated with nails and how they split open whatever they were driven into.

Above his head they placed the written charge against him: THIS IS JESUS, THE KING OF THE JEWS. Two robbers were crucified with him, one on his right and one on his left. Those who passed by hurled insults at him, shaking their heads and saying, "You who are going to destroy the temple and build it in three days, save yourself! Come down from the cross, if you are the Son of God!"
In the same way the chief priests, the teachers of the law and the elders mocked him. "He saved others," they said, "but he can't save himself! He's the King of Israel! Let him come down now from the cross, and we will believe in him. He trusts in God. Let God rescue him now if he wants him, for he said, 'I am the Son of God.' " In the same way the robbers who were crucified with him also heaped insults on him. Matthew 27:37-44

Then the insults started up again. It's one thing to hurl insults at a man who thinks he's so great and strong. It's another to insult a man when he's down, beaten and bloody. And the insults came from every one, all around him.

- The sign over his head put there by the Roman guards and Pilate had a condescending tone to it. While it declared truth, it said it in a nah-nah-nah-nah way. Pilate wrote it in Aramaic, Latin and Greek, the predominant languages of the world.
- The cocky religious elite mocked Jesus.
- Locals who passed by and tossed an insult this way, clucking their tongues and shaking their heads.
- The robbers. These guys had a lot of room to talk. They were being crucified too, but looked at Jesus as one more pitiful than themselves.

Jesus allowed himself to be mocked by every possible aspect of the world. The political system, the religious system, the common man with rights and the convicted sinners without any rights. Jesus was a master at debate and wise comebacks. He said nothing.

When they came to the place called the Skull, there they crucified him, along with the criminals—one on his right, the other on his left. Luke 23:33

Just weeks ago, Jesus stood on the Mount of Transfiguration with Moses and Elijah at his right and left. Now he hung with two criminals on his right and left. The positioning of Jesus in the middle and Moses and Elijah at each hand, symbolically put Jesus in a position of authority.

On the mount of Transfiguration, Jesus was the King of all Prophets. Now he symbolically represented the King of all sinners. Jesus had almost every sin committed to him in these final hours and he was about to take every sin upon him to his death. It was as if hell threw everything it had at him.

Norman Geisler

If Jesus were here today, how would we react to Him? And my answer to that is we'd crucify Him again because we couldn't stand somebody that perfect around. Just His very presence shows up our imperfections, you know, just the light brings to light all of the things we want to do in darkness.

I missed this at previous visits to the Holy Land, but it leapt out at me now here, looking at the rock Skull.

It was the third hour when they crucified him.
At the sixth hour darkness came over the whole land until the ninth hour. Mark 15:25, 33

Six hours? Six hours he hung on a cross. Is Jesus tough or what? The Bible says that even the Roman guards had to sit down to watch over him. They couldn't even stand on their feet for one hour and Jesus hung by nails for six.

When news arrived to Pilate about Jesus' death, Pilate could not believe Jesus died so quickly. Maybe he had no idea how efficient his

271

guards worked him over in the morning. Maybe Pilate had no idea how painful crucifixion could be.

There they offered Jesus wine to drink, mixed with gall; but after tasting it, he refused to drink it. Matthew 27:34

      Wine-gall-vinegar acted as an anesthetic, to bring a little relief for the pain. We get anesthesia for shots, cavities, child birth and surgeries. Jesus refused it for something a hundred times worse than filling in a cavity. He seemed to want to feel and receive every ounce of wrath being poured on him. No shortcuts here.
      The sacrificial lambs did not get anesthesia before they died. Why should he?

When they had crucified him, they divided up his clothes by casting lots. Matthew 27:35

      Dead men don't need clothes. This is proof that these experts at execution who stood around him knew he wouldn't be back. No one wonder ever survived a day in their torture spa.
      Receiving as much pain as he can stand—physically, emotionally, mentally, relationally—Jesus began to die, but he had a few things to say. His words reflect his heart:

About the ninth hour Jesus cried out in a loud voice, *"Eloi, Eloi, lama sabachthani?"*—which means, "My God, my God, why have you forsaken me?" Matthew 27:46

Joel Hunter
The absolute loneliness of the cross, even, "why hast thou forsaken me?" The moment that He pronounces the psalm that at the same time announces His Messiahship from the cross
That's Psalm 22, "My God, my God, why hast thou forsaken me?"
That's both a pronouncement of the pain of abandonment and the announcement of the Messiah.

      A sacrifice on an altar became the "sinner" as the one bringing the sacrifice transferred his sin into the sacrifice. The sin caused a separation between the person and God. The sacrifice took on the separation from God, taking the blame for the sin. Jesus, at that moment, knew what it felt like to be a sinner, living with a broken relationship with God. While he never sinned and it was impossible for him to break his relationship with himself, Jesus felt it for the first time.

Paul Young

He even experiences the sense of the loss of His relationship with the Father on the cross. I don't believe that Father ever separates Himself from the Son but He who is baptized in the Spirit, born of the Spirit, filled with the Spirit suddenly no longer senses the presence of the Father. And He cries out, 'Why have you forsaken me?' But then He makes the greatest human statement of faith ever. In the midst of all that absence of the presence He says, 'But into Your hands I commit My Spirit, I know You're still here.' And in that little scenario you have Him identifying with the deepest sense of loss that all of us have felt where we don't sense the presence and the affection of the Father.

Norman Geisler

One of the great mysteries of Christ being on the cross is His statement, 'Why have You forsaken Me?' And I think that there are some things that cannot be true and there are some things that can be true. It cannot be true that there was an actual breech between Him and the Father. That somehow there was a break in the Trinity, that's an eternal relationship, that's an unbreakable relationship. So there was nothing in terms of the actuality of the Trinity that was affected by that. There wasn't a temporary cessation of fellowship between the Father and Son. So, it must mean something else, what else could it mean? Well, like 2 Corinthians 5:21, 'He was made to be sin for us who knew no sin that we might be made the righteousness of God in Him.' Well He wasn't actually made sin because He was actually sinless. But judicially, legally, officially, our sins were place on Him. And I think that's the same thing you have in 'My God my God why have You forsaken Me?' Legally, judicially as the sins of the world were placed on Him, God had to officially express His disapproval because He can't look on sin, Habakkuk 1:13, with approval. So as the sins of the world were placed upon Him there had to be a relational, judicial break. Not an actual ontological break.

It was probably the most painful thing Jesus ever felt. No whip, no nail, no betrayal ever compared to the pain of the separation with his Father.

Then how come I don't cry out every time I sin and hurt my relationship with God? I guess I just grow used to living at arm's distance from God. How sad.

Jesus said, "Father, forgive them, for they do not know what they are doing." And they divided up his clothes by casting lots. Luke 23:34

After all these people did to him, Jesus forgave them. Jesus never whined or complained or blamed others, like Adam and Eve did, pointing fingers in the garden, the incident which started this whole mess that Jesus had to come fix.

It's hard to forgive, especially while you are being killed. I can't imagine someone forgiving his murderers as they are murdering him. This breaks my heart if I dwell on it too long. I can think of hundreds of smaller "evils" done to me that I still dwell on years after they have happened:

- Not giving me credit when I deserved it
- Passing me over for a job
- Giving me an office without a window
- Disrespecting me in front of others
- Cutting me off when I drive
- Questioning my loyalty
- Not giving me enough attention on my birthday

How petty a list. I think Jesus allowed every possible hurtful thing to happen to him so when he forgave them, I would look at every hurtful thing that ever happened to me and say "Why am I holding on to my hate?"

Joel Hunter
The cross breaks my heart. There's absolutely nothing enjoyable about that experience. There's not a shred of pleasure. He has lost everybody that's loved Him. He's completely alone. He's losing His breath slowly. He's reviled upon by voices down below that He is dying for and they're mocking him. And He sees people who are killing Him and He's praying

274

for their forgiveness and He's praying for forgiveness for them, you know. He's even having to do work on the cross, I mean, it's not even like He can even suffer in peace. And so, there's just something about the cross that absolutely destroys every bit of pretention that I have.

It's as if he forgave them so they wouldn't live with the guilt and shame of killing an innocent man. No executioner ever heard that before. Jesus saw this as an opportunity to help others and not as an excuse or reason to ask for people's pity.

One of the criminals who hung there hurled insults at him: "Aren't you the Christ? Save yourself and us!"
But the other criminal rebuked him. "Don't you fear God," he said, "since you are under the same sentence? We are punished justly, for we are getting what our deeds deserve. But this man has done nothing wrong." Then he said, "Jesus, remember me when you come into your kingdom.'"
Jesus answered him, "I tell you the truth, today you will be with me in paradise." Luke 23:39-43

Just like Simon of Cyrene, another story happened around the main story. The criminals watched everything and how Jesus reacted. They both had the same vantage point, yet, by the end of their time, both had different perspectives on Jesus. One criminal rejected and mocked him. The other, once a mocker, now accepted him. Jesus' demeanor and "Christ-like" attitude changed the heart of the one criminal.

Jesus reaches out his hands in the same way today. On the one hand, some will accept Jesus and on the other hand, some will reject Jesus. They all have the same information, they just choose to process it differently. That choice, though, means the difference between life and death.

Joel Hunter
The cross was picturesque of not only His life down here, of those that would believe and those that would turn against Him and not believe. But it was picturesque of all of the history that would follow Him. He was literally in the middle of history. On the one hand, there were those that were always looking forward to the Messiah, and on the

275

other, there were those that finally witnessed his fulfillment of Scripture.

Jesus began to die with the sadness that this one criminal would die without any hope of salvation. Even at his death, the thief rejected the truth in his heart, only two arm's length away from the heart of Jesus.

Near the cross of Jesus stood his mother, his mother's sister, Mary the wife of Clopas, and Mary Magdalene. When Jesus saw his mother there, and the disciple whom he loved standing nearby, he said to his mother, "Dear woman, here is your son," and to the disciple, "Here is your mother." From that time on, this disciple took her into his home.   John 19:25-27

Dying on a cross, Jesus thought of others. Pain is an excuse to be self-centered, but Jesus wanted to make sure his mom was taken care of. A widow without the provision of her oldest son could mean poverty for her, so Jesus gave her over to another "believer." He honored his mother as his body suffocated and his wounds bled.

Later, knowing that all was now completed, and so that the Scripture would be fulfilled, Jesus said, "I am thirsty." A jar of wine vinegar was there, so they soaked a sponge in it, put the sponge on a stalk of the hyssop plant, and lifted it to Jesus' lips. John 19:28-29

His final earthly taste in his current body, Jesus accepted hyssop. This pointed to Psalm 69, a chapter rich in biblical prophecy, specifically verse 21 which says "they…gave me vinegar for my thirst." For those doubting the prophetic fulfillment of Jesus' death, Jesus wanted to make sure they knew he was the real thing.

When he had received the drink, Jesus said, "It is finished." With that, he bowed his head and gave up his spirit. John 19:30

I think Jesus wanted this statement heard loud and clear.

Max Lucado

I think when Jesus said, "It is finished" He was saying, "It is paid. It is paid. It is complete." If I understand correctly that phrase, *Tetelestai* is kind of a commercial word. That, if you were paying off a house or I was paying off a debt and I wanted to make a big deal about making my last payment I could say something like *Tetelestai*, it's paid, it is completely paid. And it's at that point when Jesus made that call from the cross that the curtain of the temple was torn in two from top to bottom as if to say there's no more need for sacrifice, no more need for any sacrifice to be made. He was the once and for all sacrifice that's given for the forgiveness of sins.

Norman Geisler

I think when Jesus said, 'It is finished ', it means that all that the Father had asked Him to do on behalf of our salvation was completed on the cross. 'It is finished', means that I have finished the work which you gave me to do which He said in His high priestly prayer, anticipating it in John 17. I think it means what Hebrews 10 says, 'By one sacrifice forever, died for our sins, it forever put away sin. So you only need one sacrifice forever, by one person and it's final. Everything that was necessary for Jesus to do on the cross, to suffer and to die for our sins, and then and then only can He say, 'It is finished', and of course that was the end of His time on the cross.

"It's done, people! You don't have to do anything to earn salvation! I did it all! My work here is done! And when God starts something, he finishes it!"

However, religions and cults will spring up throughout history adding more things that people must do to finish the work Jesus started. They mock him by saying,

"Thanks Jesus for all you did. I'll take it from here."

Max Lucado

What separates Christianity from any other world religion is that phrase, "It is paid". Every other religion says, "Pay up". Jesus says, "It is paid". In certain, it's not pure Christianity but living under the umbrella of Christianity are religions that say, "You've got to pay, keep paying, keep paying, keep paying". That's exhausting, that's exhausting. And it's fruitless and unnecessary. Jesus paid the debt once and for all, it

277

doesn't have to be paid anymore and everything we do is a simple response of gratitude to his once and for all gift.

Joel Hunter
When Jesus said, "It is finished", it was the absolute sense of accomplishment. It's like when the marathoner breaks through the ribbon. It's like when the artist paints the last dab on the canvas. One more dab would be too much, you know. It is the accomplishment that has been now set in place for all of history to be fulfilled in that moment. And so when Jesus says, "It is finished", He means that salvation is accomplished. None of us can add to it or subtract from it. He means that we don't earn it or deserve it; it's all done in what His death accomplishes on that cross. He means that Satan is now defeated because all the dominions and principalities and all of their victories are destroyed in that moment. All of history comes to the point of accomplishment in that moment.

People want some credit for their salvation. However, "It is finished" should give us some relief, since we don't have to do anything to make ourselves righteous, just believe what in Jesus has already done. He took on the burden so we don't have to. Why would we want to add more burden by thinking we have to earn our salvation?

Norman Geisler
We want to add to what Christ has finished because we want a part of the action and we want a part of the credit. That's why in Ephesians 2:8-9 there's a little phrase stuck in there, 'For by grace are we saved through faith that not of ourselves; it is the gift of God; not of works, lest any man should boast.' If we had any part of it we'd want to take credit for it. We don't have any part in it and we can't take any credit for it.

What a sense of relief on Jesus' part to finish the job. I can't wait to finish this book and say, "It is finished." We all like to complete projects. Jesus could not wait for death to come and life to begin.

Then Jesus, ever in charge of the supernatural world, gave up his spirit. Death did not have control of the time and place of his expiration, nor did the executioners. Jesus did. Jesus decided when his spirit could depart his body. Jesus decided the manner and length of his execution.

278

The Romans and the Pharisees thought they were calling the shots. Sorry.

It was now about the sixth hour, and darkness came over the whole land until the ninth hour, for the sun stopped shining. And the curtain of the temple was torn in two. Luke 23:44-45

> What a dark day when the world kills an innocent man.
> What a darker day when it crucifies God on a cross.

At that moment the curtain of the temple was torn in two from top to bottom. The earth shook and the rocks split. The tombs broke open and the bodies of many holy people who had died were raised to life. They came out of the tombs, and after Jesus' resurrection they went into the holy city and appeared to many people. Matthew 27:51-53[21]

Because of Jesus' death, there was no longer any separation between God and man. No curtain had to keep the sinfulness of man from spilling into the presence of God. Jesus took care of all that. The sacrifice completed his ultimate, eternal mission.

No longer did a little thing like death have to keep people in their tombs. Resurrection was promised to all.

Finally, people took notice. This was no ordinary crucifixion.

When the centurion and those with him who were guarding Jesus saw the earthquake and all that had happened, they were terrified, and exclaimed, "Surely he was the Son of God!" Matthew 27:54

The centurion had seen a lot of people die on a cross. It was his job. This one died differently. Jesus forgave. He counseled. He expressed love to his family. Whatever Jesus had inside him, the centurion wanted it too, having witnessed hate and regret from so many before Jesus and finding none of that in him.

---

[21] Some believe these incidents did not actually happen, but the authors wanted to express themes like darkness, separation, resurrection.

It's never too late to recognize Jesus as the Son of God. The centurion got it.

As the curtain went down and darkness filled the world stage, Jesus breathed his last. His pain ending. The humiliation over.

And the world was changed forever.

Exactly as Jesus desired.

His innocence makes the abuse unjust, yet his action brought justice. For those who believe in what the cross did, their sins are judicially paid for and God now views them as righteous. Hard to imagine that out of all this injustice comes justice.

If he were just a man in the wrong place at the wrong time, this would be tragic. Instead he asked for it. He accepted it. This isn't a sadomasochistic human being, but God himself willing to suffer to save others.

Paul Young

In "The Passion", there is this scene that I love. And that is where Jesus is crawling onto the cross. And it's not like He is trying to hold Himself away and resisting. He is crawling with all the energy He's got left to get onto that. And to me that's His love, that He's crawling on there because this is the humanity that is pouring out all of its hatred and vengeance against God on Him.

What happened to Jesus Christ on the cross is what we do to others. We hurt each other. We draw blood. We mock. We reject. We steal. We lie. He died for those who are hurting and those who cause the hurt. Jesus suffered because sin causes pain. He wanted us to see it as he experienced it. Romans performed crucifixions in public, on the main highways, so people would know that law breaking was punishable by death. People cleaned up their acts when they entered a Roman town.

The crucifixion should do the same thing to us today. Our sins should break our hearts. We should witness the brutality our sins cause and never want to return to them again.

The day is called Good Friday, yet it hardly seems like a "good" day for Jesus, but for us it's a Great Friday. The Greatest Friday. The Greatest Friday ever because on this day, Jesus chose a painful death so I could have a wonderful life.

Paul Young
Why would He do it for me? There's only one answer. Because He loves me, that's all. Because He loves me.

TIME TO JOURNEY

1. **Watch "Crucifixion" from "In His Shoes: The Life of Christ"**

2. **Discussion Questions**

- What is so good about Good Friday? Can we come up with a better name for that day?

- Do you prefer to see an empty cross or one with Jesus on it at your local church?

- Was Jesus able to choose this death? If we do, what's it called? What's the difference?

- Why did Christ allow so much hurt to happen to him?

- List all of the atrocities that happened to Christ. What parallels do you see between them and how we treat others?

- How do you view these atrocities in light of Jesus' innocence?

- Do you use suffering as an excuse or an opportunity?

- If Jesus went through so much to die for our sins, how do you view your sins differently?

- Would you be so forgiving in Jesus' situation?

- What did Jesus mean when he said "It is finished"?

- Why do people want to add more burden to their life to pay for their sins?

- Is there anything you are trying to add to your life to help "finish" what Christ did?

- Of all the things Jesus said on the cross, which means the most to you?

- How can Jesus be so unselfish while he died on the cross?

Resurrected
The Garden Tomb

I've been away on this trip for nearly a month and it will be good to get home. I miss my family, my wife and kids, my friends, my home. I miss America with all its problems, but they're MY country's problems. It's weird being away from the culture I know, the language I understand, the television shows in English. I feel disconnected from my simple support systems.

Jesus wanted to get home too, I imagine. He had been away for thirty years, from his Father, his angels, that comfortable throne he sat on. Earth was a nice place to visit, but heaven was his home.

While I long to return to home from this trip to Israel, I have more important things to do first. I have to shoot some final segments to complete this documentary that we hope will encourage and teach people about Jesus Christ and his life on earth.

Jesus I imagine wanted to return to his father, but he too had some important things to get done first. He promised his disciples that after three days in the grave he would rise again from the dead. Nobody can keep a promise like that, unless you're God.

Through all the gory details of his crucifixion, the Bible wants to make clear that we know for certain that Jesus was dead.

This was not the Resuscitation of Christ...or the Miraculous Healing of Christ...or the Misdiagnosis of Christ...this was the Resurrection of Christ from death.

I found myself at Gordon's Calvary, the place of the Golgotha Skull. The garden area, just yards from the spooky rock, was peaceful, well-manicured and perfect for reflection. They too provide ample evidence as to why this is the place of Jesus' resurrection. Most archaeologists, including Avner, point to the Holy Sepulchre as the true location for the death and resurrection of Christ, based on tradition, Constantine's confirmation and history.

However, it's too noisy at the Holy Sepulchre. The tension is thick. I wanted to go to a place where I could relax. I found myself sitting on benches and pondering the power of this place, whether it was the real location or not. Avner was there, but this wasn't a time to talk to him. I didn't need archaeology now.

Joseph from the Judean town of Arimathea, a rich man, was a member of the same religious Council that voted to have Jesus crucified (Joseph voted against the decision, seen in Luke 23:51). Now, Joseph, at great risk to his reputation, had the guts, and obviously some clout, to address Pilate publicly for the body of Jesus. Pilate agreed, so Joseph took Jesus' body, with the help of another prominent member of the Sanhedrin, Nicodemus, the man who heard the most famous verse ever spoken by Jesus, the John 3:16 speech.

Joseph was obviously rich since he owned a tomb that he had cut out of rock, also called a sepulcher. Families carved a tomb so they could be buried together. Then, once the body had decomposed, they put the remains in an ossuary, or small chest.

Jesus never made it to total decay.

Since it was Friday and the Sabbath began at sundown, Joseph and Nicodemus had to work fast before their day off. Dead bodies needed to be covered with myrrh, aloes and spices, nearly seventy-five pounds of it, wrapped in a clean linen cloth – both attempts at preserving the body. The myrrh was a reminder of the gift given by the wise men, a foreshadowing to this day.

A huge rock was rolled in front of the tomb, to lock in the smell and to keep robbers from desecrating the graves. Roman guards, the elite fighting force of their day, positioned themselves outside the tomb to make sure the disciples did not steal the body. They knew that Jesus predicted his resurrection and they wanted to make sure the body stayed put and no deceptions occurred.

All Saturday, the Jewish Sabbath, nobody did anything. The disciples probably couldn't if they wanted to. They were numb from the pain of seeing the nicest, kindest, holiest guy they had ever met, their best friend, die brutally on a cross after hours of suffering. While their enemies celebrated with feasts, they sat locked in a room, scared and full of despair. They probably had not slept much, waiting, hoping this would all die down and they could go back out in public and start over their lives again. It was hardly a day of rest, but a Sabbath couldn't have come at a better time.

Sunday morning came, releasing them from the confines of Sabbath regulations, so the women followers of Christ went to the tomb to cover Jesus' body in more spices. Obviously they did not believe Jesus *literally* meant that today, the third day, he would resurrect since they were preparing his body for more death. After all the brutality they had seen, nobody came back from that kind of treatment.

They had seen Jesus raise Lazarus from the dead, but raising someone himself from the dead…it had never been done.

The women entered the tomb to get to work and instead they met some angelic greeters:

In their fright the women bowed down with their faces to the ground, but the men said to them, "Why do you look for the living among the dead? He is not here; he has risen! Remember how he told you, while he was still with you in Galilee: 'The Son of Man must be delivered into the hands of sinful men, be crucified and on the third day be raised again.' "

Then they remembered his words.

When they came back from the tomb, they told all these things to the Eleven and to all the others. It was Mary Magdalene, Joanna, Mary the mother of James, and the others with them who told this to the apostles. But they did not believe the women, because their words seemed to them like nonsense. Peter, however, got up and ran to the tomb. Bending over, he saw the strips of linen lying by themselves, and he went away, wondering to himself what had happened. Luke 24:5-12

The women ran and told the men back in the upper room who did not believe them. Why? Because they were women. Nobody in that day ever believed the testimony of a woman. These women are just being emotional, the men were thinking, after the death, so they were seeing things, freaking out. Sorry to say that, but that was the mindset of the day. The testimony of women did not verify anything. It could be true, but not until a man confirmed it. So Peter and John decided to check it out, just to make sure.

John, in his Gospel, said the moment he ran to the tomb, he believed Jesus had resurrected, but Peter did not believe right away. They went back to the room with the other disciples.

The Gospel story says the women stood outside the tomb, crying after all the rejection that just occurred. Their emotions caught up after the startling events.

Then Jesus appeared to Mary Magdalene[22]:

---

[22] Matthew indicates that other women were present too, but John just focuses on Mary Magdalene.

At this, she turned around and saw Jesus standing there, but she did not realize that it was Jesus. "Woman," he said, "why are you crying? Who is it you are looking for?"
Thinking he was the gardener, she said, "Sir, if you have carried him away, tell me where you have put him, and I will get him."
Jesus said to her, "Mary."
She turned toward him and cried out in Aramaic, "Rabboni!" (which means Teacher).
Jesus said, "Do not hold on to me, for I have not yet returned to the Father. Go instead to my brothers and tell them, 'I am returning to my Father and your Father, to my God and your God.' "
Mary Magdalene went to the disciples with the news: "I have seen the Lord!" And she told them that he had said these things to her.   John 20:14-18

Mary thinks he's the gardener. Anyone but Jesus, right? How could it be Jesus?
Matthew adds another point to this encounter with the women.

Suddenly Jesus met them. "Greetings," he said. They came to him, clasped his feet and worshiped him. Then Jesus said to them, "Do not be afraid. Go and tell my brothers to go to Galilee; there they will see me." Matthew 28:9-10

As I stand outside this rock hewn grave, imaging the scene, I had to wonder, after all Jesus said and did and proved, and only a few woman showed up at his tomb on the third day? The greeting party feels too small. Jesus had to relay a message to the men through a handful of women.
Why wasn't everyone camped out in front of the grave with their lawn chairs and cameras, ready for the big event? People have more faith and excitement over getting tickets to see a concert or fireworks on the Fourth of July. A Founder's Day celebration at a small Missouri town gets more attention than the resurrection of Jesus Christ.
Jesus told them what would happen, but nobody showed up. Instead they all hid, embarrassed that they followed Jesus, some great

leader who allowed himself to be crucified. Some superstar he turned out to be…

Norman Geisler

If I had been Jesus and gotten the response that He got, I would have been disappointed. Because He told them from Matthew chapter 12 on that He was going to die. Well actually in John chapter 2 in the early ministry He told them He's was going to resurrect three days later. Matthew 12 He told them. In Matthew 17:18 He told them again repeatedly. He told them, 'I'm going to die and rise from the dead.' And it never seemed to get through their thick skulls. He dies, so they think it's all over. I would have been really disappointed. I spent three and a half years with these guys. They called me the Son of God and the Messiah and they didn't even get the main thing, you know. I would have really been disappointed. And what was the response? Disbelief, doubt, okay you guys saw Him but I don't believe until I can see Him and stick my finger in His hand and my hand in His side…I'm not going to believe. The women came back, and they say, 'Oh yeah some emotional, excited women, you know, see an angel and all that but, I don't believe it.' So they run down to the tomb and don't see anything in the tomb, except John. John saw the head cloth folded up by itself and he believed. He's the only one to believe before that Jesus had resurrected, before he saw Him.

Every Easter we retell this story, reflect on its beauty and majesty, then sing glorious hymns of praise for what this day signified. However, as I look at these accounts, I wonder if Jesus was frustrated.

Jesus then showed up and told the women to tell the men to go to Galilee. And what do the men do?

Stay in Jerusalem. More frustration?

Same day, at another part of town, two disciples out for a walk to Emmaus (running away, maybe), one named Cleopas, were talking about the weeks' events. Suddenly a stranger showed up and walked with them. They tell him about the crucifixion of Christ and the mysterious disappearance of the body.

The stranger fired back:

He said to them, "How foolish you are, and how slow of heart to believe all that the prophets have spoken! Did not the

287

Christ have to suffer these things and then enter his glory?"
And beginning with Moses and all the Prophets, he
explained to them what was said in all the Scriptures
concerning himself. Luke 24:25-27

I'm going to be as diplomatic as I can with Jesus' tone, but it's
like Jesus said, "You fools! The prophets predicted this! The scriptures
proclaim it! Don't you get it? Do I have to explain it all over again!
You people!"

Jesus ate with them, repeating the communion and their eyes
were opened. "It's him!" they cried. So they turned around and went to
Jerusalem to talk to the other disciples.

The disciples, not in Galilee as they were told, STILL weren't
buying this story about Jesus. So, Jesus had to show up himself, making
a house call.

While they were still talking about this, Jesus himself stood
among them and said to them, "Peace be with you."
They were startled and frightened, thinking they saw a ghost.
He said to them, "Why are you troubled, and why do doubts
rise in your minds? Look at my hands and my feet. It is I
myself! Touch me and see; a ghost does not have flesh and
bones, as you see I have."
When he had said this, he showed them his hands and feet.
And while they still did not believe it because of joy and
amazement, he asked them, "Do you have anything here to
eat?"
They gave him a piece of broiled fish, and he took it and ate
it in their presence.
He said to them, "This is what I told you while I was still with
you: Everything must be fulfilled that is written about me in
the Law of Moses, the Prophets and the Psalms."
Then he opened their minds so they could understand the
Scriptures. He told them, "This is what is written: The Christ
will suffer and rise from the dead on the third day, and
repentance and forgiveness of sins will be preached in his
name to all nations, beginning at Jerusalem. You are
witnesses of these things. I am going to send you what my

288

Father has promised; but stay in the city until you have been clothed with power from on high." Luke 24:36-49

Jesus responded, "Why are you so upset? Why do you doubt? Look for yourself. You can't touch a ghost. Look, I'm eating food. Ghosts don't eat food. I told you everything from the scriptures and yet you don't believe."

Finally their minds were opened. They got it.

IT'S HIM! IT'S REALLY HIM! HE'S REALLY ALIVE! HE'S RESURRECTED! HE HAS COME FROM THE DEAD!

Later, Thomas missed this meeting and doubted. So Jesus made a re-appearance to him. But we always attacked Thomas and his doubt when the truth is EVERYONE doubted. He was just the last to doubt.

I imagine Jesus enjoyed the reunion that came from the resurrection, but it's like telling everyone you are coming home and nobody's expecting you. Nobody's at the airport to pick you up. No "Welcome Home" signs in hand. No appetizers prepared.

"We know you said you were coming home for Christmas, but we didn't think you were really coming home. We thought that was a metaphor."

Frustrating day?

All that explanation.

All those miracles.

All that time.

All those promises.

Forgotten. Rejected. Not believed.

Jesus showed up and nobody recognized him, and he only went away for three days.

Joel Hunter

Resurrection day must have been like everything else in Jesus' life, a mix of heaven and earth. First of all, there was the absolute triumph but second of all there was the initial disbelief. And Jesus is just going, "Now let me ask you again, why are you looking for the living among the dead?" And, so I do believe that there was probably some frustration on Jesus' part. On the other hand, He'd lived with these guys, He knew they were slow and so He knew they would ultimately get it. He knew they would grow in to it. It was the greatest moment in all of history, when we're talking about life and the extension of life. But it, like

289

everything that takes place on earth, it's always mixed with our limitations.

Today, compound that frustration a billion times over with all the information God has provided throughout history to people and they still don't believe. God has made himself clear through his creation and in our hearts[23]. He provided prophets to proclaim his reality. Miracles. Changed lives. Prophecies that came true and yet...

Nothing.

Driving this doubt and disobedience were feelings of fear and hopelessness. The disciples lost faith and became afraid of death by the hands of the very people who killed Jesus. If they could kill him, the disciples were easy targets.

Yet Jesus resurrected to take away their fears and hopelessness. By having faith in him, we need not be afraid of death. His resurrection proved his power over our biggest fear. Jesus knew they were weak. If they only believed...

Look at what they were asked to believe—that a man who healed people and brought them back to life could heal himself after his own death. It's easy for us to believe because we know the story. At the time, it was unfathomable.

While I detect that tone of frustration in Jesus and the angels, I also recognize something else. Grace.

The women were given two chances to believe, through the angels then through the clandestine appearance by Jesus Christ.

The disciples were given multiple chances to believe, through the women, through Peter and John, through the two appearances of Jesus in the upper room.

Thomas was not there when Jesus showed up the first time, so Jesus showed up again.

Two guys walking along a road were given a special live appearance by Jesus himself.

The Apostle Paul writes that Jesus appeared to around 500 people.

Only grace gives people first, second or third chances to believe. He won't punish you because you were late, missed an opportunity, stubbornly refused once or your schedule just didn't work. Jesus will do everything he can to make sure the people believed.

Scriptural proof.

---

[23] Romans 1 & 2

Physical proof.

Reasonable proof.

What more does Jesus have to do to prove that he rose again from the dead? It seems he's done enough, but if someone won't believe, he'll always do more. Resurrection is a difficult concept to grasp. People need reviews and do-overs all the time.

Is seeing believing? For Thomas, did he have to see? Seeing isn't always believing, but believing is seeing—seeing through the lies, distortions, fears and doubt of this world into an eternity of life, love and relationship in the next.

As I wrap up my time here at Gordon's Calvary, I thank God that, through all the frustration I caused him, he gave me hundreds of chances to believe until I finally saw the proof, in my own upper room, my mind opening up and I received him as the Risen Lord.

Paul Young

I don't think it surprised Him in the least that they didn't do anything that He had asked them to do. I don't see the frustration; I see the invitation, constantly in those conversations. I see the warmth and, I mean, the first thing you see really is, in terms of the disciples, is the situation with Peter. Do you see any frustration in that conversation? I don't. I see huge restoration and reconciliation, and love. Reaching to where Peter is. Helping Peter to see where he is. But, even before that He makes them some fish, cooks them up some fish and we're going to eat around a meal. He totally understands what human beings are like and what being human is so I don't see the frustration there at all.

TIME TO JOURNEY

1. **Watch "Resurrected" from "In His Shoes: The Life of Christ"**

2. **Discussion Questions**

- Think of a time you really wanted to go home. How long were you away? What was that feeling like?

- Do you think Jesus had similar feelings? Why or why not?

- How do you think the disciples were feeling that morning? What plans were going through their heads?

- Why was the resurrection so important for Jesus?

- Do you think, under the circumstances, you would have run to the tomb and believed?

- Why didn't anyone go to Galilee when they were first asked?

- Why was the resurrection so frustrating for Jesus and the angels?

- Why didn't anyone want to believe that Jesus had returned after all he had done?

- How do you think Jesus felt seeing everyone again?

- Why did Thomas get a personal visit? Would you have needed one?

- Why did Jesus give so many second chances for people to believe?

- Do you sense times in your life that God came to you over and over again with proof of his existence?

- What does "belief" mean according to this story?

- If you could resurrect someone, who would it be?

- Why is death so troubling for us?

Goodbye
Mount Arbel / Mount of Olives

When I leave this earth, I want to say something very profound. I want to tell my family something that will reverberate through their lives. Something they will always remember, ponder on and actively pursue until their dying breath. And then, pass that on to their family. Something like…

- *Buy low, sell high.*
- *Don't take wooden nickels.*
- *Look both ways before you cross the street.*

Good advice, but not profound. How about…

- *Love others.*
- *Reach the world.*
- *Teach whenever you can.*

While those would be profound last words, they aren't very unique. In fact, all of them are copied straight from Christ's final message to his followers. Paul says in 1 Corinthians 15 that Jesus appeared to over five hundred people after the resurrection saying both "hello" and "goodbye."

Jesus wanted his followers to know for sure that the resurrection he spoke of was a reality. Why? His resurrection guaranteed their resurrection, so "goodbye" is for now on never in the vocabulary for two believers in Christ. "I'll see you later" is much more fitting, thanks to the resurrection.

But before Jesus left this earth he had some things to take care of, some things to say, and a gift to leave them with.

Taking Care of Business: Before Jesus departed the earth, he needed to repair a relationship damaged by events over the past few days. Many abandoned and betrayed Jesus. Jesus didn't want to leave without making sure these matters were addressed. Out of all those relationships that Jesus connected with, there was one in particular he needed to focus on—Peter—and it occurred in the region of Galilee.

Afterward Jesus appeared again to his disciples, by the Sea of Tiberias. It happened this way: John 21:1

293

Peter and the others picked up their things and finally went to Galilee as Jesus originally asked. Galilee (Tiberias) was well away from the maelstrom of religion and politics. Here they could safely get together, like the old days, strategize then move on to the next phase of God's plan.

It was also the place where he called many of them three years before, proclaiming that they would be fishers of men. So they returned to the region and became fishers of…fish.

While they waited for Jesus to show up, they passed the time by doing the thing they knew the best. They went fishing. While in the boat, a stranger on the shoreline told them to cast their nets on the right side of the boat, the exact same net trick Jesus said when he first met Peter. Peter jumped into the water and swam to Jesus, while the others followed.

Jesus cooked breakfast and three times told Peter to take care and feed his sheep, a direct reference to Peter getting engaged in ministry. Why did Jesus give Peter direction instructions and why press him three times?

Peter had betrayed him, denying any acknowledgment of knowing Jesus three times to the people around the fire in the courtyard of the High Priest's home. In Caesarea Philippi, Peter committed to stand by Jesus to the death. Then he turned coward when cross-examined by a little girl.

Now Jesus singles him out around the campfire. "It's okay, it's okay, it's okay, Peter, I have something for you to do." Jesus didn't even ask for an apology. Peter was forgiven before he said "I'm sorry."

Joel Hunter
It was so important for Jesus to talk with Peter that one last time. First off, because Peter needed to be redeemed emotionally from his betrayal of Jesus. He didn't want Peter to doubt His love for Peter, His mission through Peter or Peter's self-identification as a strong leader. All of us who are strong, when we fall, our regrets take us down to the depths, you know. When we have failed, those of us who are high achievers, you know, we feel failure. And it's not until someone else comes to us that we love and respect and say, "Don't go there, I got a mission for you here, and these people who I'm sending you to really need your strength. Feed My lambs, Feed My sheep, they need a shepherd". And so he is being re-empowered for that mission.

I appreciate Jesus extending the scepter of forgiveness instead of waiting for Peter to say he was sorry. Peter was a prideful man. Jesus probably knew Peter wouldn't step up and ask for forgiveness, so Jesus offered it first. This was unfinished business that would nag at Peter as he wondered if he was fit to be in the ministry.

"You're forgiven. Now move on."

Jesus moves first when it comes to forgiveness and he restores our relationship to him. Jesus gets the tough stuff out on the table, refusing to let it fester, then pushes us to move beyond this. I can't tell you how many times on this project I've doubted my worthiness and every sin from my past has come to the surface.

I need to acknowledge them, confess them, accept forgiveness and move on.

Something to Say: When Jesus told his disciples to meet him in Galilee, he specifically mentioned the place as a mountain. The mountain is believed to be Mount Arbel.

Entering Galilean area, you can't miss Mount Arbel. It's a huge cliff with a spectacular view of the Sea of Galilee, overlooking the ministry area Jesus and disciples frequented for three years. We climbed to the top and Avner pointed out all the places we had journeyed together while in Galilee.

Capernaum. Bethsaida. Mount of Beatitudes. The non-Jewish areas of Kursi. It seemed so small up here. It's almost a God's eye view of their world.

Then the eleven disciples went to Galilee, to the mountain where Jesus had told them to go. When they saw him, they worshiped him; but some doubted. Matthew 28:16-17

They doubted? Really? Still? Let's give them credit for coming along and climbing the mountain. While there, Jesus made his famous statement:

Then Jesus came to them and said, "All authority in heaven and on earth has been given to me. Therefore go and make disciples of all nations, baptizing them in the name of the Father and of the Son and of the Holy Spirit, and teaching them to obey everything I have commanded you. And surely

I am with you always, to the very end of the age." Matthew 28:18-20

Jesus began by stating his credentials as Commander in Chief. By saying "all authority," Jesus did not speak to them as a friend, but put on a crown on his head and said, in essence, what I'm about to say is not optional. "I'm the boss."

Jesus gave them a mission that summarized the question "why" he came to them in the first place while they fished on this sea spread out before them. He did not come to earth to entertain them and give them stories to tell around the dinner table. He came to kick start a ministry and they needed to get busy.

This statement, known as the Great Commission, basically says this:

- Go. Get busy. Create interest. Start talking.
- Make students of God.
- Baptize them.
- Teach them all those things I taught you.

From Mount Arbel you can see for miles in all directions. Jesus said to them, "Remember everything I said as we traveled through this area. Remember the feeding of the 5,000 over there? Remember when I healed the demoniac over there? How about the teaching on that mountain? Or when I walked on water? Remember that? Now go and tell all those other regions, as far as the eye can see and even further, what I showed you told you and we experienced together."

Mount Arbel has another meaning especially for Jews who lived in this area. Avner showed me some caves along the sides of the cliff. The look down the side of the mountain dizzied me. As we stood on the edge of cliff, gusts of wind wanted to pick me up and throw me over the side. Was I willing to sacrifice my life for this project? Apparently sacrifice is the theme of this mountain.

"Mount Arbel has cliffs from both sides facing north and east towards the sea," Avner said, calmly standing just inches from the 360 foot drop. "Those are sheer cliffs and make it almost impossible to climb up. In the cliffs are caves and people many times found shelter on those caves, especially during time of revolts and fighting against authorities. When King Herod gained the throne, that was at the year 40 BC, many of the people that were here, the Jews, revolted against him. Here there was a very bitter resistance and many of the people of the Galilee fought against him, finding shelters in the caves."

The Hasmoneans (140-37 BC) grew from the Maccabean revolt during the time between the Old and the New Testament. They considered themselves an independent state with their own authority. Herod didn't like them. Avner went on to explain.

"He gathered his army and even built here not far from us, on the mountain over there, an army camp." Avner pointed a smaller mountain just across from us. "Some of the remains of it can still be seen. And from this very point he lowered his soldiers in large wooden boxes using chains, metal chains, and brought them to face the caves and those soldiers used huge hooks, just pulled the people out of the caves and dropped them down the cliff and killed them. Not a very pleasant story but, typical to King Herod."

I looked at the drop and imagined the sickening thuds and screams of people falling to their death, all for a cause. "So, this mountain, before Jesus was here, represented sacrifice."

Avner agreed. "It represented sacrifice. It represented fighting for being Jews and belief in God in this country. Since for them Herod symbolized more the Roman world than the Jewish one."

This location, as I scanned the horizon during a beautiful sunset, had more to offer than just a view. But a viewpoint. "So it seems really appropriate, if you were going to stand somewhere and talk about risking your life and giving for a cause that was for God, this would be the mountain."

"That would be a mountain, that's for sure, and was remembered well by everybody around here."

This was a mountain of sacrifice, where people died for their belief. The cries of death still echoed from these hills as Jesus commissioned them to enter the enemies' territory. Jesus was telling them that their mission would involve sacrifice and probably death.

This had to be frightening, maybe discouraging. Jesus, knowing this, wanted to comfort them. He told his followers "I'm going to be with you always. Until everything ends."

He wanted them to know that they would not be alone. I'm grateful he gave those disciples such confidence. They needed it. Their sacrificial efforts brought the gospel to the world and eventually thousands of years later to me.

A Departing Gift: Finally, Jesus instructed them to go to Jerusalem. It's where the final goodbye (see you later) will occur.

After his suffering, he showed himself to these men and gave many convincing proofs that he was alive. He appeared to them over a period of forty days and spoke about the kingdom of God. On one occasion, while he was eating with them, he gave them this command: "Do not leave Jerusalem, but wait for the gift my Father promised, which you have heard me speak about. For John baptized with water, but in a few days you will be baptized with the Holy Spirit."

So when they met together, they asked him, "Lord, are you at this time going to restore the kingdom to Israel?"

He said to them: "It is not for you to know the times or dates the Father has set by his own authority. But you will receive power when the Holy Spirit comes on you; and you will be my witnesses in Jerusalem, and in all Judea and Samaria, and to the ends of the earth."

After he said this, he was taken up before their very eyes, and a cloud hid him from their sight. Acts 1:3-9

The final location was the Mount of Olives (stated in verse Acts 1:12), with a perfect view of the entire area where Jesus taught, suffered, was crucified and resurrected.

The traditional spot of Jesus' ascension, with the best view of the Old City, is a just a simple pathway on the mountain with a couple churches as a backdrop. The place is overrun by pushy vendors trying to get you to buy maps and pictures of the very place where you are standing. There's even a camel which you can sit on for a fee.

Was there a camel on this mountain when Jesus ascended?

Jesus wanted to meet up with the apostles one more time before he left, so he chose the Mount of Olives as his final departure. It's clear he chose the place for the view of the temple, as a reminder, once again of the sacrifice he did for them and the sacrifice they were going to give others, but was there more to this mountain? As always, Avner, my faithful guide on this trip, understood why.

"The Mount of Olives is dominating Jerusalem, also dominating the Temple Mount. It's above the Temple Mount from the east, where the sun is rising. The temple faces the east. That's a very strong connection there. It is the end of the green area and beyond that starts the Judean wilderness, dropping dramatically down to the lowest place on earth - the Dead Sea. After the Romans destroyed Jerusalem it was forbidden for centuries for Jews to get into the city and the only place they could watch the area with what was the temple mount and the holy city in general was the Mount of Olives. So the Mount of Olives has a very strong association with feelings, faith and belief."

Once again we picked a sunset to stand on this mountain, 70 miles away from the other mountain, and the view is breathtaking, as the warm glow of the sun cast across the temple. Once again I could see all the important spots I had visited with Avner: the Temple Mount, the Temple stairs, the Garden of Gethsemane, the Holy Sepulchre.

Between the two mountains, you had the best views of the two most important areas of Jesus' ministry. The two places he made the most impact. These mountains summarized it all.

What a farewell message he was sending to his followers. It was the perfect spot to leave them with a perfect gift – the Holy Spirit. The Holy Spirit would have a dispersing effect on them, pulling them in all directions from the immediate area, Jerusalem, outside to Judea, Samaria and the ends of the earth, wherever that may be.

Norman Geisler

Well He said, 'If I go not away the Holy Spirit won't come. If the Holy Spirit doesn't come you're not going to be empowered to do the work that you've got to do because not many days hence you're going to receive the power to be witnesses to me in Jerusalem, Judea, Samaria and the outer most parts of the earth.' Furthermore the fact that Jesus departed and went to the Father is where He ever lives to make intercession for us which is another stage of our salvation called sanctification. All the rest accomplished our justification but Satan accuses us before the Father day and night and Christ is our advocate, 1 John chapter 2, 'Ever pleading our case before the Father right now', so that when I sin right now Christ is there saying, 'Hey my blood takes care of that too, it takes care of that sin and that sin.' So it was necessary for Him to enter into His priestly intercession, Hebrews 7 – 9, where He ever lives to make intercession for us as a great high priest. And that's a very neglected part of the Christian life today. Our sanctification and His intercession makes it possible.

Paul Young

I think there's got to be some sense of separation in the sense that, 'I'm not going to be walking with you every day, not in a tangible physical way. But I'm so excited because the Holy Spirit is going to deliver me into you every single day.' So I think there is huge exaltation in the sense of, 'Okay here we go' I mean 'What I did finished everything in terms of what needed to have happen. Now we're going to watch this little stone, that is made without human hands, that comes from off the scene, roll in and knock over the systems of the world and begin to grow and grow and grow and grow.'

And He totally believes in the life that's in these men. He totally believes in it because it's His life. So I don't think there's any worry on His part, I don't think there's any concern. I think He's excited for the adventure that they're about to go on. And we sense that excitement in each other's lives when we talk about transformation and change that happens in our lives. As we begin to see the realities that we're a part of. Aren't you excited for that person? Even though there is pain involved? Even though that's part of the sorrow that would have been there. 'You guys don't know the baptism that you're going to be baptized with. But I'll be there; I will not leave you or forsake you. This is not a leaving or forsaking. I will never leave you or forsake you. Nothing will ever separate you from My love.'

We all like presents, especially when someone comes back from a long trip. Jesus promised he would be with them always and this fulfilled that promise. His Holy Spirit could do things Jesus could not do in his limited earthly form – be at more than one place at a time and live in their hearts.

He told them to wait patiently for that present…

Norman Geisler

When Jesus gave His farewell to the apostles, the Mount of Olives, and just before that, He'd given them the great commission. He told them that the Holy Spirit is going to come; He called the Holy Spirit a Comforter. Empirically someone is going to come along side so He knew they'd be fully equipped, they'd be fully comforted. He knew that if He didn't go, not only would the Holy Spirit not come and His intercessory ministry not incur but that they wouldn't be empowered to take this to all the world. And what's His ultimate goal?

Arching back to Genesis 10, 'through you Abraham, that all the earth will be blessed.' Remember in John 12 where the Greeks came and said, 'Sir we would see Jesus.' And He in essence said, 'No, I am not coming to Greece now, but if a corn of wheat, a grain of wheat die, fall on the ground and die, it abides alone but if it dies it brings forth much fruit.' In other words, after the ascension and after I have died in Jerusalem from the dead then my message is going be taken to all the world including Greece, so just hang on, I can't be detoured now but I'll be there later.   So I think He felt optimistic. He knew what was going to happen. He knew that they were going to be empowered. He knew the gates hell would not prevail against the church. He knew they would go into all the world and preach the Gospel to every creature and they would have the power to do it.

Then he ascended into heaven – a miraculous finish to his ministry. Whoosh! Gone. For Jesus, it was homecoming, returning to the presence of his loving Father.

For the others, it was see you later and anticipation for the Holy Spirit.

As I stood on the Mount of Olives, a tremendous wind blew over us, offering some evidence that maybe Jesus ascended with a strong gust. That wind reminded me of Acts Chapter 2 and the strong wind that would blow over this disciples, a supernatural force that would disperse them in all directions.

For the disciples, it was the beginning of a whole era in history. What they would do would change the world forever.

Unfortunately, they were just standing around.

They were looking intently up into the sky as he was going, when suddenly two men dressed in white stood beside them. "Men of Galilee," they said, "why do you stand here looking into the sky? This same Jesus, who has been taken from you into heaven, will come back in the same way you have seen him go into heaven."

Then they returned to Jerusalem from the hill called the Mount of Olives, a Sabbath day's walk from the city. Acts 1:10-12

Marveling at the sight of Jesus ascending, the disciples were caught staring off into the sky.

"Wow. Cool. Did you see that?"

The angels wondered, "Why are you standing around? He's coming back. Now get prepared, for the best part is yet to come."

As I looked out over the Mount of Olives, I wonder if I'm just standing around, marveling at all the supernatural sights and the amazing testimonies of God. Am I comfortably nestled in my Christian afghan, all warm and snuggly with fellow disciples, or am I out in the streets doing what God directs me to do, awaiting those divine encounters inspired by the Holy Spirit?

Max Lucado

When I leave this earth, give me 5 minutes before I die to tell people some things. I'll gather my closest family and I'll tell them that I genuinely am excited, I really cannot wait, I really cannot. I think it's going to be the adventure of eternity. I think it's just going to be something just beyond words. That's been kind of a recent development in my life. Maybe it's because I have more and more people already over there. But, I would want people to know I'm really okay with this, it's alright. I think that the idea of any physical pain that I might have to go through when I die, I'm not excited about that but I'm genuinely intrigued about what's awaiting us on the other side. So I would want them to know I'm fine with it and that I'll miss them but we really will be together real quickly, we really will.

A long life span here is really short by comparison and so for them to just live in peace, love life and enjoy it. Jesus' final commission, you know, going to all world to preach the Gospel to every creation. I try not to read that as some type of formal commissioning, but more of a, go do good things, let everybody know about me, make a difference in the world. Live for something bigger than you.

TIME TO JOURNEY

1. Watch "Goodbye" from "In His Shoes: The Life of Christ"

2. Discussion Questions

- How are you with goodbyes? Do you cry or keep a stiff upper lip?
- Who would you invite to your final goodbye?
- What final words would you tell people before you die?
- Where would you take people for your final goodbye? What places are significant for you and why?
- Why did Peter need this special visit by Jesus?
- If Jesus made a visit to you, what would you want him to say?
- If you've been to a mountain, describe the experience. How did it feel?
- What was Jesus trying to say on each mountain they visited?
- What instructions did Jesus give to his followers? What would those activities require on the part of the disciples?
- Do you sense the presence of Christ with you always or do think you're all alone sometimes?
- How hard was it for Jesus to say goodbye even though he knew he would see them again?
- This wasn't so much a "Goodbye" as what?
- When you see Jesus again, it will be "Hello." What do you want Christ to say to you?

3. Wrap up your Small Group time by watching the next episode "Fire" from "In His Shoes: The Life of Christ."

Fire
Temple Stairs

We visited a lot of places during our visit to Israel, places that have been venerated with a mixture of legend, tradition and truth. We never really knew where Jesus actually set foot or where he really visited. Everything from the star marking his birthplace to the tomb marking his resurrection were all in question.

Except for one place...

"Avner, is there somewhere that we know for sure that Jesus set foot? The actual place, the actual stone that he would have touched."

Avner thought for a second. "Well, I would say that Jesus actually set foot on the stairs leading up to the temple."

The area Avner referenced is called the Southern Temple Mount, on the south side of the Old City, leading up to the original entrance of the temple. Mikvahs, "baptismal" areas that once prepared and cleansed Jewish worshippers before they set foot on the Temple Mount, line the massive stone stairs. The stairs took worshippers to the Triple Gate and a partially exposed Double Gate, entrances and exits to the temple area. Those stairs date to the first century.

That means your foot can touch the stairs that Jesus set his foot on.

As I walked up those stairs, I pondered walking in the shoes of Jesus one last time. God, Emmanuel, came as a human, with a human foot, wearing a human shoe and walked right here. The moment was ethereal. Supernatural.

Yet I realized this was where another significant event took place.

There is some solid speculation that Pentecost happened right here on the stairs leading up the temple. It was a common area where people of all nations would gather. Traditionally rabbis taught and discussed issues here. And since it was Pentecost, this would be a very busy area.

Peter spoke to a large group of gatherers in Acts 2 and made the first public presentation of the Gospel.[24]

---

[24] Acts 2 states that they were in house. Now maybe this all started in a house, but it had to end somewhere that would accommodate over 3,000 people and baptize them. So at some point in this story, at Pentecost, scholars believe, it

Peter replied, "Repent and be baptized, every one of you, in the name of Jesus Christ for the forgiveness of your sins. And you will receive the gift of the Holy Spirit. The promise is for you and your children and for all who are far off—for all whom the Lord our God will call." With many other words he warned them; and he pleaded with them, "Save yourselves from this corrupt generation." Those who accepted his message were baptized, and about three thousand were added to their number that day. Acts 2:38-41

These stairs could easily accommodate a large crowd of thousands of people. Plus for 3,000 to be baptized, you would need multiple baptismal areas. The mikvahs solve that problem.

This is where the Holy Spirit touched down and touched the lives of those new believers, within a good hard stone's throw from the temple where God also touched down in the Holy of Holies. Now his home was going to be franchised and portable.

In Acts 2:1-4, when the Holy Spirit miraculously debuted in the hearts of the new believers, two things happened.

1. Fire burned over their heads
2. They began to speak in other languages

What did this symbolize?

Their hearts were passionately set on fire for God and they started talking in whatever language they could about Him.

As I stood on those stairs, I watched groups of tourists, talking in their own languages – Norwegian, German and Hebrew – discussing the significance of the stairs they sat on, while teachers and tour guides instructed them on history.

I thought…not much has changed here. The area is still used to gather and to teach people from all around the world, filling them with passion to go back out into the world and tell others about God.

This is the place where everything changed. The Jesus chapter of history closed and the Holy Spirit's chapter began.

---

moved to these stairs.

While these stairs represented a beginning for Christianity, for me, it was an ending of my journey in Israel.

I had the privilege of visiting the Holy Land and reflecting on Jesus coming to us in the flesh, dwelling among us. As much time as I have had to explore the places where Jesus walked and comprehending his thoughts using the Bible, history and archaeology as my guide, I only have one thing to say. I want it to be a profound summary of weeks of study and walking in deep discussions with experts such as Avner. So here goes…

Wow.

That's it. Not very profound. Just an exclamation from the gut, spawned by an overwhelmed mind trying to understand it all.

Wow. Really? He came to earth? To be close to us?

And to think that everything I examined was only the surface of the story of Jesus Christ coming to earth.

Jesus did many other miraculous signs in the presence of his disciples, which are not recorded in this book. But these are written that you may believe that Jesus is the Christ, the Son of God, and that by believing you may have life in his name.   John 20:30-31

This is the disciple who testifies to these things and who wrote them down. We know that his testimony is true. Jesus did many other things as well. If every one of them were written down, I suppose that even the whole world would not have room for the books that would be written.   John 21:24-25

As I conclude my journey, I realize there's so much more to know and to explore. Whole books, written for years to come, will examine the many facets of Jesus Christ, God who came as a man, in the flesh, and walked among us.

The very notion of knowing more set my heart on fire.

I needed to take this passion and spread it around.

Pass it on.

Tell others.

Why?

He's coming back soon!

I pondered my "death" when I started this journey and now realized that the death of myself at the beginning—sacrificing my time, energy and maybe my life by coming here to walk in the shoes of Jesus—only led to a new passion, new perspective, a new life for Him in the end.

Every step on the stairs of life only lead us one step closer to a reunion with our Savior, our Redeemer, our Friend—Jesus.

It's time to strap on my shoes and continue my journey for Christ, wherever I go.

TIME TO JOURNEY

1. **Watch "Fire" from "In His Shoes: The Life of Christ"**

2. **Discussion Questions**

- Are you *on fire, lukewarm, chilly or ice cold* when it comes to your passion for reaching others for Christ?

- What is keeping you from reaching the world?

- Why do you need to die first before you go?

- Are you ready to strap on your shoes and go?

ABOUT THE AUTHOR

Troy Schmidt began writing animation in Los Angeles in 1985 (*Dennis the Menace, Heathcliff, Flintstone Kids*). In 1992, he moved to Orlando to write for *The Mickey Mouse Club,* for three seasons. He adapted a Max Lucado children's book *Hermie* into a video, then created and wrote all the future video installments and twenty Hermie books. Troy directed documentary footage in Israel for iLumina Gold, then returned in 2008 to host a documentary entitled "In His Shoes: The Life of Jesus" for GLO Bible software. Troy was also a producer for the GSN game show "The American Bible Challenge" starring Jeff Foxworthy and wrote the board game based on the show.

Troy is married to Barbie and they have three grown boys, Riley, Brady and Carson. He is a campus pastor at First Baptist Church Windermere, Florida.

MORE IN THE PRAYING THROUGH THE BIBLE SERIES

Genesis	Exodus	Leviticus	Numbers	Deuteronomy
Matthew	Mark	Luke	John	Praying Through the Gospels
Galatians/Ephesians/Philippians/Colossians			Praying Through the Law	

BOOKS

The Best 100 Bible Verses About Prayer (Baker)
This Means War: A Prayer Journal (B&H Kids)
The American Bible Challenge Daily Reader: Volume 1 (Thomas Nelson)
Chapter by Chapter: An Easy to Use Summary of the Entire Bible (Amazon)
Reason for Hope: Answers to Your Bible Questions (Amazon)
Reason for Hope: MORE Answers to Your Bible Questions (Amazon)
Reason for Hope: Answers to Your Questions about Heaven (Amazon)
40 Days: A Daily Devotion for Spiritual Renewal (Amazon)
Saved: Answers That Can Save Your Life (Amazon)
Release: Why God Wants You to Let Go (Amazon)
In His Shoes: The Life of Jesus (Amazon)
Laughing Matters (Lillenas Publishing)

BIBLE STUDIES

Foundations: A Study of God (Amazon)
Living the Real Life:
12 Studies for Building Biblical Community (Amazon)

WEBSITES

Personal writing page – **www.troyeschmidt.com**
Apologetic/Bible Q&A – **www.reasonhope.com**
Church dramas – **www.churchscriptsonline.com**

Made in the USA
Las Vegas, NV
09 February 2022

43566354R00177